W9-BTM-772

TO

HOUSE" ESPECIALLY
THE MEN

FROM NORM &
KAY

the STANLEY CUP

A COMPLETE PICTORIAL HISTORY

the STANLEY CUP

A COMPLETE PICTORIAL HISTORY

JOHN DEVANEY AND BURT GOLDBLATT

RAND McNALLY & COMPANY

Chicago · New York · San Francisco

Acknowledgments

A number of people were extremely helpful to the authors in preparing this book. We thank Clarence Campbell, President of the National Hockey League, Vice-President Don Ruck, and Public Relations Director Bob Casey, who gave us every cooperation. We are also indebted to Lefty Reid, curator of the Hockey Hall of Fame in Toronto, for his advice and background information. New York Ranger Public Relations Director John Halligan, assisted by his wife, Janet, provided us with a great deal of valuable material from their files. Dave Barbour of Molson's Brewery was most kind, and we wish to thank Molson's for loaning us motion picture film of a number of the playoffs. Helping us to cover recent Stanley Cup finals were Philadelphia Public Relations Director Joe Kadlec and Boston Public Relations Director Herb Ralby. The always sympathetic Pete Sansone of United Press International was invaluable in providing photos, as was Fred Canty at Wide World. The authors owe special thanks to Warren Chaisson, who translated the sound tracks of playoff films from French to English. Also extremely helpful were Judy Epstein of the National Hockey League office in New York, Marty Appel of the New York Yankees, and a great many anonymous people at the New York Public Library, the Columbia University Library, and the New York University Elmer Bobst Library. And as with our previous book for Rand McNally, we are again in debt to Mary Chiaro and her staff for their diligence and understanding.

Photo Credits

Jacket photos: front cover, Ron Mrowiec; back cover, National Hockey League; front flap, Clifton Boutelle; back flap, National Hockey League

Detroit (Red Wings) Hockey Club: 157

John Devaney: 268, 272 bl, 277 b

Burt Goldblatt: 2, 6 bl, br, 17, 272 t, br, 273, 274, 275, 276, 277 t

Molson's Brewery: 11, 26, 40 t, 62, 176, 178–179, 181, 194, 196, 197, 200, 202, 203, 205, 212, 214, 215, 218, 220, 221, 223, 230, 232, 233, 234–235, 236, 238, 239, 241, 242, 244, 245, 247, 248, 250, 251, 252, 253, 256, 258–259

New York Rangers: 6 tr, 8, 9, 10, 12, 18, 20, 21, 24, 25, 28, 32, 33, 36, 38, 40 b, 41, 46, 65, 66, 68, 69, 74–75, 80, 84, 86, 91, 94, 95, 96, 97, 103, 108, 109, 115, 120, 122, 124, 125, 126, 128, 132, 133, 134, 145, 151, 162, 163, 175, 187, 193, 199, 217, 229

New York Yankees: 22, 29, 30, 34, 49, 53, 61, 92

Al Ruelle: 70

United Press International: 3, 42, 45, 50, 54, 56–57, 76, 104, 106–107, 116, 138, 139, 142–143, 146, 148–149, 152, 154–155, 158, 160–161, 164, 166–167, 169 b, 170, 172–173, 182, 184–185, 188, 190, 191, 206, 208, 209, 224, 226–227, 262, 265

Wide World: 14, 58, 72–73, 78–79, 82, 88–89, 98, 100–101, 110, 112–113, 118–119, 130–131, 136–137, 140, 169 t, 264

Copyright © 1975 by Rand McNally & Company
All rights reserved
Library of Congress Catalog Card Number: 74-16838
Printed in the United States of America
by Rand McNally & Company

ISBN 0-528-81855-4

Designed by Burt Goldblatt

First printing, 1975

For Sal and Marietta,
who are wild about hockey,
and
In memory of Ruth Goldblatt,
who loved it all . . .

"That Battered Old Mug"

Bobby Orr sat on the stool in the hushed dressing room, glaring at the floor. An inner anger made the muscles around his mouth quiver. A few minutes earlier the Boston Bruins had lost the third game of the 1974 Stanley Cup final to the Philadelphia Flyers. One of the many reporters encircling the half-dressed Orr asked him what had gone wrong with the Bruins, now trailing in the series, two games to one.

"We're not hungry enough," he said in a low growl. "We got to work harder."

Orr glanced upward, then reached out his right hand and held it about three feet above the floor. "There it is," he said. "The big thing, the Cup, there it is for us to win. If you need anything else to get yourself up when the big thing is there . . ."

He looked down again at the floor, no longer able to speak about the big thing, the Stanley Cup, that these other Bruins did not seem hungry enough to win.

Some 40 feet away, in another dressing room at the Philadelphia Spectrum, Flyer goalkeeper Bernie Parent was trying to explain why the underdog Flyers had outplayed the Bruins in the first three games. "Look around this room before a game," he said, "and what do you see? You see 20 guys and not one of them—*not one*— has ever had his name written on the Stanley Cup. That's what gives us something extra . . ."

Every Canadian boy dreams about it from the first time he goes out to play shinny on a pond. He dreams about seeing his name on the Stanley Cup.

 —New York Islander coach Al Arbour, whose name is on the Stanley Cup four times

The Stanley Cup is uniquely Canadian. We have nothing in this country that transcends how the Canadians feel about the Stanley Cup as an ultimate goal—not the Super Bowl, not the World Series, nothing . . .

 —Hockey writer Gerald Eskenazi of the *New York Times* during a telecast of the 1974 Stanley Cup finals

"Hockey, more than any other sport, I think, has placed its emphasis on trophies and cups," says Clarence S. Campbell, president of the National Hockey League. "In baseball or football you call your most valuable player the winner of the MVP award. In hockey we say that our most valuable player is the winner of the Hart Trophy. We say that our leading scorer is the winner of the Art Ross Trophy. In baseball or football a team wins a pennant or a championship. In hockey the NHL team that finishes first wins the Prince of Wales Trophy.

"There is something especially Canadian in the way we put our emphasis on trophies that are named for people. I think we try to connect a concept with an identity, a famous identity. We are not content to say that someone was this year's best goaltender. We say that he is the Vezina winner, identifying him with Georges Vezina, who was the first of the great goaltenders. In hockey, we try to give character to someone or something by identifying them with someone or something that already has character.

"Of course, Lord Stanley did not bring that same sense of identification with greatness to the Stanley Cup that Vezina brought to the Vezina Trophy. Stanley was just another governor-general sent over from England. But as the league has grown, the Stanley Cup has grown in importance. Ever since 1893 the world of hockey has revolved around the Stanley Cup. And the history of pro hockey is the history of the Stanley Cup. I would say that the Cup is the best-known trophy in North American sport today."

Sir Frederick Arthur Stanley, Baron Stanley of Preston, arrived in Ottawa in 1888. He resided at Rideau Hall, where his two sons learned the game of ice hockey on a flooded outdoor rink. The sons helped form a team, the Rideau Rebels, and one year the Rebels played the Ottawa City Club for the championship of Canada (the Rebels lost).

One of the Rideau Rebels was Lord Kilcoursie, an aide to Lord Stanley. After he returned to En-

7

Today's Stanley Cup (far l.) consists of a bowl and descending "collars," or bands, on which the names of winners are engraved. The bands have been widened over the years to hold more names. The bowl is an exact copy of the Cup donated by Lord Stanley (top) in 1893. Bottom: A drinker's view of the Cup, with winners' names engraved inside.

gland, Lord Stanley wrote to Lord Kilcoursie, offering to provide a hockey challenge cup. The letter was perhaps prompted by something he had seen in the eyes of his sons after the loss of that game for the championship of Canada. Whatever actually did prompt the suggestion, the idea was expressed this way in Lord Stanley's letter, which Lord Kilcoursie read on March 18, 1892, at a banquet for the Ottawa Hockey Club:

"I have for some time been thinking it would be a good thing if there were a challenge cup which could be held from year to year by the leading hockey club in Canada. There does not appear to be any outward visible sign of the championship at present. Considering the interest that hockey matches now elicit and the importance of having the games fairly played under generally recognized rules, I am willing to give a cup that should be annually held by the winning club . . ."

The offer was accepted. The Cup was made by a London silversmith (at a cost of about $50) and packed off to Canada. Two trustees were named to pick the teams that would challenge each year for the Cup. After the 1893 season the trustees awarded the Cup to the Montreal Amateur Athletic Association team, which had finished first in the Amateur Hockey Association. That year there was no playoff for the Cup, but there has been a playoff every year since.

The 1894 AHA season ended with four teams tied for first. Three of these chose to play off for the league title—and the silver Cup from England that went with the title. The first Stanley Cup playoff game was held on St. Patrick's Day night, 1894, at the rink of the Montreal Victorias, who met the Montreal AAA team. The AAAs won, 3-2, then beat the Ottawa Capitals, 3-1, to retain the league championship—and Lord Stanley's Cup.

Through the first decade of the new century, the Cup's trustees considered challenges for the trophy from amateur and not-so-amateur teams from all over Canada. To win that ultimate piece of silver—the Cup—newly rich gold and silver miners of the north stocked their teams with the best players they could lure, paying unheard-of salaries: as much as $4,000 a season. Out of this frenzied competition for the Cup emerged the first great hockey pros—Frank and Lester Patrick, Art Ross, Fred ("Cyclone") Taylor, Edouard

The two stars of the Ottawa Senators, winners of the Cup in 1909 and 1911: Percy LeSueur (above), a goaltender who used the same stick for five straight seasons, and Fred ("Cyclone") Taylor. Photo of Taylor may have been taken while he was playing for the Vancouver Millionaires, who won the Cup with him in 1915.

8

("Newsy") Lalonde, Georges Vezina. They jumped from one "amateur" team to another. In 1906 Lester Patrick came from the west coast to play for the Montreal Wanderers in a two-game challenge round for the Cup against the Ottawa Silver Seven, which had won the trophy an unprecedented three years in a row.

The winning team would be decided by the total number of goals scored in the two games. Lester Patrick's Wanderers won the first game, 9-1, but Ottawa came back to take the lead in the second 9-0. Then in the closing minutes Patrick slammed in two goals that won the series and the Cup.

By 1910 some of the mining titans had formed an unabashedly pro league—the National Hockey Association. One of the teams in the league was Les Canadiens of Montreal, who won the Cup in 1916, the first Cup for a team that some 60 years later would have won it more often than any other team.

After 1912 the trustees limited the challenging teams to the champion of the NHA and the champion of some other pro league. (Amateur teams competed for the Allan Cup.) In 1914 the NHA and the Pacific Coast Hockey Association, organized by the Patrick brothers, agreed to annual playoffs between their two champions. In 1917 the NHA reorganized as the National Hockey League, adding one new team—the Toronto Arenas (later the Maple Leafs)—winners of the Cup more often than any team except the Canadiens.

In the 1920s the NHL flourished. There were now two leagues on the west coast, and for a while the Cup winner was decided by a series among the three league champions. But neither west coast league did well, finally merging into one, the Western Hockey League, owned by the Patricks.

For the 1925–26 season the NHL had added three U.S. franchises: the Boston Bruins, Pittsburgh Pirates, and New York Americans. The west coast league meanwhile continued having financial problems. Intent on further expansion, the NHL needed experienced players, and in 1926 it purchased the Western Hockey League with all its players for $250,000. Boston got Eddie Shore, known as the Edmonton Express, and several others; the rest were parceled out

9

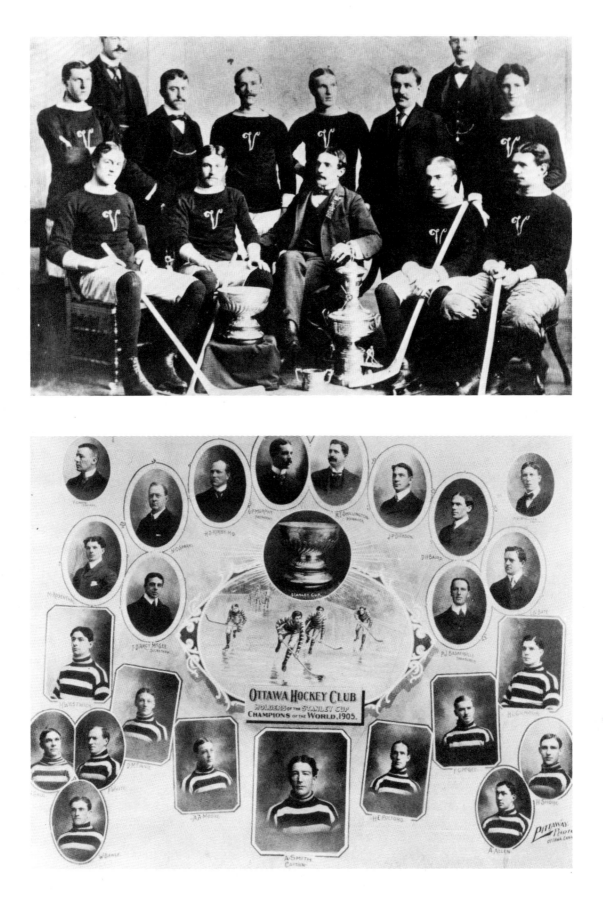

Above: The 1896 Montreal Victorias pose behind the Cup, another trophy on the right. They had won the Cup in 1895 and defended it successfully in 1897 and 1898. Bottom: Photos of the 1905 Ottawa Silver Seven players circle the Cup that they had also won in 1903 and 1904.

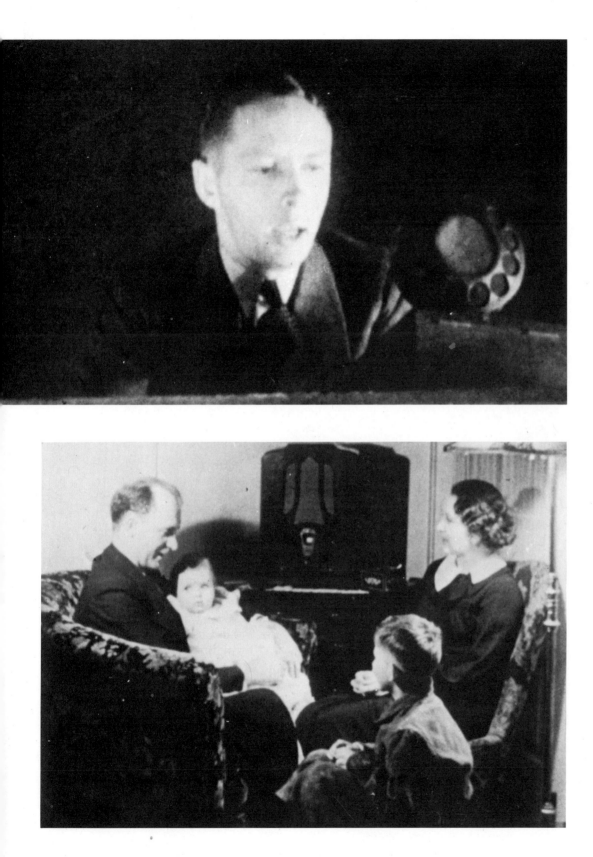

The Voice of Hockey in Canada for
decades, Foster Hewitt (top) broadcasts
a Cup game. A Canadian family (bottom) is
one of millions who listened to Foster
Hewitt Hockey Night broadcasts, some
Canadians first hearing of the Cup
while babes in arms.

11

Georges Vezina: The first of the great
goaltenders, he stood in goal for the 1916
Canadiens—the first Flying Frenchmen
to win the Cup.

among the other teams, including three new ones: the Chicago Black Hawks, Detroit Cougars (later the Red Wings), and New York Rangers. Beginning with the 1926–27 season, the Cup—already being called "that battered old mug" in U.S. newspapers—has been in the sole possession of the NHL, awarded to the NHL team that won a playoff with other NHL teams.

Today's Cup is not the Cup that Lord Stanley donated more than 80 years ago. On Lord Stanley's Cup the names of the first winners were inscribed on the outside and inside of the bowl. When there was no more room on the bowl, the names were engraved on silver bands, or "collars," added one under another to form a stovepipe-like base. Pushed upward by band after band, the Cup rose almost three feet in height. By 1956 the base had been broadened to allow for the addition of many more teams.

Lord Stanley's Cup was hoisted high by winners until the late 1960s, when metallurgists advised the league that in time the Cup would become so brittle it could shatter if dropped during a clubhouse celebration. The bowl was taken off the base in 1967, and by 1970 a Montreal silversmith had finished creating a duplicate of the bowl so painstakingly exact that it includes the thinnest of scratches on the side of the Cup and the teeth marks on its rim made by exuberant sippers.

Lord Stanley's original Cup, and the bands that were underneath it, are now on display at the Hockey Hall of Fame in Toronto. "One day," says Lefty Reid, the Hall's curator, "we may reassemble the Cup, mounting it above its bands again, but it will always have to be kept in a showcase."

For the 1926–27 season the ten NHL teams divided into two divisions. In the American Division were the Boston Bruins, Chicago Black Hawks, Detroit Cougars, New York Rangers, and Pittsburgh Pirates. In the not-quite-accurately named Canadian Division were the Ottawa Senators, Montreal Canadiens, Montreal Maroons, New York Americans, and Toronto St. Pats (renamed the Maple Leafs midway through the season). The teams would play a 44-game schedule, double the number of games played by the teams when the league was organized in 1917 (all team records in this book, incidentally, date back to 1917 unless stated otherwise). Recalling Lester Patrick's dictum—"playoffs are the lifeblood of hockey"—the NHL Board of Governors decided that even 44 games were not enough to choose the teams that would play off for the Cup. Six of the league's ten teams would go into the playoffs, the two division champions determined in preliminary rounds that were won by the team scoring the most goals in a two-game series. The two division champions then went at each other in a best-of-five series for the Cup.

That system, with slight variations, continued until 1939. By then hard times had thinned the league to seven clubs, which were grouped into one division. With every team needing infusions of that lifeblood, six of the seven teams were still eligible for the playoffs after five months of battling. Tickets for the playoffs sold quickly even in depression days, the sales hyped by a tag hung onto the playoffs by newspapers—"The World Series of Hockey."

Luckily for the reputation of the Cup and the league, these "World Series" never ended with a sixth-place team winning the Cup. After 1942, with only six teams left in the league, the top four played off for the Cup. That playoff system continued until 1967–68, when the league expanded to 12 teams. Again the league split into two divisions—East and West. To win the Cup a team had to labor through three best-of-seven rounds.

By the 1974–75 season, with 18 teams divided among four divisions, a team might have to struggle through four rounds and as many as 24 games to win the Cup—more games than the first NHL teams played in a season. After an 80-game schedule, 12 of 18 teams are eligible to compete for "that battered old mug." Despite crowded arenas during the season, NHL owners —burdened by soaring player salaries—need that playoff lifeblood perhaps as much now as they did when the first all-NHL playoffs began late in March of 1927 . . . . .

Stanley Cup Winners, 1893–1926

1893—Montreal AAA	1904—Ottawa Silver Seven	1915—Vancouver Millionaires
1894—Montreal AAA	1905—Ottawa Silver Seven	1916—Montreal Canadiens
1895—Montreal Victorias	1906—Montreal Wanderers	1917—Seattle Metropolitans
1896—Winnipeg Victorias (February)	1907—Kenora Thistles (January)	1918—Toronto Arenas*
1896—Montreal Victorias (December)	1907—Montreal Wanderers (March)	1919—No winner**
1897—Montreal Victorias	1908—Montreal Wanderers	1920—Ottawa Senators
1898—Montreal Victorias	1909—Ottawa Senators	1921—Ottawa Senators
1899—Montreal Shamrocks	1910—Montreal Wanderers	1922—Toronto St. Pats*
1900—Montreal Shamrocks	1911—Ottawa Senators	1923—Ottawa Senators
1901—Winnipeg Victorias	1912—Quebec Bulldogs	1924—Montreal Canadiens
1902—Montreal AAA	1913—Quebec Bulldogs	1925—Victoria Cougars
1903—Ottawa Silver Seven	1914—Toronto Blueshirts	1926—Montreal Maroons

* Now the Maple Leafs
** Called off during series between Seattle Metropolitans and Montreal Canadiens because of flu epidemic

BOSTON BRUINS
OTTAWA SENATORS —1927

"Kill 'em," Shouted the Boston Fans, Looking for Eddie Shore to Oblige

Only once had a U.S. team won the Cup, the Seattle Metropolitans beating the Montreal Canadiens in the 1917 final. As the new playoff system began in the reorganized National Hockey League, Canadian fans had reason to worry that the Cup would cross the border again, and this international rivalry added an extra dash of excitement to the playoffs. The New York Rangers and Boston Bruins, finishing first and second in the new American Division, were loaded with former western stars. New York's Bill Cook led the league in scoring, with 33 goals in 44 games; for the Bruins that dreadnaught on skates, Eddie Shore, the Edmonton Express, bowled over opponents with manic dashes up and down the ice.

In the American Division playoffs the second-place Bruins beat the third-place Chicago Black Hawks, 6-1, in the first game of their quarter-final series, then tied the Hawks, 4-4, to win the series, 10 goals to 5. The Bruins took on the first-place Rangers, the total goals for two games again determining the winner. On a Saturday night in Boston some 9,000 fans packed the old Arena. They left disappointed after seeing a cautious 0-0 tie game, each player knowing a trip to the Stanley Cup final was at stake. A small knot of Bruin fans entrained for New York with the team for the game the next night at Madison Square Garden. The Garden lobby, wrote one reporter, "looked like a green lawn" with crisp $100 bills being bandied between Bruin and Ranger supporters. Before a filled Garden the Bruins won, 3-1, to take the series, 3 goals to 1, and go on to

the final. One writer estimated that $50,000 left Penn Station with the Bruin fans.

Up north in the Canadian Division the second-place Montreal Canadiens met the third-place Montreal Maroons. The teams' rivalry reflected the linguistic split within the country. The Maroons were popular among English-speaking Montrealers, the Canadiens ("The Flying Frenchmen") the favorite among French-speaking fans. Amid bilingual cheering by some 11,000 enthusiasts, the first game was another cautious affair and ended in a 1-1 tie. In overtime of the second game the Canadiens' Howie Morenz, the famous Stratford Streak, flailed the rubber by veteran goaltender Clint Benedict for a 1-0 victory that won the quarterfinal series for the Flying Frenchmen, 2 goals to 1.

Ottawa's Senators had finished first in the Canadian Division. In goal for Ottawa was slender, somber Alex Connell. He shut out Montreal in the first game, 4-0, then held the Canadiens to a 1-1 tie in the second, Ottawa winning 5 goals to 1 to go into its seventh final since 1909.

The final, a best-of-five affair, matched Boston power against Ottawa defense. For the first two games, to be played at Boston, some 30,000 fans applied for tickets to an Arena that held only 9,000. Before the games a band played "Tessie," a victory song that had stirred Boston baseball fans since the 1903 World Series, and the strains of "Tessie" added to an atmosphere that reminded visiting journalists of a World Series. Writers called the final "the World Series of Hockey,"

Eddie Shore stands forbiddingly before the nets. The combative Edmonton Express was nearly as well known as football's Red Grange and baseball's Babe Ruth. "There are people," said one writer, "who have never seen a hockey game who know who Eddie Shore is."

15

and remarked on the fervor of the "crazed" Boston fans, who shouted "kill 'em" when the Senators skated onto the ice.

Again seemingly awed by the importance of each game in the short playoffs, both teams played close-to-the-cage hockey. Neither scored in three periods of regulation play and two sudden-death overtime periods. Near the end of the second overtime, Frank Calder, the league president, decided that the ice was too rough to continue play, and he called the game a tie. To silence critics who might claim the teams tied on purpose to sell tickets for a sixth game, Calder ruled that the series could go no more than five games. The team with the best record, based on two points for a victory and one point for a tie, would be awarded the Stanley Cup.

Both teams opened up their attacks in the second game, Eddie Shore in so violent a manner that he drew five penalties for various assaults. That didn't help the Bruins, who lost, 3-1.

In Ottawa, fans waited in lines at six in the morning for tickets. An estimated 10,000 spectators filled the Auditorium, the crowd called a record for a hockey game in Canada.

Whipped on by the enthusiasm of the crowd, the two teams sailed into each other, Boston scoring in the first period, Ottawa in the second. Tied 1-1, the game went into overtime, the two squads, each with only ten skaters, showing their exhaustion. Shots were longer and longer, feebler and feebler. Again called because of rough ice, the game was ruled a 1-1 tie, each team gaining a point. Ottawa now led, 4 points to 2. If Ottawa won the fourth game it would clinch the Cup, 6 points to 2.

Ottawa won the game handily, 3-1. At the end of the game Boston's Bill Coutu punched referee Jerry Laflamme. Other Bruins piled onto Laflamme. Newspapers called the attack "disgraceful." Again acting decisively to erase any possible blemish on the rebuilt league and its playoffs, Calder expelled Coutu from the league for the rest of his life.

Ottawa's Senators, the oldest team in Stanley Cup competition, had won it a sixth time, more often than any other team. This Cup would be their last, the Senators extinct eight years later, but the Senators' record of six Cups would stand in the record book until 1948 when Toronto won its seventh.

Harry Oliver:
"Hooley just took a notion..."

After leading the Calgary Tigers of the west coast league in scoring for five years, forward Harry Oliver came to the Bruins in 1927. Now living in Winnipeg, he recalled the first "modern" Stanley Cup final.

It was near the end of that last game and I was handling the puck and [Ottawa's] Hooley Smith clobbered me. I never saw him coming and I never knew what hit me until much later. He hit me across the nose and forehead with a stick or elbow. I went down and I didn't come to until they'd dragged me to the boards. They helped me into the dressing room. There were two minutes to go. So I missed the ruckus when some of our boys got after the officials at the end. Our boys took it that the officials, especially Laflamme, had made some raw decisions against us. But I wasn't there. I was hors de combat, *as they say, which was just as well, because our Billy Coutu never did come back to the National Hockey League for hitting Laflamme.*

But why Smith clobbered me, I'll never know. We didn't have any fuss before that. He was supposed to have taken me for Eddie Shore, but that was hardly creditable. Shore was a rugged player and I was more of a skater than a hitter. Hooley just took a notion, I guess. No, I never asked him.

16

FIRST GAME (April 7, at Boston)
  Senators 0, Bruins 0

FIRST PERIOD
  No scoring
SECOND PERIOD
  No scoring
THIRD PERIOD
  No scoring
FIRST OVERTIME
  No scoring
SECOND OVERTIME
  No scoring; game called with one minute left of overtime; ice too rough to continue

SECOND GAME (April 9, at Boston)
  Senators 3, Bruins 1

FIRST PERIOD
  Ottawa—Clancy 6:37
  Ottawa—Finnigan 11:23
SECOND PERIOD
  No scoring
THIRD PERIOD
  Boston—Oliver 16:45
  Ottawa—Denneny 19:55

THIRD GAME (April 11, at Ottawa)
  Senators 1, Bruins 1

FIRST PERIOD
  Boston—Herberts 7:24
SECOND PERIOD
  Ottawa—Denneny 15:50
THIRD PERIOD
  No scoring
OVERTIME
  No scoring; game called; rough ice

FOURTH GAME (April 13, at Ottawa)
  Senators 3, Bruins 1

FIRST PERIOD
  No scoring
SECOND PERIOD
  Ottawa—Finnigan 5:10
  Ottawa—Denneny 7:55
THIRD PERIOD
  Ottawa—Denneny 11:55
  Boston—Oliver 16:45

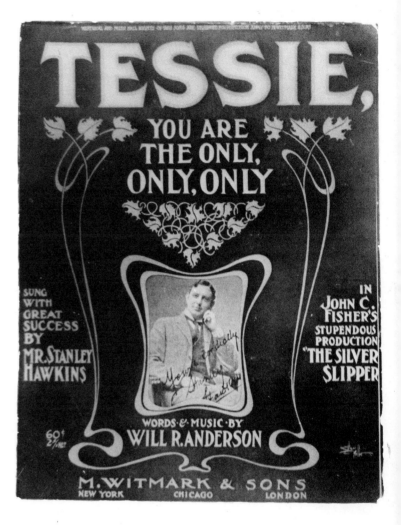

Cover of the music sheet for "Tessie," the rallying song of Boston fans at World Series going all the way back to 1903. In playing the song, bands gave the Cup final a Series flavor.

MONTREAL MAROONS
NEW YORK RANGERS
1928

To the Rescue: The Silver Fox and Red Light Miller

Whenever Stanley Cup tales are told, there is nearly always the one about how, at the age of 45, the Rangers' Silver Fox, Lester Patrick, stepped into the goalie's cage and shut out the Montreal Maroons to win the Cup. Time and too many retellings have blurred the truth of the affair unnecessarily; the hard truth of this story contains as much drama as any piece of embroidered fiction.

This Ranger team, coached by the Silver Fox, possessed some high and mighty scorers. Its top line—center Frank Boucher and wingers Bill and Frederick ("Bun") Cook—ranked among the league's top ten scorers. Clarence ("Taffy") Abel and Ivan ("Ching") Johnson (at 6-foot-2 he was a mountain alongside the bantam-sized hockey players of the time) stood rocklike on defense in front of goaltender Lorne Chabot. New York came in second behind Boston in the American Division. Outscoring third-place Pittsburgh 6 goals to 4 in the opening two-game round, the Rangers surprised the Bruins, tying the first game, 1-1, and winning the second, 4-1, to go into the final.

In the Canadian Division the Canadiens breezed home first, with Howie Morenz and Aurel Joliat finishing one-two in league scoring, and George Hainsworth, the league's stingiest goaltender, yielding only a goal a game. But the second-place Maroons, after beating third-place Ottawa, 3 goals to 1, tied the Canadiens in the first game, then won the second, 1-0, for a place in the final against New York.

The Rangers had to pack up their sticks and leave Madison Square Garden, displaced by the circus. Although they could have played their "home" games on Boston or Detroit ice, the Rangers chose Montreal's spacious Forum, its large rink giving their speedy skaters room to maneuver.

The Maroons won the first game of the best-of-five series. In the second period of the second game, Montreal's Nels Stewart slugged a liner that struck Lorne Chabot in the eye. "He dropped like a man hit by a firing squad," wrote a New York reporter. Chabot was taken to a hospital, where his vision was saved. Back at the rink Lester Patrick was looking for a goaltender.

Ottawa goaltender Alex Connell, sitting in the stands, told Patrick he would step in for Chabot. This was a not-unusual custom of the time, borrowing another team's goalie in an emergency, and Patrick sent a *pro forma* note across the ice to the Maroons' coach, Eddie Gerard, asking for permission to use Connell. The reply came back as cold as the ice: No. The Maroons insisted that the Rangers adhere strictly to a league rule which allowed only players under contract to sub for an injured player.

An angry Patrick donned Chabot's sweaty uniform and pads and strode onto the ice, the Montreal crowd applauding when they saw his silvery

The Silver Fox, Lester Patrick, shows how he guarded the New York cage against the Maroons. Red Light Miller, who succeeded Patrick in goal, refused to go to New York for a victory party. "Lorne Chabot and I are pals," he said. "I don't want to take any glory from him."

head. A former defenseman, he hadn't played in two years, but he staved off shot after shot, mostly by scrambling crablike on his hands and knees. Early in the third period Bill Cook whipped the puck by Clint Benedict to put New York ahead, 1-0. But the Silver Fox didn't get his shutout, Nels Stewart lifting the puck over him to tie the game 1-1. In overtime Frank Boucher poked a puck by Benedict to win the game, 2-1, and the Rangers mobbed the Silver Fox. But the Silver Fox quickly went back to retirement, signing another goalkeeper as soon as he caught his breath.

He signed Joe Miller, a former New York American goalie best known in the Garden as Red Light Miller; he got the nickname because the red light, signaling a goal, flashed so often when he played. The red light flashed twice above Joe in the third game, won 2-0 by the Maroons, who now led, two games to one. But Red Light shut out the Maroons in the fourth game to even the series at two victories apiece. In the fifth and final game Frank Boucher, who scored four of the five New York goals in the series, socked in two goals while Miller kept the red light dark until the closing minutes. At the bell the Rangers were 2-1 winners and owners of the Cup in only their second year of competition. The Cup's new home was a showcase in the lobby of Madison Square Garden, New York City, USA.

Murray Murdoch:
"Lester said, 'I will, by God, I will' "

An original Ranger, joining the team when it was formed in 1927, forward Murray Murdoch later coached the Yale hockey team and now lives in Connecticut. He recalled the moments after Chabot's injury.

We were all standing around trying to decide what to do. Lester was looking around at us to see who could play goal, and I said to him, "Not me, Lester, not me." The Maroons' coach sent over a note saying, "If you need a goalkeeper, why the hell doesn't Lester play?" Lester said, "I will, by God, I will." He put on the pads and out he went. Well, we made sure they didn't get too close to him. We went out to the blue line and made them shoot from way out. The officials were kind to us; we may have held [the Maroons] a

little bit to keep them out. Anyway, Lester stayed low on the ice, on his hands and knees, and they got only that one by him, and after Boucher's goal, we really did mob him.

We were very close to Lester. In those days there was an NHL general manager, and if you got 31 points in a season and a winger on another team got 32, he wanted to get that winger and get rid of you. Not Lester. He always told us, "Just win more games than you lose and we'll get into the playoffs. That's all I ask: win more than you lose." But we knew if we ever lost more than we won, we'd be out of jobs as Rangers. I tell you, if we lost in Toronto on a Saturday night and the next night we were playing in Detroit, those Red Wings would catch hell.

We liked to play jokes on Lester. One night we got on the train as it left Toronto and sneaked back to the observation car and stayed there while Lester was looking all over the sleeping car for us. After a couple of hours we finally showed up. He was walking up and down. All he said was, "Boys, I sure am glad to see you."

Frank Boucher (opposite page) led the New York scoring and later became a Ranger coach. Above: Nels Stewart, who put in two of the Maroons' six goals. Photo may have been taken of young Nels as a minor leaguer with Cleveland.

FIRST GAME (April 5, at Montreal)
Maroons 2, Rangers 0

FIRST PERIOD
No scoring
SECOND PERIOD
Montreal—Dutton........................10:50
THIRD PERIOD
Montreal—Phillips........................ 7:50

SECOND GAME (April 7, at Montreal)
Rangers 2, Maroons 1

FIRST PERIOD
No scoring
SECOND PERIOD
No scoring
THIRD PERIOD
New York—Bill Cook..................... 0:20
Montreal—Stewart........................14:20
OVERTIME
New York—Boucher...................... 7:05

THIRD GAME (April 10, at Montreal)
Maroons 2, Rangers 0

FIRST PERIOD
No scoring
SECOND PERIOD
Montreal—Stewart........................ 9:00
THIRD PERIOD
Montreal—Siebert........................17:20

FOURTH GAME (April 12, at Montreal)
Rangers 1, Maroons 0

FIRST PERIOD
No scoring
SECOND PERIOD
New York—Boucher...................... 6:15
THIRD PERIOD
No scoring

FIFTH GAME (April 14, at Montreal)
Rangers 2, Maroons 1

FIRST PERIOD
New York—Boucher.......................17:05
SECOND PERIOD
No scoring
THIRD PERIOD
New York—Boucher.......................15:15
Montreal—Phillips........................17:50

BOSTON BRUINS
NEW YORK RANGERS 1929

Tiny Has a Lax Moment,
New York Minutes of Joy

Grumbling was heard around the league after the 1928 playoffs when both first-place teams—Boston in the American Division and Montreal's Canadiens in the Canadian Division—were erased from the playoffs before the final round. It seemed both unfair and illogical that a team should finish first after 44 games and then be eliminated in two or three games by a team that finished lower in the standings. The league devised a new playoff system: The first-place teams of each division would meet in a best-of-five series, the winner going to the final to meet the team that survived the brawling among the lower-placed teams. Thus one of the first-place teams was certain to be in the final, which was changed from a best-of-five to a best-of-three series.

The Canadiens ("The Flying Frenchmen") finished first again in the Canadian Division, losing only one game of their final 25. Boston finished first in the American Division. Montreal was favored over Boston, primarily because of the high scoring of Howie Morenz and Aurel Joliat and the goaltending of George Hainsworth, who rang up 22 shutouts in 44 games. But Boston's rookie goaltender, Cecil ("Tiny") Thompson, twice shut out the Flying Frenchmen and Boston won three straight games to go into the final.

In the two-game, total-goal series between the second-place teams of each division, the light, speedy Rangers squeaked by their Manhattan rivals, the star-spangled-uniformed Americans, with a scoreless tie in the first game and a 1-0 victory in the second. The Canadian Division's third-

place Toronto Maple Leafs eradicated the American Division's third-place club, Detroit (then called the Cougars), 7 goals to 2. In the semifinal, a best-of-three affair between the Maple Leafs and the Rangers, the Rangers won 1-0 and 2-1, going on to the final to defend the Cup they had won a year earlier.

It was the first all-U.S. final. The Bruins were favorites after having walloped the Rangers five of six times during the season. The Bruins were showing a new line—Ralph ("Cooney") Weiland at center and Aubrey ("Dit") Clapper and Norman ("Dutch") Gainor on the wings. The line would later become famous as the Dynamite Line. The rambunctious Eddie Shore was charging out of his end often enough to score 12 goals and 7 assists, the 12th highest point total in the league. The Bruins led the league in scoring, with 89 goals in 44 games, and Tiny Thompson ranked second among the league's goaltenders, allowing little more than a goal per game.

The Rangers showed up with much the same crew that had won the Cup a year earlier, except that Johnny Roach, something of a playboy, had replaced Lorne Chabot in goal. No line slithered the puck through defenses with more deftness than the one centered by Frank Boucher with the Cook brothers, Bill and Frederick ("Bun"), on the wings. As good a scoring club as this was, it backchecked with efficiency: in four playoff games so far, the Rangers had given up only one goal.

Some 18,000 enthusiasts filled the new Boston Garden for the first game. Bruin fans blared

The 1928–29 Bruins. Standing (l. to r.): Cooney Weiland, Harry Oliver, Eric Pettinger, Dit Clapper, Lloyd Klein, Percival ("Perk") Galbraith, Eddie Rodden, and Redvers Green. Seated: Tiny Thompson, Frank Fredrickson, Eddie Shore, Lionel Hitchman, Cy Denneny, Dutch Gainor, and Hal Winkler, who retired before the season began. Missing are Duncan ("Mickey") MacKay, Bill Carson, and manager-coach Art Ross.

trumpets when Dit Clapper batted in his own rebound to put Boston ahead, 1-0, and they snowed
paper onto the ice five minutes later when Dutch
Gainor banged in another. The Rangers couldn't
put anything by Tiny Thompson, and the Bruins
were 2-0 victors.

The next night about 15,000 fans streamed into
Madison Square Garden to see the first Stanley
Cup final in the big city. Midway through the third
period the Bruins led 1-0. The Rangers' Melville
("Butch") Keeling ripped off a long shot that
seemed to catch Tiny Thompson at a lax moment.
The puck blew by him, the game was tied 1-1, and
suddenly aroused Ranger fans were fluttering rolls
of paper from the balconies.

Their joy didn't last long. The Bruins' Harry
Oliver crossed into Ranger territory with the puck
and sucked the Ranger defense toward him. He
shuttled the puck to Bill Carson, who veered in on
Roach's open side. Carson swatted at the puck before Roach could swivel to face him, and the puck
blurred past Roach's hip and into the cage for the
goal that won the game, 2-1, and Boston's first
Stanley Cup.

Harry Oliver:
Wingo!

The hero of the 2-1 victory over the Rangers that
brought the Stanley Cup to Boston for the first
time was forward Harry Oliver. At his home in
Winnipeg he recalled the winning goal.

*I was going down the right side. I saw Bill Car-
son loose on the left side. I passed him the puck
and wingo! It was in on the left side. Today they
make a big fuss about a goal, hugging each other
. . . jumping up and down. We just gave a tap on
the shoulder, nice going, and that was all. Today
they're more emotional after a goal.*

*The Cup didn't have all those bands at the bot-
tom. It had just one or two bands. We had a team
dinner in Boston the next night and went home.
The Bruins gave us each a bonus of five hundred
dollars in twenty-dollar gold pieces. And the
Stanley Cup playoff money was around a thousand
dollars . . .*

FIRST GAME (March 28, at Boston)
  Bruins 2, Rangers 0
FIRST PERIOD
  No scoring
SECOND PERIOD
  Boston—Clapper 5:13
  Boston—Gainor 10:48
THIRD PERIOD
  No scoring

SECOND GAME (March 29, at New York)
  Bruins 2, Rangers 1
FIRST PERIOD
  No scoring
SECOND PERIOD
  Boston—Oliver 14:01
THIRD PERIOD
  New York—Keeling 6:48
  Boston—Carson (Oliver) 18:02

Cooney Weiland (opposite page), the
center of the Bruins' Dynamite Line, met
the Rangers' top line of Bill Cook,
Frank Boucher, and Bun Cook (above).
All four were shut out.

BOSTON BRUINS
MONTREAL CANADIENS 1930

The Flying Frenchmen
Play with Dynamite

In the average 1928–29 NHL game, three goals were scored. Some U.S. audiences thought the game was dull; "not enough runs" was a common complaint among fans fascinated by Babe Ruth's home runs and a climbing Dow Jones average. The NHL decided to make the scoreboards whir faster in the 1929–30 season. It passed a rule that, in effect, erased the off-side rule. Now a player could cross the blue line into the other team's zone before the puck. He could "hang" near the opposing cage, then take a pass from a teammate and stuff the puck by the goalkeeper before a defenseman could knock him away.

Average goals per game soared to seven. A noted "hanger," Boston's Ralph ("Cooney") Weiland, was rapping in a goal a game. To stop runaway scores, the NHL revised the rule: The puck had to precede the player into the attacking zone; otherwise he was off-side. But Cooney Weiland had gained enough of a head start to lead the league in scoring, with an unheard-of total of 43 goals in 44 games, almost double the 22 goals that had led the league the previous season and a rate per game that has never been equaled.

Boston's Dynamite Line—Weiland, Aubrey ("Dit") Clapper, and Norman ("Dutch") Gainor

—scored 102 of the Bruins' league-leading total of 179 goals. With a clenched-fist defense—Cecil ("Tiny") Thompson in goal and the rambunctious Eddie Shore, the Edmonton Express, up front—the Bruins finished with a 38-5-1 record, 30 points ahead of second-place Chicago.

The Montreal Maroons finished first in the Canadian Division, Montreal's big S Line—Albert ("Babe") Siebert, Nels Stewart, and Reginald ("Hooley") Smith—bulling its way through defenses to cannonade at goalkeepers from short range. But in the best-of-five first-place playoff with the Bruins, the S Line came in hobbled by injuries and the Bruins won, three games to one.

In the second-place playoffs the Canadiens beat the Black Hawks, 1-0, in the first game of the two-game, total-goal series, but were losing the second game, 2-1, at the end of regulation time. With the series tied at two goals apiece, the game stretched into three overtimes before Howie Morenz, the Stratford Streak, drove on Chicago goalkeeper Chuck Gardiner and slammed the puck by him for the goal that won the series, 3 goals to 2.

In the opening game of the third-place playoff, the Rangers tied Ottawa 1-1, then won the second game, 5-2, to take on the Canadiens in the best-

The Canadiens' magic duo, Howie Morenz (l.) and Aurel Joliat, wrap gloves around each other's shoulders. The fiery, 140-pound Joliat played left wing with Morenz at center. In 1937, while recuperating in a hospital with a broken leg, Morenz died of a heart attack. He was 35.

of-three semifinal. In the first game the two teams battled through what was then a record 68 minutes of overtime before Montreal substitute Gus Rivers slugged the puck by Ranger goalkeeper Johnny Roach for a 2-1 victory. The Canadiens won the second game, 2-0, to enter the first final for the Flying Frenchmen since they last won the Cup in 1924.

The defending-champion Bruins, with their Dynamite Line and tight defense, were solid favorites against a Canadien team that had won only 21 games during the season while losing or tying 23. In the entire season the Bruins had never lost two games in a row. But Boston appeared lethargic in the first game of the best-of-three contest, and Eddie Shore was having trouble bumping the Stratford Streak out of the way. "I was as fast as any man in hockey except Morenz," Shore said years later. "He was that little extra bit faster. I could never get even with him to give him a good check." The Flying Frenchmen dazzled the Bruins in the first game, winning 3-0, and Morenz put in the winning goal in Montreal's 4-3 triumph in the second game. It was the Canadiens' third Cup since 1916, the second and next to last of the Morenz Era.

Cooney Weiland as a youth: "Clapper and I would bust in...taking a chance because we left the wings open."

Cooney Weiland:
But Morenz was no Bobby Orr

Ralph ("Cooney") Weiland joined the Bruins in 1929 and later coached them and the Harvard University hockey team. Living in Wayland, Massachusetts, he recalled the upset of a Bruin team that had lost only five games during the season.

It was a terrific shock to all of us. It seemed we got most of the penalties, especially in the second game. The Bruins always felt they were outmaneuvered. Imagine, of 44 games, losing only five at home and away. And there were no soft touches in those days. Whether we were overconfident or not, I don't know, but Morenz was a great player, unquestionably the fastest skater of his time, no doubt about it. I usually tried to cut him off at his net, before he got started. If he got to center ice without being checked, he'd fly right by you. And he had a terrific shot. With his speed, naturally, it added momentum to his shot. But you can't compare him to Bobby Orr. Morenz wasn't a stop and start fellow or as good a stick-handler as Orr is.

That was the year I led the league. You could cross the blue line ahead of the puck, but the guy carrying the puck had to carry it across the blue line. He couldn't pass it across to you. So you needed a great stick-handler to stick-handle the puck in, and our Dutch Gainor was an amazing stick-handler. Clapper and I would bust in, across the line, taking a chance because we left the wings open, but Gainor would manage to hold onto the puck and get it across the line, then pass it to us.

You can see what the new rule did to the defensemen. They didn't know whether to go for the puck-handler or cover the wingmen busting in, and they were all confused.

But too many guys abused the rule. Some never came out of the zone. They stayed there, just like basket-hangers in basketball, exactly. And halfway through the season they cut out the rule and went back to the old way. But I scored as many goals in the last half of the season as I did when it was in effect. I thought it was a good rule. It sure opened up the game.

FIRST GAME (April 1, at Boston)
Canadiens 3, Bruins 0
FIRST PERIOD
No scoring
SECOND PERIOD
Montreal—Leduc........................ 8:43
Montreal—S. Mantha (Joliat)............12:00
THIRD PERIOD
Montreal—Lepine (Leduc).................15:27

SECOND GAME (April 3, at Montreal)
Canadiens 4, Bruins 3
FIRST PERIOD
Montreal—McCaffrey (Lepine).............. 9:08
Montreal—Wasnie (Burke)..................16:46
SECOND PERIOD
Montreal—S. Mantha (Wasnie).............10:05
Boston—Shore.........................16:50
Montreal—Morenz (Leduc).................17:55
THIRD PERIOD
Boston—Galbraith (Oliver)................. 5:55
Boston—Clapper (Weiland)................ 8:00

The 1930 Cup winners. Standing (l. to r.):
Gus Rivers, Gerry Carson, Sylvio Mantha,
Marty Burke, coach Cecil Hart, Albert
Leduc, Nick Wasnie, Armand Mondou, Bert
McCaffrey. Seated: Alfred Lepine, Georges
Mantha, George Hainsworth, Aurel Joliat,
Howie Morenz, and Wildor Larochelle.

CHICAGO BLACK HAWKS
MONTREAL CANADIENS —1931

After a Long, Long Wait, Here Comes Howie

Trailing 1-0 in the closing minutes of a 1931 play-off game with the Canadiens, Bruin manager Art Ross astonished the spectators by taking out his goaltender and sending six skaters flying down the ice, leaving the cage empty. No one had ever attempted this dicey maneuver before in big league hockey. It didn't work for Ross as it hasn't worked for countless coaches since, the Canadiens fending off the Bruins' last-gasp assault. But the idea was so intriguing that other coaches were employing it by 1932—and finding that every once in a while those six skaters could overwhelm a defense and score the goal that turned a galling one-goal defeat into a tie.

The Bruins won often enough in 1930–31 to capture the Prince of Wales Trophy for the fourth straight year by finishing first in the American Division. (The trophy had been awarded from 1924 to 1927 to the league champion; from 1928 to 1938 it was awarded to the first-place team in the American Division.) In the Canadian Division the Canadiens won the O'Brien Trophy by finishing first, their Stratford Streak of a forward, Howie Morenz, leading the league in scoring.

The first-place Bruins and Canadiens faced off in a best-of-five series. With the series tied at two games apiece and some 19 minutes gone in the first overtime of the fifth and final game, Montreal defenseman Marty Burke sped in on Cecil

("Tiny") Thompson, took a pass from Wildor Larochelle, and winged the puck by Thompson's knee for the goal that won the game, 3-2, rocked the Forum, and sent the Flying Frenchmen into the final to defend the Cup they had won 12 months earlier.

In the second-place series the Chicago Black Hawks, directed by new coach Dick Irvin, ousted the Maple Leafs, while the Rangers eliminated the Maroons in the third-place series. In the best-of-three semifinal the Black Hawks' Irvin spewed out a stream of forwards who wore down the Rangers while his goalkeeper, happy-go-lucky Chuck Gardiner, was batting down all the rubber New York could fling at him. The Black Hawks won, 2-0 and 1-0, to earn a place in the final, which had been restored to a best-of-five series.

Observers speculated that the young Black Hawks would crumble in the spotlight of a Stanley Cup final. This was a team without a star, with the possible exception of goaltender Gardiner. Its top scorer, Johnny Gottselig, had finished only 12th in league scoring. But Dick Irvin could roll out a series of speedy lines that dizzied opponents with the slickness of their skating and stick-handling.

Montreal's Canadiens came to the final with some walking wounded, notably Howie Morenz, whose shoulder was sore and his mood sour after having failed to score a goal so far in the playoffs.

The 1931 Canadiens. Top (l. to r.): George Hainsworth, Howie Morenz, Johnny Gagnon, Marty Burke, Sylvio Mantha, Georges Mantha, and Art Lesieur. Bottom: Pit Lepine, Gus Rivers, Albert Leduc, Wildor Larochelle, Armand Mondou, Nick Wasnie, and Aurel Joliat. Not shown are Jean Pusie and Bert McCaffrey.

At Chicago Stadium in front of 17,000 shrill fans, the Canadiens won the first game, 2-1. The second game went into overtime, tied 1-1. Instead of crumbling, the young Black Hawks fended off drive after drive by Montreal. In the second overtime Chicago's Johnny Gottselig beat George Hainsworth with a drive to the corner, the goal winning the game for the Hawks, 2-1, and tying the series at a game apiece.

In the cauldron of the Montreal Forum, some 13,000 Canadien fans pounding noise at their ears, the Black Hawks kept their composure even after falling behind 2-0. They rallied to tie, 2-2, and after 53 minutes of three overtimes—a record for a final series that still stands—Marvin ("Cy") Wentworth drove the puck by Hainsworth for a 3-2 Chicago victory. The young Black Hawks led two games to one and needed only one more victory to take home their first Cup. Chicago had one hand on the Cup, ahead 2-0 in the fourth game, when Montreal's Johnny Gagnon snapped two drives by Gardiner to tie the score, and Alfred ("Pit") Lepine whacked home two more for a 4-2 Canadien victory that tied the series at two games apiece.

The deciding fifth game was also played at the Forum. The Canadiens worried about Morenz, who had now failed to score in nine straight games. After an opening period played cautiously by both sides, Gagnon beat Gardiner with a shot for a 1-0 Montreal lead. In the third period Morenz electrified the crowd by seizing the puck at his own end, then weaving through the Chicago defense to ram the puck by Gardiner for his first goal of the playoffs. The Canadiens won, 2-0, to take the Cup for the fourth time in their history and the second year in a row, the first back-to-back victories since the Ottawa Senators' triumphs of 1920 and 1921.

Eddie Shore:
The way we were

Retired and living in Springfield, Massachusetts, Eddie Shore talked about his days as the big bad Bruin, the most feared player of his time.

They always said I was vicious. I wasn't. I just knew how to hit. When did you ever see a hockey player who was a good fighter? Never. And why? Because they carry their weight forward when they skate. When they throw a punch, they don't have their weight behind a punch. I skated with my knees bent and with my weight behind me and when I hit I put all my weight behind the swing. But I was never vicious. I knew how to swing. I'm 71 years old and I can still hit a golf ball 280 yards because I know how to swing.

Three stars of the 1931 playoffs: Boston's Eddie Shore (above), Montreal's Johnny Gagnon (r.), and the most famous Flying Frenchman of his time, the ill-fated Howie Morenz (far r.).

32

FIRST GAME (April 3, at Chicago)
 Canadiens 2, Black Hawks 1

FIRST PERIOD
 Montreal—G. Mantha (Gagnon)............ 4:50
SECOND PERIOD
 No scoring
THIRD PERIOD
 Montreal—Lepine...................... 2:20
 Chicago—Ripley (Gottselig, Couture)....... 6:00

SECOND GAME (April 5, at Chicago)
 Black Hawks 2, Canadiens 1

FIRST PERIOD
 No scoring
SECOND PERIOD
 Chicago—Adams........................11:45
THIRD PERIOD
 Montreal—Wasnie (Larochelle)............12:10
FIRST OVERTIME
 No scoring
SECOND OVERTIME
 Chicago—Gottselig..................... 4:50

THIRD GAME (April 9, at Montreal)
 Black Hawks 3, Canadiens 2

FIRST PERIOD
 Montreal—Gagnon..................... 5:15
SECOND PERIOD
 Montreal—G. Mantha (Lepine)............. 7:29
THIRD PERIOD
 Chicago—March (Gottselig)................16:20
 Chicago—Adams (Cook)..................16:38
FIRST OVERTIME
 No scoring
SECOND OVERTIME
 No scoring
THIRD OVERTIME
 Chicago—Wentworth.....................13:50

FOURTH GAME (April 11, at Montreal)
 Canadiens 4, Black Hawks 2

FIRST PERIOD
 Chicago—Gottselig (Ripley)................ 1:33
 Chicago—Arbour (Ingram).................13:58
SECOND PERIOD
 Montreal—Gagnon (Leduc)................ 4:34
THIRD PERIOD
 Montreal—Gagnon (Wasnie)............... 4:25
 Montreal—Lepine (Gagnon)...............10:55
 Montreal—Lepine (Joliat).................17:25

FIFTH GAME (April 14, at Montreal)
 Canadiens 2, Black Hawks 0

FIRST PERIOD
 No scoring
SECOND PERIOD
 Montreal—Gagnon (Joliat)................ 9:59
THIRD PERIOD
 Montreal—Morenz.......................15:27

NEW YORK RANGERS
TORONTO MAPLE LEAFS **1932**

Dick Gets Revenge,
Johnny Gets the Gate

"Johnny Roach has got to put more in front of the net than a bundle of jangled nerves."
—New York writer during the final

Lines at box offices were disappearing, while lines at soup kitchens were stretching longer in these depression days. The Philadelphia Quakers (formerly the Pittsburgh Pirates) dropped out of the league after a record-setting 4-36-4 season, and the Ottawa Senators withdrew from competition for the year. So there were only eight NHL teams for the 1931–32 season. But since the owners badly needed playoff revenue, they continued to make six teams eligible for the playoffs, creating the comic situation where eight teams played a 48-game schedule to eliminate two teams.

Toronto celebrated the opening of the new Maple Leaf Gardens by booming in 155 goals, a total exceeded since the reorganization of the league only by the 1930 Bruins. Thudding the rubber against the back iron most often was Toronto's Kid Line, led by Harvey ("Busher") Jackson, only 21 and called "the greatest natural athlete hockey has ever known." Jackson led the league in scoring while his partners on the Kid Line—Joe Primeau and Charley Conacher—ranked second and fourth.

Trouble with Toronto was a porous defense, Lorne Chabot in goal as likely to give up as many goals in a game as the Kid Line could score. The Leafs finished second in the Canadian Division behind the Canadiens, who—with Aurel Joliat and Howie Morenz—were still the same powerful

unit that had won two straight Cups and were looking to be the first to win three straight since the Ottawa Silver Seven of 1903–05.

Finishing first in the American Division were the Rangers. Lester Patrick had inserted only one new name in the starting lineup that had won the Cup in 1928, young Earl Seibert replacing Clarence ("Taffy") Abel on defense. In goal was Johnny Roach, of whom it was said that Broadway's bright lights sometimes dazzled his eyes. The line centered by Frank Boucher, with the brothers Bill and Frederick ("Bun") Cook on the wings, played a deft passing game, dearly loved by Lester Patrick and still a Ranger trademark 40 years later.

The Ranger swifties were underdogs in the best-of-five first-place series with the Canadiens, but they surprised Morenz and his crew by winning one of the two games at the Forum. In New York there were surprisingly long lines waiting to buy tickets for the next two games, but most tickets were being sold at bargain-basement levels, way below the $4 prices of the Roaring Twenties. With some 17,000 fans crammed into the Garden, for example, gate receipts toted up to little more than a reported $20,000.

The Rangers shot down the Canadiens at Madison Square Garden, winning 1-0 and 5-2, to take the series, three games to one, and go into their third Stanley Cup final. The Canadiens went home to say adieu to the old mug they had held these 24 months.

In the second-place series the Maple Leafs op-

The 1931–32 Maple Leafs. Standing (l. to r.): trainer Tim Daly, King Clancy, Andy Blair, George ("Red") Horner, Lorne Chabot, Alex Levinsky, Joe Primeau, Harvey Jackson, Hal Darragh, and Hal Cotton. Seated: Charley Conacher, Frank Finnegan, Clarence ("Hap") Day, general manager Conn Smythe, coach Dick Irvin, public relations director Frank Selke, Irvine ("Ace") Bailey, and Bob Gracie.

posed the Chicago Black Hawks in what had to be a grudge affair for Maple Leaf coach Dick Irvin. A year ago he had coached the Black Hawks into the playoff final, but he had been fired when the team got off to a wobbly start this season. Hired by Toronto, he got his revenge when his Maple Leafs blasted the Black Hawks off the ice in the second game of their two-game, total-goal series, 6-1, to win the series, 6 goals to 2.

The Maroons' big S Line—Reginald ("Hooley") Smith, Nels Stewart, and Albert ("Babe") Siebert —helped Montreal edge Detroit in the third-place playoffs. In the two-game, total-goal semifinal, the Maroons opposed the Maple Leafs with two brothers lined up on opposite sides: Charley Conacher for the Maple Leafs and Lionel Conacher for the Maroons. With the series tied at three goals apiece, the second game went into overtime, Maple Leaf Gardens reverberating with noise as the teams swayed up and down the ice, a trip to the final for the one who scored first. After almost 18 minutes of tumult, Toronto sub Bob Gracie rapped the puck by Jim ("Flat") Walsh, and the Maple Leafs were on their way to their first final since they were called the St. Pats way back in 1922.

The best-of-five final opened in New York. Lester Patrick assigned the swift Murray Murdoch to shadow Charley Conacher, and Conacher growled at Murdoch what every shadowed star has thought before and since: "Why don't you try to get a goal yourself?" Conacher broke away from his shadow to score once, and Busher Jackson whaled three past Johnny Roach, who was described as "befuddled." The Maple Leafs won, 6-4, their defense no better than usual.

The circus elephants again were padding into the Garden, and the kids could not be disappointed, so the Rangers had to move, choosing Boston Garden as "home" ice for their second game. They gave Johnny Roach a 2-0 lead, but Toronto's Kid Line threw three pucks by him and even the venerable defenseman Francis ("King") Clancy socked in two as the Leafs won again, 6-2.

After the game Lester Patrick told the press that Roach had broken training on the eve of the final. "If our goalkeeper had done that," snorted King Clancy, "I'd have kicked his head off. We hated to score. It was like tossing a puck into an open net."

36

Joe Primeau: "Mixed with a feeling that you're so doggone glad it's over with...like a load off your shoulders."

"Roach is through for next season," announced a grave Lester Patrick.

That must have reduced to zero what little confidence Johnny had left. In the third game, with Foster Hewitt perched above Maple Leaf Gardens to describe the action by radio to millions, Roach gave up another six goals, making a total of 18 for the series, and the Maple Leafs won, 6-4, to bring the Cup to Toronto for the first time in a decade.

The victory in three straight games, the first by any team, was hailed by Toronto manager Conn Smythe as an example of hockey's honesty. "Two extra games," he said, "would have brought in at least $40,000 to Maple Leaf Gardens, but we played it straight and won in three."

Joe Primeau:
Glad it's all over

Coach of the Maple Leafs in the early 1950s and now a Toronto businessman, Joe Primeau—one of the members of the high-scoring Kid Line—talked about his emotions after winning his first Stanley Cup.

To win the Stanley Cup, it's the top prize and the feeling you get is a little hard to describe. It's a great feeling but it's mixed with a feeling that you're so doggone glad it's over with. You have spent so much of yourself by this time, you're glad you don't have to spend any more. You have this combined feeling: You have this sense of accomplishment after reaching what you have been driving for so long, and you have this feeling of relief —like a load off your shoulders—that now you are going to be able to get some rest.

FIRST GAME (April 5, at New York)
Maple Leafs 6, Rangers 4

FIRST PERIOD
Toronto—Day (Cotton). 4:25
New York—Bun Cook (Bill Cook). 17:25
SECOND PERIOD
Toronto—Jackson (Day). 3:35
Toronto—Jackson (Horner). 10:20
Toronto—Conacher. 10:50
Toronto—Jackson. 17:05
New York—Dillon (Murdoch). 18:20
THIRD PERIOD
New York—Johnson. 2:35
New York—Bun Cook (Boucher). 6:30
Toronto—Horner (Jackson). 18:32

SECOND GAME (April 7, at Boston)
Maple Leafs 6, Rangers 2

FIRST PERIOD
New York—Bun Cook (Bill Cook). 3:53
SECOND PERIOD
New York—Brennan. 1:09
Toronto—Jackson. 2:06
Toronto—Conacher. 8:58
THIRD PERIOD
Toronto—Clancy. 1:39
Toronto—Conacher (Jackson). 9:56
Toronto—Clancy (Primeau). 10:51
Toronto—Cotton (Primeau, Finnigan). 17:10

THIRD GAME (April 9, at Toronto)
Maple Leafs 6, Rangers 4

FIRST PERIOD
Toronto—Blair (Clancy). 5:44
Toronto—Blair (Gracie). 6:11
SECOND PERIOD
Toronto—Jackson (Primeau, Conacher). 10:57
New York—Boucher (Heller). 15:24
THIRD PERIOD
Toronto—Finnigan (Day). 8:56
Toronto—Bailey (Conacher). 15:07
New York—Bun Cook (Boucher). 16:33
Toronto—Gracie (Finnigan). 17:36
New York—Boucher (Bun Cook). 18:24
New York—Boucher (Bill Cook). 19:27

NEW YORK RANGERS
TORONTO MAPLE LEAFS
1933

$100 a Man If the Silver Fox Doesn't Have to Take a Fifth

Late in the season the New York Rangers looked lackadaisical playing a 3-3 tie against a tail-end team. Talk spread that the Rangers were dilly-dallying in third place, not interested in finishing first in the American Division and having to tangle in the first-place series with the Maple Leafs, who were leading the Canadian Division.

If the rumors were true, the Rangers showed good sense if not good sportsmanship. For what happened to the Maple Leafs in that first-place series was proof again that one can win a battle and lose the war.

Boston came in first in the American Division and matched its splendid defense—the bruising Eddie Shore in front of Cecil ("Tiny") Thompson in the nets—against Toronto's sharpshooting Kid Line: Harvey ("Busher") Jackson, Charley Conacher, and Joe Primeau, who were pumping in a goal a game.

Few playoff series before or since have provided as much sudden-death tension. After 14 minutes of overtime in the first game, Boston's bantam center, Marty Barry, beat Toronto cagekeeper Lorne Chabot to put Boston one game ahead. After 15 minutes of overtime in the second game, Busher Jackson beat Tiny Thompson when the Bruins were a man short, and the series was tied at a game apiece. The third game went into four

minutes of overtime and ended when Eddie Shore took off on one of his pell-mell dashes the length of the rink to blast the puck by Chabot, putting Boston ahead two games to one.

More agonizing moments were to come for both goalkeepers. Toronto tied the series at two games apiece by winning the fourth game in regulation time, 5-3. The fifth and final game stretched through three 20-minute periods of regulation play without a goal being scored, then one 20-minute overtime period . . . followed by a second . . . a third . . . a fourth, and still a goal had yet to be scored, the 14,000 people in Maple Leaf Gardens now nearly as wilted as the players.

At this point, after a Stanley Cup record of 140 minutes of hockey without a goal, league president Frank Calder suggested that a coin be tossed to decide the winner.

The exhausted Bruins agreed. At first the Maple Leafs said yes, but a loud roar of protest from their fans changed their minds and the game resumed.

The tired players could put out only occasional bursts of speed as they skated through a fifth overtime, the clock crawling toward two o'clock in the morning. In the sixth overtime the smallest player on the ice, Toronto's Ken Doraty, cut around a wobbly Boston defenseman and shot point-blank

Receiving the Cup from Frank Calder, NHL president, are six of the 1933 Rangers (l. to r.): Albert ("Babe") Siebert, Andy Aitkenhead, Ivan ("Ching") Johnson, Frank Boucher, Bun and Bill Cook. The Rangers placed the Cup in a showcase in the lobby of Madison Square Garden for viewing by the public.

Two of Toronto's Kid Line, Busher Jackson
(above) and Charley Conacher (below),
during moments when they were
better rested.

at Thompson. The puck billowed the nets, welcomed by a pistol-shot of a roar from the fans.
After a record 104 minutes of overtime, the Maple
Leafs had won, 1-0, to gain the final. Within an
hour after the game they were clambering aboard
a sleeper bound for New York, the first game of
the final series only 18 hours away.

The Rangers had reached the final by clobber-
ing the Canadiens in the Garden 5-2, then tying
them at the Forum to win the third-place series,
8 goals to 5. In the semifinal the Rangers beat the
Detroit Falcons (formerly the Cougars), who had
won the second-place series against the Maroons.
After playing four easy games, the rested Rangers
awaited the arrival in Manhattan of the hockey-
weary Leafs.

In goal for New York was Andy Aitkenhead,
called the Glasgow Gabber; the little Scot chattered
constantly during games to keep calm. Winger Bill
Cook, on the top-scoring Ranger line with his
brother Frederick ("Bun") Cook and Frank
Boucher, had led the league in scoring. Ranger
fans, anxious to avenge the loss to Toronto in the
previous year's final, were looking for a scoring
shootout between Bill Cook and Toronto's Busher
Jackson, who had finished second in scoring.

Neither played a scoring role in the first game
as the Rangers skated through the sleepy-eyed
Leafs to win, 5-1. The teams went to Toronto for
the remainder of the games, the circus again having kicked the Rangers out of the Garden. In the
second game the Maple Leafs still looked weary,
the Rangers winning 3-1.

With Toronto only one game away from extinction, little Ken Doraty kept the Maple Leaf cause
alive by punching two pucks by the Glasgow Gabber, Toronto winning 3-2. Before the fourth game
Lester Patrick promised his Rangers $100 each if
he didn't have to sweat through a fifth game. The
Silver Fox did have to sweat through three scoreless periods and seven minutes of overtime. Then,
with two Leafs in the penalty box and the Leafs
obviously fatigued after one overtime session too
many, Bill Cook shoved the puck by Lorne
Chabot for a 1-0 victory and New York's second
Cup. The third-place Rangers were the lowest-
finishing team to win the Cup since the league was
reorganized in 1926.

Ching Johnson:
Tit for tat

At his home in Takoma Park, Maryland, former Ranger defenseman Ivan ("Ching") Johnson talked about the goal that won the Stanley Cup for the Rangers in 1933.

At the time they had a rule that you couldn't raise your hands above your shoulders. It was a silly rule—it was in effect for only one year. It meant you couldn't raise your hands to protect your face and stop a puck from hitting you. In the overtime of that fourth and final game, I threw up my hands to stop a puck and they put me in the penalty box. We raised hell, but there was nothing we could do about it. Anyway, while I was still in the penalty box, I guess the officials thought they had to return the compliment because they put Clancy [Francis ("King") Clancy of Toronto] in the penalty box for doing the same thing. That made them shorthanded by two men, and Bill Cook scored to win the game, 1-0. Oh, Lord, were those Maple Leafs sore at those officials.

Ching Johnson (who left the Rangers to play for the New York Americans): "We raised hell but there was nothing we could do about it...Oh, Lord, were those Maple Leafs sore."

FIRST GAME (April 4, at New York)
Rangers 5, Maple Leafs 1

FIRST PERIOD
New York—Bun Cook (Boucher, Bill Cook)...12:18
New York—Dillon (Murdoch)..............13:11
SECOND PERIOD
New York—Heller (Asmundson, Somers).....8:31
New York—Dillon........................14:25
THIRD PERIOD
Toronto—Levinsky.......................15:53
New York—Murdoch (Dillon).............16:55

SECOND GAME (April 8, at Toronto)
Rangers 3, Maple Leafs 1

FIRST PERIOD
Toronto—Doraty (Gracie, Clancy)..........1:11
New York—Heller (Somers)................8:16
New York—Bill Cook....................11:39
SECOND PERIOD
No scoring
THIRD PERIOD
New York—Siebert.......................14:40

THIRD GAME (April 11, at Toronto)
Maple Leafs 3, Rangers 2

FIRST PERIOD
New York—Dillon........................2:21
SECOND PERIOD
Toronto—Doraty (Primeau, Clancy)........7:21
THIRD PERIOD
Toronto—Doraty.........................5:30
New York—Keeling (Somers)..............7:43
Toronto—Horner (Sands, Cotton)..........8:29

FOURTH GAME (April 13, at Toronto)
Rangers 1, Maple Leafs 0

FIRST PERIOD
No scoring
SECOND PERIOD
No scoring
THIRD PERIOD
No scoring
OVERTIME
New York—Bill Cook (Keeling)............7:34

41

CHICAGO BLACK HAWKS ─1934
DETROIT RED WINGS

Something to Think About on a Summer's Night

I was having my afternoon steak before a game. I poured a hell of a lot of ketchup on it. I'd just started to eat when my wife Beulah made some casual remark. For no good reason, I picked up my steak and threw it at her. She ducked and the steak hit the wall. The ketchup splattered and the steak hung there on the wall. Slowly it began to peel, and I stared at it. Between the time that steak hit the wall and then hit the floor, I decided I'd been a touchy goalkeeper long enough. By the time it landed, I'd retired.

> —Veteran goaltender Wilf Cude
> after his retirement in the 1940s

The pressure is unreal. Most of the goalkeepers, they feel the pressure. The only ones that don't worry are the ones too dumb to understand what's happening to them.

> —Chicago goalkeeper Tony Esposito in 1972

The freshly named Detroit Red Wings soared to the top of the American Division, winning the team's first Prince of Wales Trophy. Toronto's Maple Leafs finished first in the Canadian Division and were top-heavy favorites to eliminate the Red Wings in their best-of-five first-place series for the league championship. Toronto's Kid Line —Charley Conacher, Harvey ("Busher") Jackson, and Joe Primeau—still knew how to put the puck into the cage. Conacher led the league in scoring, Primeau was second, and Jackson seventh.

Francis ("King") Clancy was picked as an All-Star defenseman, and only veteran goalie George Hainsworth seemed a weak spot as Toronto coach Dick Irvin and manager Conn Smythe sought their second Cup in three years.

They ran into two shocks at the Olympia when the Red Wings skated off with the first two games, 2-1 and 6-3, as youthful Detroit goalkeeper Wilf Cude did everything but handsprings to stop pucks, and the line of Ralph ("Cooney") Weiland, Larry Aurie, and Herb Lewis tied up the Kid Line. At Maple Leaf Gardens Toronto won the next two to even the series. Early in the fifth game Detroit's Ebbie Goodfellow slipped the puck by Hainsworth when Toronto was shy a man for a 1-0 Red Wing lead. From there on Detroit threw a blanket of skaters around the Kid Line and won, 1-0, to take its first league championship and enter its first Cup final.

In the second-place series Chicago eliminated a crippled crew of Canadiens by winning the first game at Montreal, 3-2, then tying the second, 1-1, on a goal scored in overtime by Harold ("Mush") March to win the two-game, total-goal series, 4 goals to 3.

In the third-place playoffs the Maroons beat the aging Rangers, 2 goals to 1. In the semifinal between the Maroons and the Black Hawks, the Chicago scoring line—Elwin ("Doc") Romnes at center and Mush March and Paul Thompson on the wings—peppered the Maroon cage while Chi-

Illustrating the collapsing defense of the time, five Black Hawks encircle the cage during a foray by Detroit's Herb Lewis (on ice). In goal is Chuck Gardiner, who died a few months later. Of the striped uniforms of the time, someone said, "the players look like barber poles."

cago goalkeeper Chuck Gardiner was heavily protected by defensemen Lionel Conacher and Sid Abel, and the Black Hawks won, 6 goals to 2. For the second time—the first was in 1929—two U.S. teams, Detroit and Chicago, faced off for the Cup.

Detroit's Wilf Cude was a sometimes-brilliant but always-jittery goalkeeper, and Detroit manager Jack Adams was hoping to give Cude some breathing room with goals from the Weiland-Aurie-Lewis line. His defense was suspect and Adams knew it.

The defense held up at the Olympia in the first game until 21 minutes into overtime when Paul Thompson beat Cude for a 2-1 Chicago victory. It collapsed in the second game, Chicago winning 4-1. The teams rode to Chicago amid general expectation that the Black Hawks, unbeaten now in nine straight games, would sweep the series with three victories in a row.

But Wilf Cude, his nose smashed by a stick, knocked down rubber shot at him by the horde of Chicago gunners in the third game before some 18,000 howling Chicago fans. The Red Wings' Aurie scored twice during a 5-2 Red Wing triumph that kept Detroit alive, down now two games to one.

Sniffing and snorting through his taped-up nose, Wilf stood just as stubbornly in the fourth game, batting away 53 shots while Chicago's Chuck Gardiner saw only 40 through the three regulation periods and another 30 minutes of overtime. But when Detroit's Ebbie Goodfellow went to the penalty box for tripping, Chicago unleashed its power-play line: Romnes, March, and Thompson. Twice they rushed Cude and twice he beat them back. Doc Romnes won the puck and shuttled it to March at the right boards. A Detroit defenseman tried to tie up March, but the little guy spun loose and ripped a waist-high shot at the cage. Cude shifted, too late, and the Black Hawks were 1-0 winners. When league president Frank Calder handed Black Hawk owner Fred McLaughlin Chicago's first Stanley Cup, Chicago Stadium resounded with roaring for ten minutes. Wilf Cude dressed and departed for home to think for the summer about a puck that came too fast too soon.

Mush March:
It could cost you fifty dollars

The former wingman on the Black Hawk line with Paul Thompson and center Doc Romnes, Mush March is now the vice-president and part owner of a bearings company and lives in North Riverside, Illinois.

Well, on that goal that won the series, they had a face-off in their end after 30 minutes of overtime had gone by. The puck came back to me from Romnes on the face-off. I shot it and [laughing] *it went right through Cude's legs. Wilf Cude. He was a great goaltender. I didn't realize it right at the second, you know, that we'd won the Stanley Cup, but it was great. I rushed in and got the puck and then the fellows grabbed me and wheeled me on their shoulders all the way around the rink. It was nice to see my name on it for the first time. It's always nice to be a champion. It's always easy to be a loser.*

I played in the National Hockey League from '28 to '45. I played with Doug and Max Bentley, Johnny Gottselig, Howie Morenz. I didn't miss seeing a Black Hawk game this [1973–74] *season. They play the game a little differently today. Now everybody's up the ice, even the defensemen. If you have a great defense that can pass the puck today, that's half your battle. That's why Mr. [Bobby] Orr is so terrific. I remember one night our coach told the defensemen, "You defensemen go over that blue line, it'll cost you fifty dollars." Imagine that happening today. Today they'd say, "You'd better be up there."*

FIRST GAME (April 3, at Detroit)
Black Hawks 2, Red Wings 1

FIRST PERIOD
   Chicago—Conacher.........................17:50
SECOND PERIOD
   No scoring
THIRD PERIOD
   Detroit—Lewis (Aurie, Graham)............ 4:45
FIRST OVERTIME
   No scoring
SECOND OVERTIME
   Chicago—Thompson...................... 1:10

SECOND GAME (April 5, at Detroit)
Black Hawks 4, Red Wings 1

FIRST PERIOD
   Chicago—Couture........................17:52
SECOND PERIOD
   Detroit—Lewis (Weiland)................. 9:58
THIRD PERIOD
   Chicago—Romnes (Thompson).............. 1:28
   Chicago—Coulter (Gottselig)................ 5:34
   Chicago—Gottselig.......................18:02

THIRD GAME (April 8, at Chicago)
Red Wings 5, Black Hawks 2

FIRST PERIOD
   Chicago—Thompson (March, Romnes)...... 0:28
   Detroit—Pettinger (Starr, Carson)........... 6:07
   Detroit—Aurie (Buswell)................... 8:40
SECOND PERIOD
   Chicago—Gottselig (McFayden, Couture).....18:07
THIRD PERIOD
   Detroit—Young..........................13:50
   Detroit—Weiland (Aurie, Lewis)............18:20
   Detroit—Aurie..........................19:53

FOURTH GAME (April 10, at Chicago)
Black Hawks 1, Red Wings 0

FIRST PERIOD
   No scoring
SECOND PERIOD
   No scoring
THIRD PERIOD
   No scoring
FIRST OVERTIME
   No scoring
SECOND OVERTIME
   Chicago—March (Romnes)................10:05

Chicago owner Major
Frederick McLaughlin
towers over his star
Mush March while
congratulating Mush for
the goal that won
Chicago's first Cup.

45

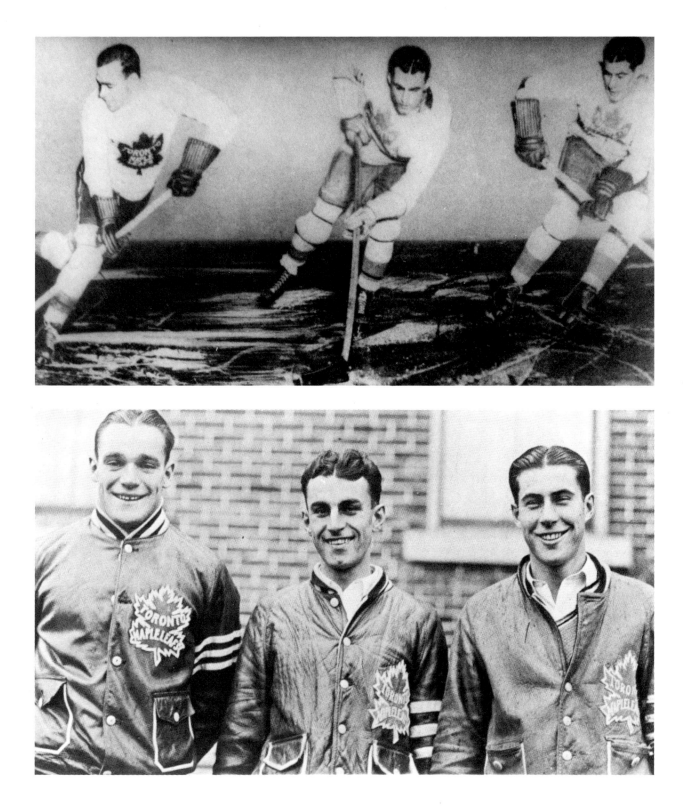

MONTREAL MAROONS
TORONTO MAPLE LEAFS
1935

Will Class Finally Show?

The validity of the Stanley Cup playoffs as a jousting place to determine hockey's best team was regularly challenged by newspaper critics. They pointed out that since the NHL began the series in 1929 between the two first-place teams for the league championship, only two league champions—the Bruins in 1929 and the Canadiens in 1931—had gone on to win the Cup in the final round against an also-ran club. If also-rans were winning the Cup in the final at least twice as often as the league champions, argued the critics, how valid was a brief three-out-of-five series in determining hockey's true best team?

Such questions only made another question more interesting as the 1935 playoffs began: Would one of the first-place clubs win the Cup? Toronto came in first in the Canadian Division, Boston in the American Division; Toronto was favored to eliminate Boston. The Maple Leafs were the league's most prolific scoring team, with Charley Conacher the league's leading scorer and his linemate on the Kid Line, Harvey ("Busher") Jackson, ranking fifth. In goal for Toronto stood the veteran George Hainsworth, bulwarked by two of the league's best defensemen, Clarence ("Hap") Day and Francis ("King") Clancy. In the Canadian Division the Maple Leafs were first in offense, second only to the Maroons in defense.

In the best-of-five first-place playoffs, Boston manager Art Ross was depending on his own stone-walled defense—Cecil ("Tiny") Thompson in goal and Albert ("Babe") Seibert and Eddie Shore on defense—to bump back Toronto pucks. In the first game he kept Shore and Seibert on-ice the full time, except for one two-minute rest, and

the Bruin defense held air-tight, Boston's Aubrey ("Dit") Clapper winning the game with a goal in overtime. But Toronto pierced the tiring Boston defense often enough to win the next three games, 2-0, 3-0, and 2-1, qualifying for its third final in four years.

In the second-place series Chicago's tall and quick-tempered goaltender, Lorne Chabot, locked into a who'll-crack-first duel with the Montreal Maroons' pale Alex Connell. The first game ended in a 0-0 tie, and neither man allowed a goal through three periods of the second. Four minutes into overtime Montreal's Larry ("Baldy") Northcott broke the stalemate, driving the puck by Chabot to win the game and the series, 1 goal to 0.

In the third-place playoffs, the Rangers and Canadiens swung sticks at skulls instead of pucks during the first game, blood flowing onto the Madison Square Garden ice, New York cops rushing out to prevent murder. The Rangers won that blood-letting, 2-1, then tied the Canadiens, 4-4, at the Forum to attain the semifinal against the Maroons.

In the first game the Maroons' Reginald ("Hooley") Smith and Baldy Northcott ping-ponged the puck between them long enough to confuse Ranger goalie Davey Kerr and beat him on a short drive for a 2-1 victory. At Montreal for the second game the Rangers could do no better than tie, 3-3, and the Maroons took the series, 5 goals to 4.

For the first time since 1926, there would be an all-Canada final: Montreal vs. Toronto. After two years south of the border, the Cup would

Toronto's Kid Line, on and off the ice
(l. to r.): Charley Conacher, Joe Primeau,
and Harvey Jackson. For Maroon manager
Tommy Gorman the triumph over Toronto
was especially delicious: A year earlier
he had coached Chicago to the winning of
the Stanley Cup and then had been
fired by Chicago's fiery owner,
Major Fred McLaughlin.

come back to the Dominion—most likely, in most minds, to Toronto, since the Maple Leafs had whipped the Maroons in five of six games during the season. The underdog Maroons looked to little Alex Connell to fend off the big Toronto shooters and hoped some good young Maroon marksmen—Herbie Cain, Hooley Smith, Russ Blinco, and Dave Trottier—could get the puck by Hainsworth.

Again season-long form wasn't matched by postseason performance, the second-place Maroons beating the league champion Maple Leafs in the first two games, 3-2 and 3-1, as Connell dived and lunged to make one spectacular save after another. In the third game, at Montreal, the score was tied 1-1 when Montreal's Baldy Northcott and Marvin ("Cy") Wentworth rammed in two goals within 12 seconds to put the Maroons ahead in a game they won, 4-1.

The Maroons had set a record by going through the playoffs in seven games without a defeat, taking their first Cup since 1926—as well as their last, the team a victim of the depression three years later.

Once again class had not shown: The league champion was the loser in the final for the fifth time in seven years.

King Clancy:
Tell me no tales of the good old days

The former Ottawa and Toronto defenseman, King Clancy is now a vice-president of the Maple Leafs.

The two teams were pretty evenly matched in that 1935 series. The difference was in the goaltending. The star of the series was Alex Connell for the Maroons in the nets. He was sensational. I used to play with him when we won the Stanley Cup at Ottawa in 1927. The only thing about Connell, you could sometimes knock in a rebound against him. My job at Ottawa was to get that puck out of there, clear those rebounds. But I remembered that about Connell, and I think that's how I scored my only goal of that series—on a rebound.

In those days most goals were scored from close up. It was a positional game, and most *every play ended up in front of the nets. In my Stanley Cup days I can't remember many of those long shots going in, as they do nowadays. You didn't see so many of those ricochet shots going in off somebody's skate. The scores were 1-0 and 2-1 affairs, none of these 5-4 and 7-6 things. Those ricochet shots make it tougher on the goalkeepers today. But the game today is much more exciting, gosh, yes. And don't let anybody tell you that the players of today aren't as good— they're probably better—than the hockey players of the old days. You wouldn't get a better checker than Bobby Clarke of that Philadelphia club. In those Stanley Cup finals in 1974, the Philadelphia club was the hardest-working hockey club I have ever seen in my life—from the goalkeeper on out. And I have never seen any hockey player the equal of the Bruins' Bobby Orr.*

FIRST GAME (April 4, at Toronto)
Maroons 3, Maple Leafs 2
FIRST PERIOD
No scoring
SECOND PERIOD
Montreal—Robinson (Blinco) 3:57
Toronto—Finnigan 14:29
Toronto—Clancy (Metz) 17:12
Montreal—Wentworth 18:24
THIRD PERIOD
No scoring
OVERTIME
Montreal—Trottier (Blinco, Robinson) 5:28

SECOND GAME (April 6, at Toronto)
Maroons 3, Maple Leafs 1
FIRST PERIOD
Montreal—Robinson 15:44
SECOND PERIOD
Toronto—Jackson 7:32
Montreal—Blinco (Shields) 16:48
THIRD PERIOD
Montreal—Northcott (Wentworth) 4:25

THIRD GAME (April 9, at Montreal)
Maroons 4, Maple Leafs 1
FIRST PERIOD
Montreal—Ward (Northcott) 19:35
SECOND PERIOD
Toronto—Thoms (Finnigan) 12:59
Montreal—Northcott (Ward) 16:18
Montreal—Wentworth (Northcott) 16:30
THIRD PERIOD
Montreal—Marker (Wentworth) 1:02

The 1935 Maroons. Top row (l. to r.): Hector ("Toe") Blake, Marvin
Wentworth, coach Lionel Conacher, Alex Connell, Stew Evans,
Earl Robinson, Bill Miller. Middle row: Dave Trottier, Jim Ward, Larry
Northcott, Hooley Smith, Russ Blinco, Allan Shields. Bottom row:
Sam McManus, Gus Marker, Norm ("Dutch") Gainor, Bob Gracie,
Herb Cain, Bill McKenzie (who left the team midway through
the season).

DETROIT RED WINGS
TORONTO MAPLE LEAFS 1936

Two of the Records Still Stand— and the Other Lasted 37 Years

Defending the Cup, the Montreal Maroons finished first in the Canadian Division while the Detroit Red Wings were winning their second Prince of Wales Trophy in three years by finishing first in the American Division. On paper the Maroons and Red Wings seemed equal—and they proved it on ice in the first game of a three-out-of-five series. Neither team scored through 60 minutes of regulation play and another 116 minutes and 30 seconds of overtime—a Stanley Cup record for overtime that still stands. At 2:25 in the morning, after some six hours of hockey, Detroit's Modere ("Mud") Bruneteau whistled the puck by Lorne Chabot for a 1-0 Red Wing victory.

The Detroit goalkeeper, Norm Smith, won a second straight shutout in the second game, 3-0. When Gus Marker finally scored for the Maroons in the first period of the third game, he snapped Smith's shutout streak at 248 minutes and 32 seconds, another playoff record that has stood and one that's likely to stand in this era of curved sticks that dipsy-doodle the puck by the goalies. Detroit won that third game, 2-1, to sweep the series in three straight.

In the second-place playoffs the Maple Leafs' high-potency offense overwhelmed the Bruins' strong defense, 8 goals to 6. In the third-place playoffs the often-pitiful New York Americans had gained a playoff spot for the first time since 1929. With Dave ("Sweeney") Schriner scoring and tiny Roy Worters dancing all over the crease to block shots, the Amerks beat the Chicago Black Hawks, 3-0, and although the Amerks lost the second game, 5-4, they won the series, 7 goals to 5.

In the best-of-three semifinal, Toronto won the first game, 3-1, but Worters would not be budged in the second, New York winning, 1-0. In the third game the Amerks seemed on the verge of one of the decade's upsets, tied 1-1 late in the third period. But Bill Thoms and Francis ("King") Clancy ripped late-minute goals by Worters for a 3-1 Maple Leaf victory, sending Toronto to its fourth final in the past five years.

In the best-of-five final, Detroit—with Wilfred ("Bucko") McDonald posted on defense in front of the hot-handed Norm Smith—was favored to put into the bag most everything the Toronto shooters could wing at them. Detroit had enjoyed a week's rest while the Leafs, an aging team, had come out of the tough Amerk series battered and out of breath.

In the first game Toronto's defensemen, Clarence ("Hap") Day and King Clancy, looked especially tired and Detroit won, 3-1. That Toronto defense sagged badly in the second game, the Red Wings delighting a huge Olympia crowd by lacing the Maple Leafs 9-4, a 13-goal total for one game that remained a Stanley Cup record until the Chicago Black Hawks beat the Montreal Canadiens 8-7 in 1973.

The proud Maple Leafs rallied to avert a three-game sweep by the Red Wings. Down 3-0 in the third period of the third game, they tied the game

Detroit goalkeeper Norm Smith kicks away the puck during the second game, won 9-4 by the Red Wings. On paper the teams seemed evenly matched. In six games during the season, Detroit had won three, Toronto three, with each team scoring a total of 14 goals against the other.

and won in overtime, 4-3, on a shot by Frank ("Buzz") Boll. As the fourth game began, waves of optimism swept through the jammed Maple Leaf Gardens: The Maple Leafs were coming back. To bring them back, coach Dick Irvin started the now-veteran Kid Line of Joe Primeau, Harvey ("Busher") Jackson, and Charley Conacher. Playing the last game of his career, Primeau smashed a puck by Norm Smith to put Toronto ahead, 1-0, filling the Gardens with joyous roaring. But Detroit's Ebbie Goodfellow, Marty Barry, and Pete Kelly whapped shots by George Hainsworth for a 3-2 victory and Detroit's first Stanley Cup. Detroit became the first league champion to win the Cup since the 1931 Canadiens.

Hundreds of Detroiters welcomed the Red Wings at the railroad station when the team returned from Toronto. The city was celebrating its third big league championship within the past seven months. The Tigers had won the World Series the previous October, the Lions were National Football League champions in December, and now the Red Wings had completed what Detroit was hailing as "our Grand Slam."

Norm Smith:
The ending that had to come

Now an executive in Detroit, Norm Smith looked back on his streak of shutout goaltending.

Well, gee whiz, naturally everyone was tired when we started that sixth overtime in the first game for the league championship. My stuff— underwear, pads, everything—was getting heavier all the time. They fed us sugar dipped in brandy to keep us going, even though our coach, Jack Adams, was one never to touch a drop. I never did see Bruneteau score the goal that won that 1-0 game for us. But I did see the red light flash on. Everybody was so stunned there was like a ten-second pause and then they all broke loose. I had 94, 95 stops in that game, something like that. Then there was the shutout the next game so now I had almost four hours of goaltending without a goal being scored against me. It went over four hours and then [the Maroons'] Gus Marker picked up a long pass and he came in on me and beat me to the top right-hand corner. To be honest, I had really forgotten how long the streak had been going, and really you couldn't expect it to go on forever.

52

FIRST GAME (April 5, at Detroit)
Red Wings 3, Maple Leafs 1

FIRST PERIOD
Detroit—McDonald......................... 4:53
Detroit—Howe (Young)..................... 5:37
Detroit—W. Kilrea (Bruneteau).............12:05
Toronto—Boll (Thoms).....................12:15
SECOND PERIOD
No scoring
THIRD PERIOD
No scoring

SECOND GAME (April 7, at Detroit)
Red Wings 9, Maple Leafs 4

FIRST PERIOD
Detroit—W. Kilrea (Sorrell)................. 1:30
Detroit—Barry (Bowman)................... 4:25
Detroit—Lewis (Sorrell, Barry).............10:05
Toronto—Boll (Thoms).....................12:35
Detroit—McDonald (H. Kilrea).............16:55
SECOND PERIOD
Detroit—Sorrell (Barry, Howe).............. 7:15
Detroit—Pettinger (Howe, Young)........... 9:10
Toronto—Primeau (Shill)...................14:00
THIRD PERIOD
Detroit—Sorrell (W. Kilrea, Bruneteau)...... 7:30
Toronto—Thoms (Boll, Horner)............. 9:40
Detroit—Pettinger (H. Kilrea).............12:05
Toronto—Davidson (Finnigan, H. Jackson)...16:10
Detroit—McDonald.......................17:15

THIRD GAME (April 9, at Toronto)
Maple Leafs 4, Red Wings 3

FIRST PERIOD
Detroit—Bowman (Pettinger)................ 9:25
SECOND PERIOD
Detroit—Bruneteau......................., 1:06
THIRD PERIOD
Detroit—Howe (Pettinger, H. Kilrea)........11:15
Toronto—Primeau (Davidson, Horner)......13:10
Toronto—Kelly (Finnigan).................15:21
Toronto—Kelly (Primeau).................19:18
OVERTIME
Toronto—Boll (Horner, Kelly).............. 0:31

FOURTH GAME (April 11, at Toronto)
Red Wings 3, Maple Leafs 2

FIRST PERIOD
Toronto—Primeau.......................18:11
SECOND PERIOD
Detroit—Goodfellow (Sorrell).............. 9:55
Detroit—Barry (Lewis)....................10:39
THIRD PERIOD
Detroit—Kelly (Lewis).................... 9:45
Toronto—Thoms........................10:57

The 1936 Red Wings. Standing (l. to r.): trainer Honey Walker, Doug
Young, Bucko McDonald, Pete Kelly, Marty Barry, Gordon
Pettinger, Ebbie Goodfellow, Johnny Sorrell, Scotty Bowman, Wilfred
Starr, and assistant trainer Mattson. Seated: Herbie Lewis, Syd Howe,
Larry Aurie, manager-coach Jack Adams, Norm Smith, L. Took,
owner Jim Norris, Sr., Wally Kilrea, Arthur Giroux, and Hec Kilrea.

DETROIT RED WINGS
NEW YORK RANGERS 1937

"His Jaw Is Busted.
Give Him His Lumps Early . . ."

With crowds again filling the hockey arenas as the great depression seemed near an end, the number of playoff games was increased. There would still be a best-of-five series between the two first-place teams in each division to decide the league champion. But instead of those two-game, total-goal series between the two second-place teams and the two third-place teams, there would be a best-of-three series between the second-place teams and another best-of-three series between the third-place teams. The two winners would play a best-of-three semifinal, with the winner meeting the league champion in a best-of-five final. With tickets selling for as high as $4.40, the playoff purse figured to be fatter.

Detroit's Red Wings, defending the Cup, waltzed home first in the American Division. In the Canadian Division meanwhile, the Montreal Canadiens finished a whisker ahead of the Maroons and Maple Leafs. At Detroit Jack Adams had fashioned a powerhouse. Norm Smith won the Vezina Trophy for giving up the fewest goals in the league, and Marty Barry and Larry Aurie finished three-four in league scoring. Near the end of the season Aurie broke a leg and sat out the playoffs, Hec Kilrea joining Barry and Herb Lewis on the No. 1 line.

In the first-place playoffs, the Canadiens met the Red Wings with the cry, "Win it for Howie." The legendary Stratford Streak, Howie Morenz, had broken a leg earlier in the season and died in the hospital of a heart attack. In goal for Montreal was the veteran Wilf Cude, crouched behind a flimsy defense and a popgun attack, with Johnny Gagnon and Aurel Joliat the only respectable scorers.

Hec Kilrea scored twice in a 4-0 Detroit triumph in the first game. Wilf Cude was strafed from right, left, and center in the second, Detroit again winning, 5-1. But back in the Forum the Canadiens won a pair of 3-1 victories to even the series at two games apiece. The Canadiens were sudden favorites to win this one for Howie.

The fifth game went into overtime, tied 1-1, and remained locked until the third overtime when Hec Kilrea, at 12:45 in the morning, stuffed the puck by Cude for a 2-1 Detroit victory. For a second straight year the Wings were in the final.

In the second-place playoffs the Maroons beat Boston, two games to one. In the third-place playoffs the Rangers surprised the Maple Leafs, who were led by two young gunners, Syl Apps and Gordon Drillon, New York winning in two straight. In the semifinal Ranger goalkeeper Davey Kerr became the toast of Eighth Avenue saloons when he twice shut out the Maroons, 1-0 and 4-0.

The Ranger team that entered the final against Detroit was a brand-new Lester Patrick model, with Frank Boucher one of the few players left from the teams that had won in 1928 and 1933. Among the new faces were Neil and Mathew ("Mac") Colville, Alex Shibicky, Phil Watson, Art Coulter, defenseman Walter ("Babe") Pratt, and winger Lynn Patrick, the son of the Silver Fox.

Before a sellout crowd in Madison Square Garden, the Rangers won the first game, 5-1, and

In the traditional hand-shaking ceremony that graces Stanley Cup finals to this day, the Rangers' Ivan ("Ching") Johnson (l.) congratulates Detroit's Johnny Sorrell after the final game. The Rangers took home about $700 a man, the Red Wings around $1,000. The fifth game was reported over a U.S. radio network.

then, as usual, had to give up the Garden to the circus. The remaining games would be played in Detroit, where the Rangers had not won a game since 1935. But after winning five straight play-off games so far, the away-from-home Rangers were favored. Critics said the Red Wings were a one-line team and with Norm Smith out of the series with an injured elbow, replaced in goal by minor leaguer Earl Robertson, the defense did not seem formidable.

But goalie Robertson and defensemen Ebbie Goodfellow and Scotty Bowman stood firm in the second game, Detroit winning, 4-2. Davey Kerr shut out the Red Wings, 1-0, in the third game, and now the Rangers were within a single game of becoming the first third-place team to win the Stanley Cup since the Rangers of 1933.

"We're in," cried Frank Boucher. "The kids have been wonderful, and I don't mind telling you we were worried about them before the series began."

But in the fourth game Marty Barry put a puck by Davey Kerr while Earl Robertson blanked the Rangers, the Red Wings winning, 1-0, to force the final to a fifth game for the first time since 1931.

"Hit Neil Colville hard," Jack Adams told his troops. "His jaw is busted. Give him his lumps early and he won't be so strong later on."

His jaw encased in a cast, the high-scoring Colville skated time after time through the Red Wing defense but he could not toss the puck under, over, or around Robertson. Late in the first period Detroit's Barry took a pass from Syd Howe and whisked the puck off Kerr's wrist and into the cage for a 1-0 lead. The Rangers could not get anything by Robertson and the Red Wings won, 3-0, capturing their second Cup in a row, the first time a U.S. team had won two in a row.

Said Detroit owner Jim Norris, Sr., after the last game: "If we had blown this game I was ready to give New York everything in the till."

Despite the higher ticket prices and the increased attendance because of the extra games, each winning Red Wing went home with only $1,000 a man, each losing Ranger with $700.

56

Clarence Campbell:
This cat didn't meow

Clarence S. Campbell, president of the NHL, began his career with the league as an official.

The first Stanley Cup game I ever saw, I worked in—as a referee. That was one of the games in the Detroit-Montreal semifinal. It was a strange kind of series—first Detroit seemed to have it won, then Montreal, and it went that way right down to the very end, in overtime of the last game. I remember during that overtime Montreal's Johnny Gagnon, they called him The Cat, came down the ice and had Norm Smith beat. He faked and there was Smith stretched out on the ice, helpless. All The Cat had to do was ram the puck by Smith. He could have scored easily and won the game. Gagnon was so sure he would score that he flipped it over Smith's body—but somehow Smith got a foot on the puck and kicked it away. And a little later Detroit scored to win the game and the series. Even when you're a good one like The Cat, you can never be too sure.

FIRST GAME (April 6, at New York)
Rangers 5, Red Wings 1

FIRST PERIOD
New York—Keeling (Murdoch, Cooper)...... 5:23
New York—Patrick (Boucher, Coulter)....... 9:40
New York—Cooper (Keeling, Dillon).......18:44
SECOND PERIOD
New York—Boucher (Johnson)..............18:55
THIRD PERIOD
Detroit—Howe (Pettinger, Goodfellow).......17:12
New York—Patrick (Boucher)..............18:22

SECOND GAME (April 8, at Detroit)
Red Wings 4, Rangers 2

FIRST PERIOD
Detroit—Sorrell........................... 9:22
Detroit—Bruneteau (Howe)................12:07
Detroit—Gallagher (W. Kilrea, Sherf).......13:31
SECOND PERIOD
Detroit—Lewis (Howe, Goodfellow).........11:02
New York—Pratt (N. Colville, M. Colville)...15:08
New York—Keeling (Coulter)..............18:18
THIRD PERIOD
No scoring

THIRD GAME (April 11, at Detroit)
Rangers 1, Red Wings 0

FIRST PERIOD
No scoring
SECOND PERIOD
New York—N. Colville (Pratt, Cooper)...... 0:23
THIRD PERIOD
No scoring

FOURTH GAME (April 13, at Detroit)
Red Wings 1, Rangers 0

FIRST PERIOD
No scoring
SECOND PERIOD
No scoring
THIRD PERIOD
Detroit—Barry (Howe, Sorrell)..............12:43

FIFTH GAME (April 15, at Detroit)
Red Wings 3, Rangers 0

FIRST PERIOD
Detroit—Barry (Howe)....................19:22
SECOND PERIOD
Detroit—Sorrell (Barry, H. Kilrea).......... 9:36
THIRD PERIOD
Detroit—Barry (Sorrell)................... 2:33

Detroit goaltender Earl Robertson sprawls to stop a Ranger drive. He gets help clearing the puck from teammates (No. 16 and No. 18) on each side of the cage.

CHICAGO BLACK HAWKS
TORONTO MAPLE LEAFS 1938

No Blackguard Could Stop This Wonder Team

Chicago Black Hawk owner Major Fred McLaughlin had been the oddball of the league for years, once hiring a stranger he'd met on a train to coach the team. After firing the stranger and a stream of other coaches, the major hired Bill Stewart, a hockey referee in the winter and a big league baseball umpire in the summer. When Stewart tried to move lumbering defenseman Earl Seibert to wing, other coaches shook their heads and they were hardly surprised when the Black Hawks won only 14 of 48 games.

But the Black Hawks did finish third in the American Division, ahead of the Red Wings, who were out of the playoffs after winning two straight Cups. Many of the Red Wings were said to be unhappy about their salaries.

Toronto's Maple Leafs finished first in the Canadian Division, leading the league in scoring, their two young forwards, Gordon Drillon and Syl Apps, finishing one-two in scoring. Boston breezed to first in the American Division, the Bruins' defense as tight as ever with Eddie Shore bouncing people off the boards and Cecil ("Tiny") Thompson a magnet for the puck in the cage. Scoring for Boston was a trio of boyhood buddies out of Kitchener, Ontario, their names Bobby Bauer, Milt Schmidt, and Woody Dumart, later to be famous as the Kraut Line.

Toronto's Walter ("Turk") Broda turned aside the Krauts in the best-of-five series, the Maple Leafs winning the league championship in three straight games: 1-0 in overtime; 2-1 on a late goal by Drillon; and 3-2, again on a goal by Drillon, in overtime. The Leafs, the money players of their decade, were on their way to their fifth final in seven years.

All the games of the second-place series took place at Madison Square Garden: the New York Americans against the New York Rangers. In the third game the Amerks' Lorne Carr scored in the fourth overtime for a 3-2 victory that won the series, two games to one.

In the third-place playoffs the Canadiens routed Bill Stewart's Black Hawks in the first game, 6-4. But in the second game Chicago's thin-faced goalkeeper, Mike Karakas, startled even Chicago fans at the Stadium by shutting out the Flying Frenchmen, 4-0. In the Montreal Forum for the third and decisive game, the largest crowd of the season watched happily as the Canadiens seemed sure winners, ahead 2-1 with only a minute to go. But Chicago's Earl Seibert let fly a long shot from the blue line that eluded Wilf Cude and tied the score. In overtime Paul Thompson veered in on Cude and beat him from the side to win the game and the series, putting the Black Hawks into the semifinal against the Americans.

The Amerks' Dave ("Sweeney") Schriner, Johnny Sorrell, and Nels Stewart summoned enough energy from their old-timey legs to whip pucks by Karakas and win the first game handily, 3-1. But in Chicago, defenseman Alex Levinsky knocked down Amerks and stopped pucks to take some of the pressure off Karakas. The 0-0 game went into overtime. The Stadium was a bedlam— one New York goal and it would be goodnight Chicago. Black Hawk rookie Carl ("Cully") Dahlstrom sent the fans streaming home happy by taking a pass from Louis Trudel and beating Earl Robertson for a 1-0 Black Hawk victory that evened the series at a game apiece.

Back in New York before screaming Amerk fans, the New Yorkers were favored. With the score 1-1, the Black Hawks' Alex Levinsky blasted the puck by Robertson but the light did not flash red to signal a goal. Amerk fans were caught

Chicago's Harold ("Mush") March flits by the Maple Leaf cage after depositing the puck for a goal in the final game. On his knees and staring forlornly at the ice is Toronto goaltender Turk Broda. March played through the final with a guard over his broken nose.

holding the goal judge's hand so he couldn't press the button to turn on the light. Even that kind of blackguardly behavior couldn't stop the Wonder Team, as the Black Hawks were being called back in Chicago; the Hawks won 3-2 to go into the final against the high-scoring Leafs, who were top-heavy favorites.

Before the first game Mike Karakas tried to lace on a boot and couldn't: his toe was swollen and found to be fractured. The Rangers' Davey Kerr, at the game, offered to replace Mike in goal, but the Maple Leafs insisted that the Black Hawks use Alfie ("Half-Pint") Moore, a dwarfish minor league Toronto goalkeeper. An angry Bill Stewart punched Toronto manager Conn Smythe and even Half-Pint Moore thought the Black Hawks had been short-changed. "I hope I stop every puck you fellows fire at me even if I have to eat the rubber," he shouted at Smythe in the hallway before the game.

He did stop most everything without having to munch on rubber, the Hawks winning 3-1. Little Alfie was ruled out for the rest of the series, and the Hawks were ordered to use Paul Goodman, one of their minor league goalkeepers. But Goodman disappeared before the second game; he had thought Moore was going to play. Goodman was found in a movie theater, a short time before the face-off. The movie might have blurred his vision; the Leafs, with Gordon Drillon and George Parsons both scoring twice, bombed him, 5-1, to even the series at a game apiece.

The spidery Karakas came back for the third game, his toe encased in a special boot. Centering for the crippled Hawks was Elwin ("Doc") Romnes, his broken nose protected by a football helmet and special nose guard. With the score tied 1-1, he rammed the puck by Turk Broda to win the game, 2-1, and put the Black Hawks ahead, two games to one.

In the fourth game, with some 17,000 fans stacked to the rafters in Chicago Stadium, the Black Hawks went ahead 1-0 and then held off the Maple Leafs to win 3-1, the jubilant Hawks carrying the chunky Bill Stewart on their shoulders to the dressing room. During these past two weeks they had won seven games—half the number they had won all season—to win the Stanley Cup in

what is still probably the most amazing upset in Cup history.

A delighted Major McLaughlin kept pointing out that half the Black Hawks, including heroes Karakas and Romnes, were American-born, a special delight to the major, who had once put an all-American team on ice (it lost three straight games). "If I die tomorrow," Bill Stewart was shouting, "I want to say the Hawks are the greatest bunch of athletes in the world." The next season the Black Hawks won only 12 games, and Major McLaughlin fired Stewart.

Johnny Gottselig: Down at the tavern, there was Alfie

A former captain of the Black Hawks, Johnny Gottselig still resides in Chicago.

We had a noon meeting before the first game in Toronto that night, and Bill Stewart told us that Mike Karakas couldn't play, his toe was so bad. Our minor league goaltender, Paul Goodman, hadn't arrived. Alfie Moore was a minor league goaltender for Toronto and he lived in Toronto, so Stewart told me to go get him. I knew Alfie. I went to his house and his wife, Agnes, she said he's down at the tavern, you can find him there. I went down to the tavern and a guy told me Alfie just left here, you can find him at another one. I caught him at the second one, and he's sitting there with three or four other hockey players who were through for the season. I walked in and Alfie looked at me and said, "By God, am I glad to see you. I'd love to get a couple of tickets for tonight's game." And I said, "Boy, Alfie, you got the best seat in the house."

When I told him he was going to play that night, he said, "Don't give me that bull." I told him, "You are playing, for sure." And he said, "Boy, it's about time. That Connie Smythe is going to rue the day he ever sent me down to Pittsburgh. I should have been playing up here instead of Broda, I'll show that Connie Smythe."

Then he said, "Let's have one more drink on that before we go." He'd had about ten or a dozen before that. When we brought him back to the hotel, Stewart—he was a nondrinker—when he

60

saw him he said, "Get him out of here, he won't play for us tonight."

I said, "Hell, I'm not going into those nets, Bill, and I don't think Mush March will. This guy is going to play or else."

"Well," Bill said, "it's your money, fellows, if you want to use this guy, go ahead and use him."

We took him out to the rink and put some coffee into him and put him under the shower. By game time he was in pretty good shape. The first shot they threw at him, it went in, the first shot of the game. But after that they couldn't put a puck by him and I guess that night he did show Connie Smythe.

FIRST GAME (April 5, at Toronto)
Black Hawks 3, Maple Leafs 1

FIRST PERIOD
Toronto—Drillon (Davidson)............... 1:53
Chicago—Gottselig (Romnes, Dahlstrom).....17:15
SECOND PERIOD
Chicago—Thompson (Seibert)............... 1:50
THIRD PERIOD
Chicago—Gottselig........................12:08

SECOND GAME (April 7, at Toronto)
Maple Leafs 5, Black Hawks 1

FIRST PERIOD
Toronto—Drillon (Apps, Thoms)........... 1:42
Chicago—Seibert........................ 8:31
SECOND PERIOD
Toronto—Jackson (Thoms)................ 6:10
THIRD PERIOD
Toronto—Drillon (Apps, Hamilton)......... 9:44
Toronto—Parsons (Kelly, Fowler)..........10:29
Toronto—Parsons (Horner, Kelly)..........11:08

THIRD GAME (April 10, at Chicago)
Black Hawks 2, Maple Leafs 1

FIRST PERIOD
Toronto—Apps (Drillon, Davidson).......... 1:35
SECOND PERIOD
Chicago—Voss (Gottselig, Jenkins)..........16:02
THIRD PERIOD
Chicago—Romnes (Thompson, March)......15:55

FOURTH GAME (April 12, at Chicago)
Black Hawks 4, Maple Leafs 1

FIRST PERIOD
Chicago—Dahlstrom (Trudel, Shill).......... 5:52
Toronto—Drillon (Fowler)................. 8:26
SECOND PERIOD
Chicago—Voss (Gottselig, Jenkins)..........16:45
Chicago—Shill..........................17:58
THIRD PERIOD
Chicago—March (Thompson, Romnes).......16:24

Johnny Gottselig: "I walked in and Alfie looked at me and said, 'By God, am I glad to see you. I'd love to get a couple of tickets for tonight's game.' And I said, 'Boy, Alfie, you got the best seat in the house.'"

BOSTON BRUINS

TORONTO MAPLE LEAFS ―1939

No Matter How You Cut the Cards, Up Comes a Maple Leaf

A new playoff system was devised after the Montreal Maroons dropped out of the league, leaving only seven teams, which banded together into one division. The first-place finisher would get the Prince of Wales Trophy, the second-place team the O'Brien. The league decreed that after a 48-game schedule (a total of 168 games) one team would be eliminated, the other six to scrap for the Stanley Cup.

A Boston powerhouse roared home first, 16 points ahead of the Rangers. Manager Art Ross called the Bruins "the greatest team ever assembled," and he had his reasons. He had traded away the revered Cecil ("Tiny") Thompson, replacing him in goal with an American-born youngster, Frankie Brimsek, who shut out six of his first seven opponents and quickly won the nickname "Mr. Zero." Protecting him on the back line were Eddie Shore, on his last hockey legs, and Aubrey ("Dit") Clapper, the "cop" of the team; he punched out opponents who assaulted smaller teammates like center Bobby Bauer. Flanking Bauer on the high-scoring Kraut Line were Milt Schmidt and Woody Dumart, the three having played together since their shinny days back in Kitchener. Boston led the league in scoring, averaging more than three goals a game, while Brimsek was yielding fewer than two a game.

In the new playoff system the first-place Bruins opposed the second-place Rangers in a best-of-seven series. Boston whooshed into the series on an eight-game winning streak. They won their ninth straight when Mel Hill, a Ranger castoff,

rapped the puck by Davey Kerr for a 2-1 victory in triple overtime of the first game. The Bruins won a tenth straight when Hill scored again in overtime for a 3-2 victory that put Boston ahead, two games to none.

They won their 11th straight, 4-1, to lead three games to none, seemingly easy winners in the opening round, especially with the injured Davey Kerr out of action, replaced in goal by Bert Gardiner. In the fourth game Murray ("Muzz") Patrick and Eddie Shore whaled into each other, toe to toe, and Shore wobbled out of the brawl with a black eye and broken nose. That victory seemed to lift the Broadway Blues, who won that game, 2-1, and took the next two—the fifth game in overtime—to even the series at three games apiece.

In the seventh game, goals by Ray Getliffe and Muzz Patrick sent the game into overtime, tied 1-1. Some eight minutes into the third overtime the Bruins' Bill Cowley took the puck behind the Ranger cage and passed it out to Mel Hill, who was zooming in on Gardiner. Hill banged the puck into the cage for his third sudden-death goal of the series, winning the game 2-1, putting Boston into the final, and making himself famous forever after on Causeway Street as "Sudden Death" Hill.

The third-place Toronto Maple Leafs opposed the fourth-place New York Americans in a best-of-three series, the Leafs winning in two straight, 4-0 and 2-0. The fifth-place Red Wings met the sixth-place Canadiens in another two-out-of-three series, Detroit winning, 7-3 and 1-0.

In the semifinal, Detroit against Toronto, the

The Bruins receive the Cup after the final game, forming a straggly line for the cameramen. Holding the Cup is captain Ralph ("Cooney") Weiland. No. 14 is Woody Dumart, No. 19 Jack Crawford, and No. 9 Roy Conacher. Manager-coach Art Ross called this the greatest team he had seen in 37 years in hockey.

teams split the first two games of a best-of-three series. In the third game Toronto's Gordon Drillon sped the length of the ice to whiz a puck by Tiny Thompson and put the Maple Leafs into the final for the sixth time in eight years.

Before the best-of-seven final between Toronto and Boston, Leaf coach Dick Irvin said he was counting on the scoring of Syl Apps and Gordon Drillon and the goaltending of Walter ("Turk") Broda, who had played two and a half hours of hockey during one stretch of these playoffs without allowing a goal. "We'll be faster than the Bruins," he said, "but they have weight and experience."

In Boston the Bruins won the first game on goals by Dumart and Bauer, but Elwin ("Doc") Romnes scored in overtime to win the second for Toronto, 3-2. "If we can win the first game in Toronto," said Toronto general manager Conn Smythe, "they're licked." Maple Leaf fans hoped he was right: their Leafs had come out of five finals in seven years with just one Cup.

Instead, Boston won that third game, 3-1, and went on to grab the next two, winning the Cup—for the first time since 1929—after a 12-game grind, the longest in playoff history. While giant firecrackers exploded on the ice at Boston Garden, the Bruins received the Cup from NHL president Frank Calder. Art Ross was telling people that his team would dominate the NHL for the next ten years. But in Europe Adolf Hitler was telling Germans that "no power can ever again force us to our knees." Before the next face-off for a National Hockey League game, Canada would be at war and within the next two years most of Art Ross' hockey team would be scattered around the globe.

Bill Cowley:
They'll never believe me . . .

The one-time high-scoring center for Boston, Bill Cowley recalled all those overtime games in the Bruin-Ranger semifinal at his home in Ottawa.

That was the greatest series I ever played in. After that the finals were anticlimactic. The series made Mel Hill famous. He was very nervous. Of course, this was his first playoff. But I can recall him walking the streets half the night after a game, trying to calm down. The rest of us would go have a few beers.

I can remember the first overtime period of the first game. I checked someone into the corner and flipped a perfect pass onto Mel's stick right in front of the net. There was nobody for him to beat but the goalkeeper, and the goalkeeper beat him.

In the third overtime period, I made the same play except that the pass wasn't too good. It was about two or three inches off the ice. Hill knocked it out of the air and into the net for the winning goal.

Then there was that seventh game, which also went into overtime. In the first or second overtime their Neil Colville broke away from the blue line and came in on Brimsek. Now I was never noted for my backchecking, but this time I was the only guy back there. He drew Brimmy out with a fake and he had the net wide open, and he missed it. The puck slithered across the front of the net. Years later I was talking about this with Weiland [Ralph ("Cooney") Weiland], who was on the bench. He said when he saw Colville break away he ducked his head under the boards. He couldn't look. And to this day Weiland won't believe I was the only guy back there backchecking.

Toronto *Daily Star* cartoon of March 11, 1939, depicts struggle by seven NHL teams for six playoff chairs. Chicago didn't get one. Circled inset refers to a fete for Charley Conacher, a long-time Maple Leaf returning to Toronto with the Red Wings, to whom he had been traded.

FIRST GAME (April 6, at Boston)
Bruins 2, Maple Leafs 1

FIRST PERIOD
Boston—Dumart (Shore, Bauer). 16:04
SECOND PERIOD
No scoring
THIRD PERIOD
Toronto—Horner (Marker, Romnes). 13:54
Boston—Bauer. 15:31

SECOND GAME (April 9, at Boston)
Maple Leafs 3, Bruins 2

FIRST PERIOD
Toronto—Chamberlain (Kampman, Drillon). . 8:55
Toronto—Apps (Metz, Drillon). 9:29
SECOND PERIOD
Boston—Conacher (Cowley, Hollett). 15:05
Boston—Hill (Shore, Cowley). 16:18
THIRD PERIOD
No scoring
OVERTIME
Toronto—Romnes (Jackson, Marker). 10:38

THIRD GAME (April 11, at Toronto)
Bruins 3, Maple Leafs 1

FIRST PERIOD
No scoring
SECOND PERIOD
No scoring
THIRD PERIOD
Boston—Bauer (Schmidt). 1:28
Boston—Conacher (Cowley). 8:12
Boston—Crawford (Conacher, Cowley). 13:03
Toronto—Marker (Romnes). 19:11

FOURTH GAME (April 13, at Toronto)
Bruins 2, Maple Leafs 0

FIRST PERIOD
Boston—Conacher (Hill). 2:20
SECOND PERIOD
No scoring
THIRD PERIOD
Boston—Conacher (Cowley, Hill). 12:55

FIFTH GAME (April 16, at Boston)
Bruins 3, Maple Leafs 1

FIRST PERIOD
Boston—Hill (Cowley, Conacher). 11:40
Toronto—Kampman (Romnes). 18:40
SECOND PERIOD
Boston—Conacher (Shore, Cowley). 17:34
THIRD PERIOD
Boston—Hollett (Crawford, Schmidt). 19:23

New York Rangers Professional Hockey Club

LESTER PATRICK COL. JOHN R. KILPATRICK STANTON GRIFFIS

FRANK BOUCHER DAVID KERR ART COULTER CAPT. OTT HELLER

ALEX SHIBICKY MAC COLVILLE Winner of THE STANLEY CUP World's Championship 1939-1940 NEIL COLVILLE PHIL WATSON

LYNN PATRICK CLINT SMITH MURRAY PATRICK BABE PRATT

BRYAN HEXTALL KILBY MACDONALD DUTCH HILLER ALF PIKE HARRY WESTERBY TRAINER

NEW YORK RANGERS
TORONTO MAPLE LEAFS
1940

Was That the Stanley Cup
I Saw Under Your Jacket Last Night?

It's a regional game, this hilarious game of hockey. It belongs to Canada and the states that lie along the Dominion border . . . There is a territorial line beyond which hockey can never hope to gain a foothold . . .

—John Kieran,
New York Times columnist, April 1940

Boston led the league for a second straight year, advancing manager Art Ross' thesis that this was the greatest team ever. In New York Lester Patrick could have claimed that his second-place Rangers, after finishing only three points behind Ross' Bruins, had to be the second-greatest team ever.

The Bruins also led in scoring, and little wonder, with the Kraut Line—Milt Schmidt, Woody Dumart, and Bobby Bauer—one-two-three in league scoring. Aubrey ("Dit") Clapper and Jack Crawford were All-Star defensemen and Frankie ("Mr. Zero") Brimsek was the league's No. 2 goaltender behind the Rangers' Davey Kerr.

The Patrickmen, as New York writers called the Rangers, were aptly named, Lester Patrick's sons, Lynn and Murray ("Muzz"), playing for the Silver Fox, who was now a grandfather. Bryan Hextall, with 24 goals in 48 games, led the league in goals, and winger Phil Watson was generally considered the successor to Eddie Shore as the league's most pugnacious player, with Muzz Patrick perhaps a close second. This was a typical Patrick team: quick-skating, adept in its passing, mean on defense. Only Boston had scored more often, and no team had given up fewer goals than the Rangers' Vezina Trophy winner Davey Kerr.

Kerr shut out the Bruins in the first game. The Bruins won the next two. Then Kerr threw suc-

cessive 1-0 shutouts at the Bruins, and the Rangers won the next game, 4-1, to take the best-of-seven series, four games to two.

In the playoffs between the third- and fourth-place teams, Toronto beat Chicago twice. The fifth-place Red Wings took on the sixth-place Americans, who had a plethora of veterans: Harvey ("Busher") Jackson, Eddie Shore, Charley Conacher, Johnny Sorrell. All were puffing after two games, the Red Wings winning in three.

In the best-of-three semifinal, Toronto erased Detroit in two games, the second game ending in a 12-minute brawl, paid for by 17 players, each fined $25. Toronto went into its seventh final in nine years but looking for its first Cup since 1932.

With the circus lions and tigers pacing in their cages at railroad yards in the Bronx, the Rangers hastily scheduled the first two games on successive nights at the Garden. In goal for the Maple Leafs was Walter ("Turk") Broda, who had the reputation of being very good when "on" and very bad when "off." Syl Apps, out for two months with a broken collarbone, returned to center the Maple Leafs' high-scoring line with Bob Davidson and Gordon Drillon on the wings.

The Rangers won the first game of the best-of-seven series on Alfie Pike's goal in overtime, 2-1. In the second game Turk Broda was very bad, New York winning 6-2. Turk heard talk that the Rangers were laughing at him "because Turk's 20 pounds too fat."

In Toronto the Maple Leafs won the next two games. "They made Broda sore," said manager Conn Smythe. But, he added, "The Rangers are the better team."

In the fifth game the score was tied 1-1 in overtime when Muzz Patrick, often called "ugly duckling" because of his skating style, let fly a puck

The 1939–40 Ranger players and executives. Note the narrowness of the bands under the Cup. Later the bands were deepened and widened to hold more names, swelling the circumference of the base. The Cup lost its stovepipe look, as can be seen by comparing this 1940 photo with later photos, shown in the opening section of this book.

from 20 feet away that took Broda by surprise and won the game, 2-1. It was only the Leafs' fourth loss in 29 games at Maple Leaf Gardens. The Rangers now led, three games to two.

In the sixth game the Maple Leafs leaped out to a 2-0 lead on goals by Syl Apps and Nick Metz. But Neil Colville and Alfie Pike tied the game in the third period and the game went into overtime. Two minutes into overtime Bryan Hextall collected a pass from Phil Watson and flicked the puck on a rising line by Turk Broda into the right corner for the goal that won the game, 3-2, and the Cup.

The Leafs shook Ranger hands and hastily left a suddenly mournful Maple Leaf Gardens, the sixth time in eight years they had shaken hands with the winners of the Stanley Cup. That night the Rangers drank champagne as they sat in a Toronto restaurant. Someone discovered that the Cup had disappeared. It was found under the bulging jacket of a Maple Leaf fan who was halfway to the door.

Lynn Patrick:
A wire from the captain

Lynn Patrick, the former high-scoring winger of the Rangers and the son of the Silver Fox, is now a vice-president of the St. Louis Blues.

The big series for us was not the final against the Maple Leafs but the semifinal against Boston. Boston had finished first the previous year, then beat us in seven games—four of the games went into overtime—and they went on to win the Stanley Cup. Then the following year they finished first again, with us second, so they were the best team in the league. But in 1940 they had injuries and that's why we beat them in six games. We beat them in one game, 1-0, when my brother Muzz scored the only goal, and I don't think he scored four goals in his life. [Actually poor Muzz scored a grand total of nine.]

We had a very close team—Muzz and me, and there were the Colville brothers. But the leader of that team was our captain Art Coulter. He put the spirit in the team. Before one of the games against Boston when we went into the dressing room there was a telegram at each player's seat. I still have mine. We opened them and they read: DETERMINATION WAS THE PREDOMINATING FACTOR IN LAST YEAR'S STANLEY CUP CHAMPIONS. WE HAVE IT TOO. LET'S GO. ART COULTER. A real leader. He should be in the Hall of Fame. And a real tough defenseman. The first guy who came into our end, Art gave him a two-hander.

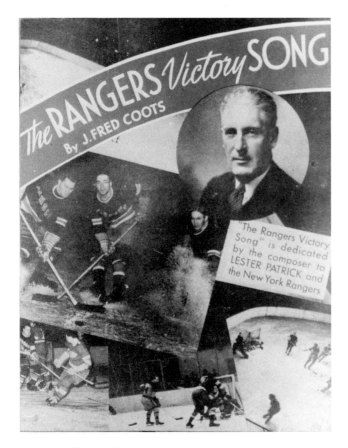

Tin Pan Alley's celebration of the return of the Cup to Manhattan was a hymn to the Rangers, dedicated to the Silver Fox.

"THE RANGERS VICTORY SONG" FREE

Fill in this coupon and give to Garden usher.

Name ....

Address ....

City ....

(A complete piano copy will be mailed with the compliments of the New York Rangers.)

FIRST GAME (April 2, at New York)
Rangers 2, Maple Leafs 1

FIRST PERIOD
New York—Coulter (N. Colville) 9:09
Toronto—Heron (Schriner) 11:10
SECOND PERIOD
No scoring
THIRD PERIOD
No scoring
OVERTIME
New York—Pike (L. Patrick) 15:30

SECOND GAME (April 3, at New York)
Rangers 6, Maple Leafs 2

FIRST PERIOD
Toronto—Taylor (Schriner, Horner) 5:01
Toronto—Goldup (Marker) 6:01
New York—Hextall (Heller, Watson) 15:14
SECOND PERIOD
New York—Pratt (N. Colville) 3:57
New York—Hextall (Heller) 19:48
THIRD PERIOD
New York—Hextall (Watson) 6:26
New York—Heller (Watson, Hextall) 12:21
New York—L. Patrick (Pratt, Heller) 13:09

THIRD GAME (April 6, at Toronto)
Maple Leafs 2, Rangers 1

FIRST PERIOD
New York—Watson 18:19
SECOND PERIOD
No scoring
THIRD PERIOD
Toronto—Drillon (Apps, Horner) 10:12
Toronto—Goldup (Metz) 13:40

FOURTH GAME (April 9, at Toronto)
Maple Leafs 3, Rangers 0

FIRST PERIOD
Toronto—Marker (Goldup, Langelle) 19:20
SECOND PERIOD
No scoring
THIRD PERIOD
Toronto—Stanowski (Church) 16:03
Toronto—Drillon (Apps, Metz) 19:26

FIFTH GAME (April 11, at Toronto)
Rangers 2, Maple Leafs 1

FIRST PERIOD
New York—N. Colville
(M. Colville, Shibicky) 12:21
SECOND PERIOD
Toronto—Apps 16:55
THIRD PERIOD
No scoring
OVERTIME
New York—M. Patrick (N. Colville) 11:43

SIXTH GAME (April 13, at Toronto)
Rangers 3, Maple Leafs 2

FIRST PERIOD
Toronto—Apps (Davidson) 6:52
SECOND PERIOD
Toronto—Metz (Schriner) 4:51
THIRD PERIOD
New York—N. Colville (Shibicky) 8:08
New York—Pike 10:01
OVERTIME
New York—Hextall (Watson, Hiller) 2:07

The Broadway Blues'
No. 1 line (l. to r.): Bryan
Hextall, Phil Watson,
and Lynn Patrick. On a
pass from Watson, Hextall
scored the goal that
brought the Cup back
to New York.

BOSTON BRUINS
DETROIT RED WINGS — 1941

Retort for a Heckler:
A Punch in the Eye

The Red Wings look like a bunch of guys named Joe to me.
—Boston's Mel Hill before the finals

We're getting tired of everybody thinking we're a bunch of lucky bums.
—Detroit's Jimmy Orlando before the finals

For the fourth straight year, the Boston Bruins won the Prince of Wales Trophy, tying the Bruins' record of 1928–31. The Bruins stormed home first with a 27-8-13 record, going undefeated for a stretch of 23 games, still an NHL record. Boston topped the league in scoring, Bill Cowley ranking first among the puck shooters, with the high-scoring Kraut Line—Bobby Bauer, Woody Dumart, and Milt Schmidt—not far behind him. Toronto goalkeeper Walter ("Turk") Broda gave up the fewest goals in the league, winning the Vezina Trophy, but Boston's Frankie ("Mr. Zero") Brimsek was a close second. Toronto's Gordon Drillon and Syl Apps finished third and fourth in scoring. With Broda, Drillon, and Apps, the second-place Maple Leafs looked every bit as strong as the first-place Bruins; the Leafs thought they were the superior of the Bruins, and this best-of-seven series was their place to prove it.

With Bill Cowley missing from the Bruins' lineup because of a wrenched knee, Toronto jumped out to a two-game-to-one lead. Cowley came back and he and Herb Cain rallied the Bruins to even the series at three games apiece. With the score tied 1-1 in the seventh game, Mel ("Sudden Death") Hill came through with another clutch goal that won the game, 2-1, and put Boston into its second final in three years.

The third-place Red Wings ousted the fourth-place Rangers, the defending Cup champions, in three games. The fifth-place Black Hawks beat the sixth-place Canadiens in three games, Carl ("Cully") Dahlstrom winning the third game, 3-2, with a pair of goals.

Detroit opposed Chicago in the best-of-three semifinal and won in two games, 3-1 and (in overtime) 2-1, the winning goal being scored by Gus Giesebrecht.

Names like Gus Giesebrecht did not impress the lordly Bruins, Mel Hill confessing the Red Wings looked like a bunch of Joes to him. "All we have to do is slow up Jimmy Orlando and Nels Stewart," Hill said on the eve of the first game.

In goal for Detroit squatted rotund Johnny Mowers, a rookie who had tied Brimsek for second-place in the Vezina competition. But on offense the Red Wings were not especially worrisome, tied for fifth in the seven-team league in scoring. And Boston seemed to have Detroit's number; not once in a year had Boston lost on Detroit ice.

In the first game, at Boston, the Red Wings could lash only eight shots at Brimsek in the first two periods, and Boston, off to an early lead, coasted to a 3-2 victory. For two periods of the second game Detroit's Johnny Mowers kept tight the gate, Detroit leading 1-0 early in the third period. But Boston's Terry Reardon tied the

Boston's renowned Kraut Line (l. to r.):
Bobby Bauer, Milt Schmidt, and
Woody Dumart. Bauer was the tricky
center, Schmidt the scorer on the wing,
the muscular Dumart the line's
"policeman" who polished off any
opponents caught bullying little Bobby.

Detroit's Syd Howe (No. 8 in dark jersey) reaches his stick for a bounding puck in front of the Boston cage during the third game. Defending for Boston are goaltender Frank Brimsek, Aubrey ("Dit") Clapper (No. 5), Des Smith (No. 8), and Jack Crawford (No. 16). Pinching in on the Bruin cage are Red Wings Jimmy Orlando (No. 4) and Alex Motter (No. 3).

game, 1-1, and with little more than two minutes remaining, Roy Conacher took a pass from Schmidt and snapped the puck by Mowers for a 2-1 Bruin victory that put Boston ahead, two games to none.

As Bruin manager Art Ross was leaving the ice, a heckler shouted at him: "Are you going to let this go to seven games the way you did against Toronto?" Ross punched the man in the eye.

In Detroit Milt Schmidt whacked in a pair of goals during a 4-2 Bruin victory, thoroughly dispiriting the Red Wing rooters. Only 8,125 fans showed up for the fourth game, but they were pleased to see Detroit leap ahead, 1-0. In the second period Boston's Bill ("Flash") Hollett tied the game and Bobby Bauer put Boston ahead, 2-1, on a pass from Schmidt. The Bruins went on to win, 3-1, to take their second Cup in three years and become the first team to win the final series in four straight games.

Milt Schmidt:
You could always call the cop

The wingman on Boston's famous Kraut Line, Milt Schmidt today is the general manager of the NHL's Washington Capitals.

Winning that series in four straight was no surprise to us. We had a great hockey club at that stage, no doubt about it. It was a wide-open series against Detroit, and that favored us, because we had a good skating club and a good scoring club. We had guys like Bill Cowley and Roy Conacher and Herbie Cain and myself and Bobby Bauer on our line. If it had been a hitting series, a heavy body-checking series, it would have taken a little away from our greatest assets —skating and moving the puck around. But we had big "Dit" [Aubrey Clapper], and after 20 years Dit was well respected around the league. They used to say he could have been the heavyweight champion of Canada if he'd wanted to. We had the muscle in Clapper—he was what they call your "policeman" today—and I guess maybe that was the reason Detroit left us alone.

Big Dit Clapper (No. 5) sits between Milt Schmidt (No. 15) and Woody Dumart. What Dit gave to the Krauts was a heavyweight's kayo punch.

FIRST GAME (April 6, at Boston)
  Bruins 3, Red Wings 2

FIRST PERIOD
  Boston—Wiseman (Smith, Conacher)........13:26
SECOND PERIOD
  Boston—Schmidt (Dumart, Crawford).......14:45
THIRD PERIOD
  Boston—McCreavy (Schmidt, Crawford)..... 9:16
  Detroit—Liscombe (Jennings, Brown).......10:55
  Detroit—Howe (Brown)....................17:45

SECOND GAME (April 8, at Boston)
  Bruins 2, Red Wings 1

FIRST PERIOD
  No scoring
SECOND PERIOD
  No scoring
THIRD PERIOD
  Detroit—Bruneteau (Howe, Orlando)........ 2:41
  Boston—Reardon (Cain, Smith)............13:35
  Boston—Conacher (Schmidt)...............17:45

THIRD GAME (April 10, at Detroit)
  Bruins 4, Red Wings 2

FIRST PERIOD
  Detroit—Jennings (Grosso, Abel)........... 3:15
  Boston—Wiseman (Conacher, Hollett)....... 3:57
  Detroit—Abel (Stewart)................... 7:45
  Boston—Schmidt (Dumart, Bauer)..........14:07
SECOND PERIOD
  Boston—Schmidt (Dumart, Clapper)........ 0:59
THIRD PERIOD
  Boston—Jackson (Reardon, Clapper)........17:20

FOURTH GAME (April 12, at Detroit)
  Bruins 3, Red Wings 1

FIRST PERIOD
  Detroit—Liscombe (Howe, Giesebrecht)......10:14
SECOND PERIOD
  Boston—Hollett (Schmidt)................. 7:42
  Boston—Bauer (Schmidt).................. 8:43
  Boston—Wiseman (Conacher, McCreavy).....19:32
THIRD PERIOD
  No scoring

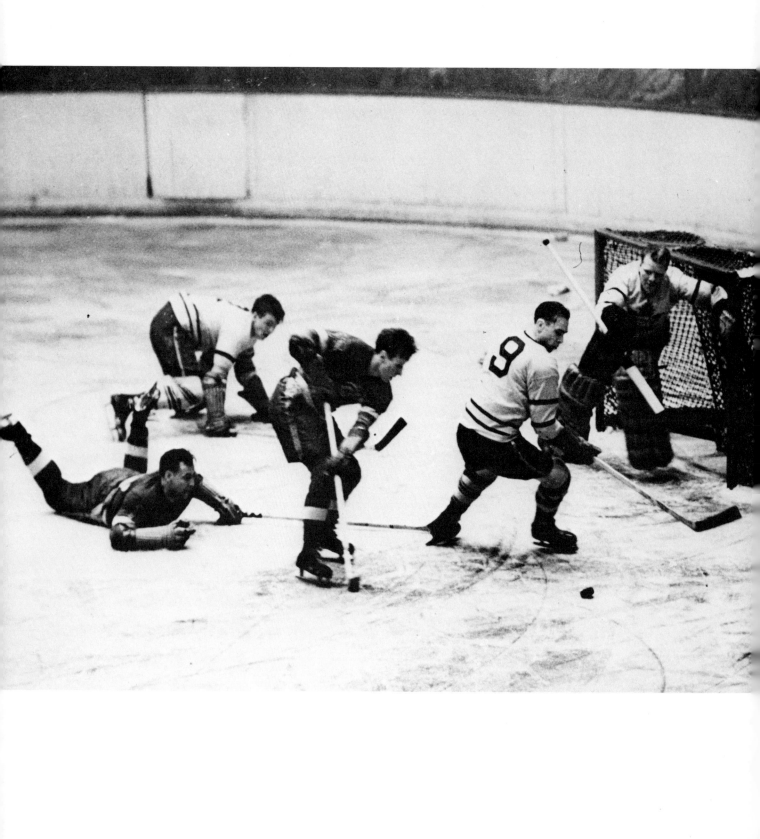

DETROIT RED WINGS
TORONTO MAPLE LEAFS
1942

Doing It the Hardest
of All Possible Ways

Detroit is unbeatable. They can't seem to do any-thing wrong.

—Toronto goalkeeper Turk Broda
after the Red Wings took the
first three games from the Leafs

Hockey players were unlacing their skates and going off to war in bunches. In one night, for example, the Bruins lost the entire Kraut Line (which had been renamed the Kitchener Line due to anti-German sentiment) as Woody Dumart, Bobby Bauer, and Milt Schmidt flew off together to join the Canadian Air Force. The Rangers held onto enough high-scoring stars to finish first, Bryan Hextall, Lynn Patrick, and Phil Watson ranking one, two, and four in league scoring. In second place were the Maple Leafs, six-foot Walter ("Turk") Broda still standing broad-hipped in goal and an array of shooters—Syl Apps, Gordon Drillon, Bob Davidson, Nick Metz, Dave ("Sweeney") Schriner, and Gaye Stewart among them—tattooing opposing goalkeepers.

That firepower blasted seven pucks by new Ranger goalkeeper "Sugar Jim" Henry in the first two games, Toronto erasing the Rangers in six games to go on to its seventh final in the ten years since it had last won the Cup.

Third-place Boston erased fourth-place Chicago while fifth-place Detroit disposed of the sixth-place Canadiens, each series lasting the full three games.

In the semifinal Detroit overpowered the Kraut-less Bruins, 6-4 and 3-1, to go into its second straight final. The Red Wings had won their last

nine games at home, but the Maple Leafs were heavy favorites.

The Red Wings came out fighting in the first game, bumping and battering the Maple Leafs all over Maple Leaf Gardens, winning 3-2. It was only Detroit's fourth victory in Toronto in five years. "We were up against the Gas House Gang," growled Toronto coach Clarence ("Hap") Day. "That wasn't hockey out there. It was hoodlum-ism."

Don ("The Count") Grosso, a flashy dresser, led the Detroit boppers in the second match, scoring twice in a 4-2 Red Wing victory. "We played the hard-checking game the Leafs don't like," said Detroit's Eddie Bush. "Wait till we get them on our own ice. We will show them checking that is checking."

In Detroit, Red Wing fans stood and roared as their team bounced back from a 2-0 deficit to win, 5-2. The Red Wings led, three games to none. No team that had lost the first two games of the final—never mind the first three games—had ever come back to win the Cup. The Maple Leafs seemed destined to be forever the Stanley Cup bridesmaid, never the bride.

Coach Hap Day and manager Conn Smythe decided some of the Leafs weren't trying hard enough. They benched Gordon Drillon and Wil-fred ("Bucko") McDonald, adding Gaye Stewart and Don Metz. An overflow crowd came to Olympia Stadium expecting to see the Red Wings win the Cup in four straight. They saw the Red Wings lead 2-0 and then 3-2, only some 15 minutes away from the winning of the Cup. But

Detroit's Modere ("Mud") Bruneteau, in dark shirt, slides along the ice after poking a puck that goes astray to the left of the Maple Leaf cage during the third game. Toronto goalkeeper Turk Broda swings to his left to block a shot by an onrushing Red Wing winding up to swat the puck.

In the first game of the
quarterfinal series
between Boston and
Chicago, Bruins Roy
Conacher (No. 9) and Bill
Cowley (No. 10) thrust
sticks high after assisting
on Des Smith's overtime
goal to beat the
Black Hawks.

Syl Apps tied the game and Don Metz fed a pass to his brother, Nick, who banged the puck by Johnny Mowers for a 4-3 Maple Leaf victory.

Detroit's Don Grosso-Sid Abel-Eddie Wares line had been knocking in goals at a steady rate in the first four games. It was shut out as Toronto won the fifth game, 9-3, a Maple Leaf Gardens crowd screaming "More!" each time another puck whistled by the embarrassed Mowers. In the sixth game Broda shut out all the Detroit marksmen, the Maple Leafs winning 3-0 to even the series at three victories apiece.

Some 16,218 fans, said to be the largest crowd ever to see a hockey game in Canada, filled the Gardens for the seventh game. The game went scoreless until early in the second period when Detroit's Syd Howe made it 1-0. The Red Wings, apprehensive now, cozied that slim lead for 26 minutes. Then Toronto's Sweeney Schriner scorched one puck by Mowers, Pete Langelle tossed in another, and Schriner batted in a third for a 3-1 Toronto victory, its fourth in a row in a comeback streak never equaled since in Stanley Cup history. No team before or since the Maple Leafs of '42 ever lost the first three games of a final and won the next four. After going all the way to the final for the eighth time in eleven years, Toronto finally had won its first Cup since 1932—doing it the hardest of all possible ways.

Syl Apps:
For a comeback, one win at a time

Syl Apps, the former Maple Leaf center and captain, is a legendary name in hockey. Now a Toronto executive, he recalled the comeback of the Leafs.

After we lost that third game, we thought: "Hey, we can't go back to Toronto after losing four straight. We got to win at least one game." So we fought like mad to win that fourth game so we could go back to Toronto with at least one victory and not be ashamed. Well, we did beat them, 4-3, and then we beat them 9-3, and we thought, "Hey, maybe we do have a chance to beat them." I can still see that clock going around in Maple Leaf Gardens at the end of the last game, with us ahead 3-1, and I remember thinking, "Well, they can't beat us now." It was a great feeling.

80

Mud Bruneteau: He helped to win three Cups for the Red Wings in 1936, 1937, and 1943. In his nine playoff years he scored 23 goals and collected 14 assists in 72 games.

FIRST GAME (April 4, at Toronto)
Red Wings 3, Maple Leafs 2

FIRST PERIOD
Detroit—Grosso (Orlando)................ 1:37
Toronto—McCreedy (Davidson, Kampman)... 6:36
Detroit—Abel (Grosso)....................12:30
Toronto—Schriner (Taylor)................12:59
SECOND PERIOD
Detroit—Grosso.........................14:11
THIRD PERIOD
No scoring

SECOND GAME (April 7, at Toronto)
Red Wings 4, Maple Leafs 2

FIRST PERIOD
Detroit—Grosso (Wares)...................11:47
Detroit—Bruneteau (Liscombe).............14:17
SECOND PERIOD
Toronto—Schriner (Taylor, Stanowski)......11:13
THIRD PERIOD
Detroit—Grosso (Wares).................. 4:15
Detroit—J. Brown (Bush, Liscombe).........10:06
Toronto—Stanowski......................14:39

THIRD GAME (April 9, at Detroit)
Red Wings 5, Maple Leafs 2

FIRST PERIOD
Toronto—Carr (Taylor, Kampman).........15:36
Toronto—Carr (Taylor)...................16:06
Detroit—J. Brown (Bush, Stewart)..........18:20
Detroit—Carveth (Bush, A. Brown).........18:58
SECOND PERIOD
Detroit—McCreavy (Grosso, Bush)........13:12
Detroit—Howe (Grosso, Bush).............15:11
THIRD PERIOD
Detroit—Bush (Liscombe)................. 7:11

FOURTH GAME (April 12, at Detroit)
Maple Leafs 4, Red Wings 3

FIRST PERIOD
No scoring
SECOND PERIOD
Detroit—Bruneteau (Motter).............. 1:32
Detroit—Abel (Wares, Grosso).............. 9:08
Toronto—Davidson (Langelle, McCreedy)....13:54
Toronto—Carr (Taylor, Schriner)...........15:20
THIRD PERIOD
Detroit—Liscombe (Bruneteau, Howe)........ 4:18
Toronto—Apps (Stanowski, N. Metz)........ 6:15
Toronto—N. Metz (D. Metz, Apps).........12:45

FIFTH GAME (April 14, at Toronto)
Maple Leafs 9, Red Wings 3

FIRST PERIOD
Toronto—N. Metz (Apps, Stanowski)....... 9:24
Toronto—Stanowski......................15:13
SECOND PERIOD
Toronto—Goldham....................... 1:59
Toronto—Schriner (Taylor)................ 4:11
Toronto—D. Metz (Apps, N. Metz).........14:11
Toronto—Apps (D. Metz, Goldham)........14:39
Toronto—D. Metz (N. Metz)...............16:43
THIRD PERIOD
Detroit—Howe (McCreavy, Liscombe)....... 3:12
Toronto—D. Metz (Apps, Stanowski)....... 5:31
Toronto—Apps (D. Metz)................. 9:20
Detroit—Motter (Howe)..................13:57
Detroit—Liscombe (Howe).................15:39

SIXTH GAME (April 16, at Detroit)
Maple Leafs 3, Red Wings 0

FIRST PERIOD
No scoring
SECOND PERIOD
Toronto—D. Metz........................ 0:14
THIRD PERIOD
Toronto—Goldham (Schriner)..............13:32
Toronto—Taylor (Schriner)................14:04

SEVENTH GAME (April 18, at Toronto)
Maple Leafs 3, Red Wings 1

FIRST PERIOD
No scoring
SECOND PERIOD
Detroit—Howe (Abel, Orlando)............. 1:44
THIRD PERIOD
Toronto—Schriner (Carr, Taylor)........... 7:46
Toronto—Langelle (Goldham, McCreedy)..... 9:43
Toronto—Schriner (Taylor, Carr)...........16:13

BOSTON BRUINS
DETROIT RED WINGS 1943

Always There Would Be
That Cry—"Remember the Leafs!"

Just a year ago we were sitting on a three-game lead and counting our championship dollars. And what happened? Toronto beat us in four straight before we could blink an eye. We've been twice in the finals for the Cup in the past two years. This time we are going to win the finals with four games in a row.

—Detroit manager Jack Adams
before the final

With the pitiful Brooklyn (formerly New York) Americans dropping out of the league—the team won only 24 games in two years—the NHL had shrunk to six teams. A new playoff system was established. The season-long schedule would eliminate the fifth and sixth teams. The top four teams would meet in two semifinal series to determine the two finalists for the Cup. Remembering Lester Patrick's dictum, "Playoffs are the lifeblood of hockey," the NHL's Board of Governors sought to create as many playoff games as possible. The two semifinal series, like the final, would be best-of-seven affairs.

By now each NHL team had contributed, on average, a dozen players to the war against Hitler and Hirohito. What was left, in the words of a popular song of the day, was "either too young or too old." Among the young ones was a flashy Montreal rookie named Maurice Richard, who broke a leg early in the season during one of his flying dashes the length of a rink.

Shooting against too-old and too-young goaltending, the Toronto Maple Leafs set a league scoring record with 198 goals. The Detroit Red Wings scored fewer goals than any team in the league except the sixth-place Rangers, but in goal Johnny Mowers could be as hard to penetrate as a snowplow. Detroit came in first, Boston second, Toronto third, Montreal fourth, only 11 points separating the first and fourth teams.

First-place Detroit met the third-place Maple Leafs; the Red Wings were anxious to avenge the previous year's disaster when Detroit led Toronto in the final three games to none, then lost the next four and the Cup. The Detroit line of Sid Abel, Don Grosso, and Eddie Wares—no ball of fire during the season—suddenly could not miss, skimming eight goals by Walter ("Turk") Broda, and the Red Wings got their revenge, winning four games to two.

Second-place Boston could put on ice a most respectable starting six: Frankie Brimsek standing in goal, Bill ("Flash") Hollett, and Aubrey ("Dit") Clapper bumping people away for the defense, with center Bill Cowley (No. 2 in league scoring) and wingers Herb Cain and Art Jackson making up a formidable scoring line. Montreal's Canadiens missed young Maurice Richard, and the Bruins overwhelmed the Canadiens in five games to go into their second final in three years.

For the first game some 12,000 Red Wing fans came to Olympia Stadium looking to cheer away the memories of last year's disappointment. They saw Detroit's Modere ("Mud") Bruneteau slice three goals by the one-time "Mr. Zero," Brimsek seeming to lack his old quickness. Detroit won, 6-2, snapping its streak of four straight losses in Stanley Cup finals. In the second game

Red Wing goaltender Johnny Mowers (No. 1) collapses on the puck during a scramble near the net in the third game. No. 11 is the Bruins' Don Gallinger, No. 2 Detroit's Jack Stewart. Detroit owner Jim Norris was said to have promised a $2,500 bonus to the Red Wings if they won in four straight.

This picture of the 1943 Red Wings, the original of which hangs in
the Hockey Hall of Fame, was probably taken during training camp
since it does not include all of the Red Wings who won the Cup
but does include some who left for the military before the start of
the 1942–43 season. Rear row (l. to r.): W. Collett, trainer Honey
Walker, Eddie Bush (who did not play in 1943), Alex Motter, Sid Abel,
Pat McCreavy (who also did not play), and C. Mattson. Second row:
Carl Liscombe, Jimmy Orlando, Mud Bruneteau, player-coach
Ebbie Goodfellow, Jack Stewart, Gerald Brown (who also left after
1942), and Adam Brown. Seated: Joe Carveth, Eddie Wares,
club official P. Haner, Johnny Mowers, manager Jack Adams, Don
Grosso, and Syd Howe. Missing are Cully Simon, Connie Brown,
Les Douglas, Hal Jackson, Joe Fisher, and Harry Watson.

84

Boston took a 2-0 lead, but Detroit whizzed four pucks past Brimsek for a 4-3 victory.

Their team behind now two games to none, Bruin fans were reminding each other of the '42 Leafs and how they came from behind to win in four straight—a once-in-a-generation feat that would be the stuff of dreams for teams trailing in Stanley Cup finals for years to come. At the Boston Garden Detroit's Don Grosso scored three times while Johnny Mowers was closing out Bill Cowley and his friends in a 4-0 shutout.

In the fourth game the Red Wings went into the third period ahead 2-0. As the Bruins volleyed shot after shot at Mowers, there had to be visions in Detroit heads of that turnaround by Toronto in the fourth game a year earlier. But this time Mowers shunted aside all the pucks thrown his way, collecting his second straight shutout. By sweeping over the Bruins in four straight to win their third Stanley Cup, the Red Wings gained another measure of revenge: two years earlier the Bruins had beaten them in four.

Sid Abel:
Hot and cold

One of the highest scorers of his time, Sid Abel later coached the Red Wings and is now the general manager of the Kansas City Scouts of the NHL.

In 1943, when I got five goals and eight assists, that was my only outstanding Stanley Cup series. Most every year Lindsay, Howe, and I were like one-two-four or one-three-five in league scoring. We would have that really hot season and then do nothing in the playoffs. The other team would send out a line against us who were exclusively checkers. They'd shadow you, check the hell out of you. I remember one year the Rangers put out three guys named Raleigh, Slowinski, and someone else. They not only checked the hell out of us, what was even worse, they got us so disorganized, they even outscored us. I always wished that I had had more than one big Stanley Cup series.

FIRST GAME (April 1, at Detroit)
Red Wings 6, Bruins 2

FIRST PERIOD
Detroit—Stewart (Abel, Liscombe)........... 1:15
Boston—A. Jackson (Cain).................18:13
SECOND PERIOD
Detroit—Bruneteau (Abel, H. Jackson).......1:12
Detroit—Abel.......................15:43
Detroit—Carveth (Douglas)................19:06
THIRD PERIOD
Detroit—Bruneteau (Abel, Liscombe)......... 1:21
Detroit—Bruneteau (Stewart, Abel)..........16:24
Boston—DeMarco (Guidolin, Gallinger)......17:53

SECOND GAME (April 4, at Detroit)
Red Wings 4, Bruins 3

FIRST PERIOD
No scoring
SECOND PERIOD
Boston—Crawford (Chamberlain)............10:16
Boston—A. Jackson (Cowley, Cain).........11:04
Detroit—Douglas (Orlando)................17:08
THIRD PERIOD
Detroit—Carveth (Orlando)................ 5:55
Detroit—Liscombe (Abel).................. 6:21
Detroit—Howe (Wares)....................13:16
Boston—A. Jackson (Cowley, Hollett).......16:38

THIRD GAME (April 7, at Boston)
Red Wings 4, Bruins 0

FIRST PERIOD
Detroit—Grosso (Wares)................... 3:26
Detroit—Grosso (Liscombe)................10:16
SECOND PERIOD
No scoring
THIRD PERIOD
Detroit—Douglas........................ 8:03
Detroit—Grosso (Wares)..................18:41

FOURTH GAME (April 8, at Boston)
Red Wings 2, Bruins 0

FIRST PERIOD
Detroit—Carveth.........................12:09
SECOND PERIOD
Detroit—Liscombe........................ 2:45
THIRD PERIOD
No scoring

CHICAGO BLACK HAWKS 1944
MONTREAL CANADIENS

For the First Time,
Eight in a Row

Wanted: Hockey Players. That sign could have been hanging from the front door of any of the NHL teams as the war continued to drain away players. One Ranger goalkeeper was giving up an average of six goals per game—and Lester Patrick was glad to have him. He'd begged the league for players and had been turned down. Defending the Cup, the Red Wings lost Sid Abel, Eddie Wares, Ebbie Goodfellow, and Jimmy Orlando.

In luck was Montreal coach Dick Irvin, who had two players medically exempt from service. One was a hulking 200-pound goaltender, Bill Durnan, a rookie at 29. The other was the swift Maurice Richard, flying up and down the ice at such velocities that he'd broken a leg and wrenched a shoulder—and earned the nickname "Rocket"—in only two NHL seasons. The Rocket was teamed on a line with the veterans Hector ("Toe") Blake and Elmer Lach, a Punch Line that would begin to rewrite the Stanley Cup record books.

Montreal whizzed home first, the Flying Frenchmen losing only five of 50 games, going undefeated on home ice, finishing a record 25 points ahead of the second-place Red Wings. Durnan won the Vezina Trophy by yielding the fewest goals in the league while the Punch Line and its cohorts were whacking home 234 goals, an NHL record.

The Canadiens took on the third-place Maple Leafs and were heavy favorites, which made their loss in the first game by a 3-1 score a shock felt in wallets all across Canada. In the second game the young Rocket showed the Maple Leafs who was boss, rapping five pucks past Paul Bibeault in a 5-1 Montreal victory. The Rocket's five goals had been exceeded only by the six scored by Seattle's Bernie Morris in 1917; the five goals are still a modern record for a single playoff game. On all five goals he was assisted by Toe Blake, another playoff record that later was tied but never exceeded.

Montreal won the next two games, then buried Toronto under an avalanche of pucks, winning 11-0, still a record number of goals by one team in one playoff game. During a two-and-a-half minute stretch of that fifth and final game, the Canadiens blistered four pucks by Bibeault, another record that still stands.

In the other semifinal, the second-place Red Wings clashed with the fourth-place Black Hawks. Spearheading the Chicago attack was a line of Doug Bentley, Clint Smith, and Bill Mosienko, who ranked second, sixth, and eighth in league scoring. With Bentley scoring seven goals, the Black Hawks ousted the Red Wings in five games and entered their first final since winning the Cup in 1938.

Chicago coach Paul Thompson talked proudly of his defense, with Mike Karakas, one of the 1938 heroes, in goal. But Thompson conceded he could send out only one scoring line while

Montreal's renowned Punch Line (l. to r.): Rocket Richard, Elmer Lach, and Toe Blake. Some 30 years after their heyday, the Punch Liners still hold or share playoff records: Lach for most assists in a period (3); Blake for most assists in a game (5); Richard for most game-winning goals (18) and most overtime goals (6), two of many for the Rocket.

Action in front of the Montreal net during
the third game: Chicago center Clint
Smith, in white shirt, sprays ice as he skids
in front of Canadien goaltender Bill
Durnan, who has kicked away his shot.
Looking on are Montreal's Emile ("Butch")
Bouchard (No. 3) and a young Rocket
Richard (behind the cage).

Montreal coach Dick Irvin could call on shooters like Buddy O'Connor, Phil Watson, Erwin ("Murph") Chamberlain, and Ray Getliffe when the Punch Line was pooped.

Irvin planned to neutralize the Bentley-Mosienko-Smith line with the Punch Line, figuring his second-line shooters could pepper Karakas with enough pucks to keep Montreal ahead. That's what happened in the first game, the Bentley line scoring only once while Montreal's Watson-Getliffe-Chamberlain line pumped in four goals during a 5-1 Canadien victory.

In the second game the Rocket burst loose to score three goals while helping to handcuff the Bentley line, which failed to score. The Canadiens won, 3-1, to lead two games to none. In Chicago the Canadiens won the third game, 3-2. The Bentley line came alive in the fourth game, scoring two goals that helped put Chicago ahead, 4-1, halfway through the third period. But the Punch Line rallied to streak three goals by Karakas to tie the game, 4-4, and Toe Blake won game and Cup with a goal in overtime. The Canadiens were hailed as the first team to win eight straight playoff games on its way to the Cup.

Maurice Richard: Lighting up the Rocket

The spectacular Rocket, living in Montreal, recalled his first of 12 Stanley Cup finals.

We had won the first three games easy and when we were behind in that fourth game, at the Forum, the fans were getting on us about not trying hard enough. Maybe they thought that with a three-game lead, we were trying to stretch out the series to five or six games. Anyway they were yelling, "Fake, fake, fake," things like that. That really roused us. I got the two goals to tie the score near the end of the game and Blake got the winner. That shut them up, those fans.

FIRST GAME (April 4, at Montreal)
Canadiens 5, Black Hawks 1
FIRST PERIOD
Montreal—Watson......................... 8:37
SECOND PERIOD
Montreal—Blake (Lach, Richard)........... 6:35
Chicago—Smith (Bentley, Mosienko)........10:11
Montreal—Getliffe (Heffernan, O'Connor)....10:58
THIRD PERIOD
Montreal—Chamberlain (Watson, Bouchard).. 4:47
Montreal—Getliffe.......................18:07

SECOND GAME (April 6, at Chicago)
Canadiens 3, Black Hawks 1
FIRST PERIOD
No scoring
SECOND PERIOD
Montreal—Richard (Lach, Blake)...........13:00
THIRD PERIOD
Montreal—Richard (Lamoureux)...........12:16
Montreal—Richard (Lach)..................15:33
Chicago—Harms (Smith, Allen)............19:59

THIRD GAME (April 9, at Chicago)
Canadiens 3, Black Hawks 2
FIRST PERIOD
Chicago—Allen (Wiebe).................... 5:14
SECOND PERIOD
Montreal—Blake (Richard)................. 2:02
THIRD PERIOD
Chicago—Harms (Johnson)................. 4:16
Montreal—McMahon...................... 5:47
Montreal—Watson (Getliffe).............. 6:42

FOURTH GAME (April 13, at Montreal)
Canadiens 5, Black Hawks 4
FIRST PERIOD
Chicago—Allen (Dahlstrom)................ 5:12
Montreal—Lach (Blake)................... 8:48
SECOND PERIOD
Chicago—Harms (Dahlstrom, Allen)........ 7:30
Chicago—Bentley (Smith)................. 9:12
Chicago—Bentley (Smith).................10:09
THIRD PERIOD
Montreal—Lach (Blake)...................10:02
Montreal—Richard (Blake)................16:05
Montreal—Richard (Blake, Bouchard)........17:20
OVERTIME
Montreal—Blake (Bouchard)............... 9:12

Maurice Richard: "Maybe they thought that with a three-game lead, we were trying to stretch out the series to five or six games...they were yelling, 'Fake, fake, fake.'"

DETROIT RED WINGS
TORONTO MAPLE LEAFS
1945

Could This Be 1942 Again—but in Reverse?

No team ever threw as long a shadow over the National Hockey League as did the Canadiens in this last wartime season. Five of the six players on the All-Star team were Canadiens: goalkeeper Bill Durnan, defenseman Emile ("Butch") Bouchard, and the Punch Line of Maurice ("Rocket") Richard, Elmer Lach, and Hector ("Toe") Blake. Finishing one, two, three in league scoring were Lach, who collected a record number of assists (54 in 50 games); Richard, who scored a record number of goals (50); and Toe Blake. The Canadiens won 38, lost only 8, and tied 4. The team scored the most goals and gave up the fewest, Bill Durnan the winner of the Vezina Trophy as the league's top goalie for the second straight year (he would win it four of the next five years).

Way back in third place were the Maple Leafs, 28 points behind Montreal. In goal was a 26-year-old former Calgary sportswriter, Frank Mc-Cool, replacing Walter ("Turk") Broda, who had gone off to war. On defense 29-year-old Walter ("Babe") Pratt was the Bobby Orr of the day. The previous season he had scored 17 goals and collected 40 assists, a record for a defenseman. On the attack, young Ted Kennedy centered a fast line with Bob Davidson and Lorne Carr on the wings. But Toronto looked puny against the Canadien heavyweights, and the Canadiens were favored to take the semifinal and go on to win a second straight Cup.

Toronto coach Clarence ("Hap") Day assigned Davidson to shadow the Rocket. Much to Richard's annoyance, Davidson blanked the Rocket and Toronto won the first two games, 1-0 and 3-2. The Canadiens won the third game, 4-2. In the fourth game Richard scored his first goal of the series, but Toronto won the game,

4-3, to lead, three games to one. They stood within one game of upsetting the mighty Flying Frenchmen.

Seeming to burst with inner rage, the Canadiens in the fifth game buried McCool in a pile of rubber, winning 10-3, the teams tying the record for total goals in a single playoff game that was set in 1936. But McCool stood steady in the sixth game, with the boulder-like Babe Pratt —the biggest man in hockey at 6-foot-3 and 215 pounds—bouncing away the Flying Frenchmen, and Toronto won, 3-2, to go into the final.

In the other semifinal the fourth-place Bruins battled the second-place Detroit Red Wings down to a seventh game at Olympia Stadium. There the dark-haired Harry ("Apple Cheeks") Lumley, at 18 the youngest goaltender in NHL history, picked off the best shots that the Bruins' riflemen, Bill Cowley and Herb Cain, could wing at him. Detroit's Carl Liscombe, meanwhile, was pushing four shots by Paul Bibeault for a 5-3 Red Wing victory, Detroit going into its fourth final in the past five years.

These were the same two teams, Toronto and Detroit, that had met in the 1942 final, won by Toronto after Detroit had taken the first three games. Toronto's McCool, who suffered from ulcers, gulped a quart of milk before each game and then shut out the Red Wings three times in succession: 1-0, 2-0, and 1-0, still a Stanley Cup record for successive shutouts.

Before the fourth game, at Toronto, flags flew at half-mast and the crowd stood in silence in memory of U.S. President Franklin D. Roosevelt, who had died several days earlier. The Red Wings won the next three games, 5-3, 2-0, and 1-0, to even the series at three games apiece. With this

The winning Canadiens shown in a montage around the Cup. Note that the Cup still has the stovepipe look which it kept until the mid-1950s.

Three of the players who helped decide the seventh game. Above: Ted Kennedy, who assisted on the first Toronto goal. Right: Nick Metz, who set up Babe Pratt for the winning Toronto score. Opposite page: Murray Armstrong, who scored Detroit's lone goal.

Best Wishes
to Gerry Jones
Sincerely
Murray Armstrong

turnaround, the Red Wings were now within one victory of doing to the Maple Leafs what the Maple Leafs had done to them in 1942—winning the last four games to come from behind and win the Cup, four games to three.

Detroit's Olympia was the site of this final shootout. Toronto's Mel ("Sudden Death") Hill, always at his best when goals were needed the most, scored early. The Maple Leafs hugged that 1-0 lead into the third period. But almost midway into the period, Detroit's Murray Armstrong slashed the puck by McCool and into the cage, tying the score at 1-1, an explosion of sound ripping through the Olympia.

With some seven minutes remaining, the Olympia now filled with roaring, Toronto's Nick Metz lined the puck at Lumley. The puck bounced off Lumley's pads and onto the stick of the Maple Leafs' Babe Pratt, that mountainous man standing just outside the crease, no more than an arm's length away from Lumley.

"I saw I had to get it under him," Babe said later. He slithered the puck under Lumley and Toronto led, 2-1, a lead they protected to capture that elusive fourth victory. The Maple Leafs skated off hugging their second Cup in four years.

The winning Leafs earned some $1,200 each for their 13 games of playoff hockey. By comparison, the world champion St. Louis Cardinals had won $4,626 each the previous autumn for playing five games of baseball in the 1944 World Series.

Babe Pratt:
"How the hell can you sleep?"

Now an official with the Vancouver Canucks, Babe Pratt played defense for the Rangers and the Maple Leafs.

I was always kind of a bad boy in those days, you know. I did some drinking then, I don't any more, but anyway the coaches always had to keep an eye on me. I used to room with [Toronto coach] Hap Day. I remember the afternoon of the seventh game, we were in Detroit, and I was with Hap Day in his suite. I went to sleep. Poor Hap, he was pacing up and down the room for hours while I was snoring away. Finally, it was about six in the evening and I guess he couldn't take my snoring any more, it finally got to his nerves. He grabbed the mattress of my bed, pulled it out, and kerplow! I landed on the floor. I woke up and I looked up at him and I said, "Hap, Hap, what's the matter, what happened?" And he looked down at me and he said, "You son of a bitch, it's two hours before the seventh game of the Stanley Cup, how the hell can you sleep?"

Heroes of the seventh game: Mel Hill (far r.), who scored Toronto's first goal, and Babe Pratt, who scored the winner, made more alert, perhaps, by that late-afternoon snooze.

96

FIRST GAME (April 6, at Detroit)
Maple Leafs 1, Red Wings 0

FIRST PERIOD
Toronto—Schriner.........................13:56
SECOND PERIOD
No scoring
THIRD PERIOD
No scoring

SECOND GAME (April 8, at Detroit)
Maple Leafs 2, Red Wings 0

FIRST PERIOD
No scoring
SECOND PERIOD
No scoring
THIRD PERIOD
Toronto—Kennedy (Pratt)..................6:05
Toronto—Morris.........................12:03

THIRD GAME (April 12, at Toronto)
Maple Leafs 1, Red Wings 0

FIRST PERIOD
No scoring
SECOND PERIOD
No scoring
THIRD PERIOD
Toronto—Bodnar (Stanowski).............. 3:02

FOURTH GAME (April 14, at Toronto)
Red Wings 5, Maple Leafs 3

FIRST PERIOD
Detroit—Hollett (E. Bruneteau)............. 8:35
Toronto—Kennedy (Hill)................... 9:19
Toronto—Kennedy (Hill)...................11:44
SECOND PERIOD
Detroit—Armstrong (M. Bruneteau)......... 9:20
Toronto—Kennedy (Davidson).............10:20
THIRD PERIOD
Detroit—E. Bruneteau..................... 1:11
Detroit—Lindsay........................ 3:20
Detroit—Carveth (Hollett).................17:38

FIFTH GAME (April 19, at Detroit)
Red Wings 2, Maple Leafs 0

FIRST PERIOD
No scoring
SECOND PERIOD
No scoring
THIRD PERIOD
Detroit—Hollett (Carveth)................. 8:21
Detroit—Carveth (Quackenbush)...........16:16

SIXTH GAME (April 21, at Toronto)
Red Wings 1, Maple Leafs 0

FIRST PERIOD
No scoring
SECOND PERIOD
No scoring
THIRD PERIOD
No scoring
OVERTIME
Detroit—E. Bruneteau.....................14:15

SEVENTH GAME (April 22, at Detroit)
Maple Leafs 2, Red Wings 1

FIRST PERIOD
Toronto—Hill (Kennedy)................... 5:38
SECOND PERIOD
No scoring
THIRD PERIOD
Detroit—Armstrong (Hollett)............... 8:16
Toronto—Pratt (Metz).....................12:14

BOSTON BRUINS
MONTREAL CANADIENS 1946

With a Cup at Stake, Forget Brotherly Love

We want to prove we are not just a wartime club ... but really a great team in any era of hockey.
—Montreal coach Dick Irvin during the playoffs

All of the big boys had returned from military service. The Krauts and Frankie Brimsek were back in Boston; Murray ("Muzz") and Lynn Patrick came home to the Garden in New York; Syl Apps returned to Toronto; Doug and Max Bentley were whirling around Chicago Stadium; and Sid Abel again was pushing pucks in Detroit. Yet even though the other teams were fortified by these returning pre-war aces, Montreal again breezed home first for a third straight year. Chicago, with its Pony Line—the Bentleys and Bill Mosienko—scored more goals than anyone else, but it was Montreal, with Vezina Trophy winner Bill Durnan in goal, who proved the toughest team to score against.

The six-foot Durnan towered over other goalkeepers, some of whom were on the dwarfish side. In the best-of-seven series against the third-place Black Hawks, he stopped most everything the high-scoring Chicago shooters threw at him. The Canadiens won in four straight games as Montreal's gang of triggermen sent 26 pucks bursting past Chicago goalkeeper Mike Karakas.

In the other semifinal, second-place Boston opposing fourth-place Detroit, the Kraut Line got a chance to measure Detroit's young wartime goalie—Harry Lumley. The two teams split the first two games. In the third game the Krauts whipped four goals by Lumley in a 5-2 Boston triumph. In the fourth game the Kraut Line's Woody Dumart and Bobby Bauer each scored, as did Armand ("Bep") Guidolin and Terry Reardon, Boston winning 4-1 to lead three games

to one. The fifth game went into overtime, tied 3-3. Boston's Don Gallinger fired a puck by Lumley for a 4-3 victory that put Boston into its second final since it last won the Cup in 1941.

Despite the presence of Brimsek and the Krauts, the Bruins seemed no match for the power of the Punch Line. Maurice ("Rocket") Richard, Hector ("Toe") Blake, and Elmer Lach were among the league's top ten scorers. When newspapers announced that the Canadiens were 3-1 favorites, Bruin manager Art Ross tried to lift his team's hopes by labeling the Canadiens as "strictly a wartime club."

Millions listened by radio to coast-to-coast network broadcasts, and they were pleasantly surprised by the feisty Bruins, who battled the Canadiens into overtime in the first two games. But Montreal won the first on a goal by Richard, and the second when Montreal's Jimmy Peters hit a puck that caromed off the skate of the Bruins' Terry Reardon and into the Boston cage.

Reardon got no sympathy from his brother, Kenny, a defenseman for the Canadiens. So far there had been no blood-letting stick-swinging between the two teams—except between the brothers Reardon, who had been whacking away at each other game after game.

After Montreal won a third straight game, Terry Reardon made up for the puck that had bounced off his skate: in overtime of the fourth game he slammed one by Durnan for a 3-2 Boston victory.

That was a last hurrah for Boston, the Canadiens winning the fifth game, 6-3, as Elmer Lach scored his fifth goal of the playoffs. He had 12 assists, breaking his 1944 record of 11, and his 17 points were only one shy of the record of 18 set by Toe Blake in 1944. The Canadiens, win-

In the semifinal series between Detroit and Boston, the Red Wings' Jim Conacher (No. 18) falls after pushing the puck by Boston goaltender Frankie Brimsek. Detroit won, 3-0, its only victory of the series.

NOTICE
Persons Sitting In Unscreened Sections
· Do So At Their Own Risk ·

It's brother against brother as Boston's
Terry Reardon (No. 7) raises his stick, his
brother, Montreal's Kenny, swinging
his glove to protect an exposed rear end.
They continued to whack away at each
other during the entire series.

ning a second Cup in three years, had nailed to the wall the lie that they would not win when the big boys came home.

Syd Howe:
More room at the top

In his career from 1930 to 1946—with the Red Wings 11 of these years—Syd Howe collected more points, 528, than any player up to that time.

The most I ever got for winning the Stanley Cup was sixteen hundred dollars. But I'm glad to see the boys today making a few dollars. In my day there were a lot of good hockey players down in the minor leagues who never made it to the top. They'd look upstairs and say, I'm never going to get up there so I might as well quit. You couldn't live very well on those salaries in the minor leagues. We lost a lot of good hockey players. Now, with expansion and the new World Hockey Association, a lot of players who develop late have a chance to get up there to the top.

FIRST GAME (March 30, at Montreal)
  Canadiens 4, Bruins 3

FIRST PERIOD
  No scoring
SECOND PERIOD
  Montreal—Bouchard........................ 0:21
  Montreal—Fillion......................... 3:19
  Boston—Guidolin (Cain)................... 5:09
  Boston—Dumart (Schmidt).................. 8:02
THIRD PERIOD
  Boston—Crawford (Guidolin)...............14:04
  Montreal—Chamberlain (Richard)...........16:23
OVERTIME
  Montreal—Richard (Bouchard).............. 9:08

SECOND GAME (April 2, at Montreal)
  Canadiens 3, Bruins 2

FIRST PERIOD
  Montreal—Lach (Richard).................. 1:06
  Boston—Egan..............................10:55
SECOND PERIOD
  Boston—Bauer (Schmidt)................... 3:04
THIRD PERIOD
  Montreal—Bouchard........................10:10
OVERTIME
  Montreal—Peters..........................16:55

THIRD GAME (April 4, at Boston)
  Canadiens 4, Bruins 2

FIRST PERIOD
  Montreal—Lach............................10:14
  Boston—Guidolin (Shill, Gallinger)..........11:01
  Montreal—Mosdell (Harmon, Chamberlain)..14:13
SECOND PERIOD
  Boston—T. Reardon (Smith, Cowley)........18:41
THIRD PERIOD
  Montreal—Mosdell......................... 2:45
  Montreal—Hiller (Lach)................... 5:18

FOURTH GAME (April 7, at Boston)
  Bruins 3, Canadiens 2

FIRST PERIOD
  No scoring
SECOND PERIOD
  Boston—Henderson (Gallinger).............. 8:05
  Montreal—Richard (Harmon)................13:46
THIRD PERIOD
  Boston—Gallinger (Cain).................. 3:01
  Montreal—Richard (Lach).................. 4:04
OVERTIME
  Boston—T. Reardon (Smith, Cowley)........15:13

FIFTH GAME (April 9, at Montreal)
  Canadiens 6, Bruins 3

FIRST PERIOD
  Boston—Cowley............................ 5:42
  Montreal—Fillion (Hiller)................ 9:55
  Boston—Bauer (Dumart)....................14:01
  Montreal—Lach (Eddolls)..................15:51
  Montreal—Mosdell (Harmon)................18:28
SECOND PERIOD
  Boston—Schmidt........................... 7:15
THIRD PERIOD
  Montreal—Blake (Lach)....................11:06
  Montreal—Chamberlain.....................14:05
  Montreal—Hiller (Lach)...................17:14

Winners of the Cup. Top row (l. to r.): Bob Fillion, Leo Lamoureux, Jim Peters, Emile ("Butch") Bouchard, Ken Mosdell, Ken Reardon, Erwin ("Murph") Chamberlain. Middle row: Trainer Ernie Cook, Frank Eddolls, Billy Reay, Joe Benoit, Wilbur ("Dutch") Hiller, Buddy O'Connor, Gerry Plamondon, assistant trainer H. Dubois. Seated: Coach Dick Irvin, Glen Harmon, Maurice Richard, Bill Durnan, Toe Blake, Elmer Lach, manager Tommy Gorman.

103

MONTREAL CANADIENS
TORONTO MAPLE LEAFS 1947

Campbell Gets a Test, the Rocket Gets the Heave-Ho

For the fourth straight year the Canadiens finished first to win the Prince of Wales Trophy, tying the record of four straight held by the Bruins. Again the Canadiens took most of the prizes: Bill Durnan won the Vezina Trophy as the best goalkeeper, Maurice ("Rocket") Richard won the Hart Trophy as the Most Valuable Player. The Rocket finished second only to Chicago's Max Bentley in scoring. But Hector ("Toe") Blake was near the end of his playing career, and Elmer Lach had to sit out the playoffs with a fractured skull. Though lacking the Punch Line in the best-of-seven semifinal with the third-place Bruins, the Canadiens needed only five games to qualify for their third final in four years.

The young Toronto Maple Leafs had finished second. There were six rookies on the 19-man squad and Nick Metz, at 33, was the team's senior citizen. Detroit had finished fourth, missing the retired Syd Howe, the league's scoring leader up to that time, but a new Howe—his name was Gordie—had taken his place on a Production Line with Ted Lindsay and Sid Abel. The 18-year-old Gordie Howe appeared in his first playoff series without distinguishing himself, the young Maple Leafs winning in five games.

For the first time ever, the Canadiens and Maple Leafs clashed in a Stanley Cup final. The young Leafs looked jittery in the first game, Syl Apps trying without success to calm them down. The Canadiens whacked puck after puck by Walter ("Turk") Broda while Bill Durnan was

invincible. Montreal shut out Toronto, 6-0, and seemed certain to win a second straight Cup.

In the second game Toronto coach Clarence ("Hap") Day assigned young Bill Ezinicki to guard the Rocket. Ezinicki's flying elbows began to irritate the easily irritated Rocket. When Richard collided with a Leaf and wrenched a knee, the Rocket swung his stick. He slashed shut the eye of one Leaf and cut open Ezinicki's skull. He was banished from the game, which was won, 4-0, by the calmed-down Leafs. The new league president was former referee Clarence Campbell, and he met his first test of nerve by suspending the popular Rocket for the third playoff game.

Richard might not have played anyway, his injured knee still stiff, but Campbell was giving warning he would not tolerate the stick fights that had so often bloodied NHL rinks.

With no Rocket to have to bottle up, the Maple Leafs seemed more buoyant on ice in the third game, whipping around the older Canadiens to take an early 3-0 lead and win, 4-2. Now they led, two games to one.

The Rocket came back for the fourth game, but he didn't score in a game which went into the third period tied 1-1. Late in the period, with sudden-death overtime looming, Toronto's Syl Apps scooted behind the Montreal cage, suddenly stopped, reversed direction, and jammed the puck by Durnan for a goal that won the game, 2-1, and put the underdog Maple Leafs ahead, three games to one.

Four men with one thought: During a game in the semifinal round, Detroit and Toronto players seem mesmerized by the puck. They are (l. to r.) Detroit's Bill Quackenbush, Toronto's Syl Apps, and Detroit's Ralph ("Red") Almas and Jack Stewart.

In the semifinal series
against Detroit, Toronto's
Syl Apps is pursued by
the Wings' Cliff Simpson
as Syl strains for the
puck, which is slithering
by Detroit goaltender
Red Almas. Toronto won
the game and the series.

107

At the Forum for the fifth game the Rocket scorched two pucks by Broda in a 3-1 Montreal victory. But this was the last gasp of a champion team that had held its fist over the league for four years. In the sixth game, at Maple Leaf Gardens, Montreal's tricky little center, Herbert ("Buddy") O'Connor, weaved through the Toronto defense to bang the puck by Broda for a 1-0 Canadien lead. In the second period Toronto's Vic Lynn lofted a rebounding puck by Durnan, tying the game, 1-1.

The young Leafs swept in on Durnan in wave after wave, tattooing him with 11 shots in the third period while Broda, at the other end, saw only five. With less than six minutes remaining, Ted ("Teeder") Kennedy flicked the puck by Durnan for the goal that won the game, 2-1, and Toronto's second Cup in three years, its third in the past six. Canadien coach Dick Irvin refused to shake hands. "I'm a tough loser," he growled. Newspapers hailed the conquering Leafs as "the youngest team ever to win the Stanley Cup."

Buddy O'Connor:
A look from the dry side

A slight, clever skater, Buddy O'Connor veered through defenses to score for the Cup-winning Montreal teams of the mid-1940s and later for the Rangers. Now a businessman in Montreal, he recalled the game that began the three-year reign of the Maple Leafs.

I was facing off against Ted Kennedy at the start of the sixth game. He was a digger, real good on face-offs. I remembered that their defensemen had a habit of rushing forward on the face-off, figuring that Kennedy would win it and would throw the puck toward our end. But this time it backfired. I flipped it toward their end and rushed after it. Their two defensemen were gone and there was only [goaltender] Turk Broda in front of me. He raced out to try to beat me to the puck but I got there first. Now he was 25 feet out, and I just pulled the puck over and slid it into the net. We had a goal after only 25 seconds and I thought, "Hell, this is it, we'll score a bunch." But you never know what is going to happen. That was all we got and we lost, 2-1. They were the better team. You do the best you can, and you take the good with the bad. The only difference in the finals of the Stanley Cup is the champagne. The losers don't get it.

Turk Broda: He lost a 25-foot race with Buddy O'Connor and after 25 seconds he was a goal behind.

Buddy O'Connor: He won the race with Turk Broda and thought, "Hell, this is it, we'll score a bunch."

FIRST GAME (April 8, at Montreal)
Canadiens 6, Maple Leafs 0

FIRST PERIOD
Montreal—O'Connor (Leger)............... 2:20
SECOND PERIOD
Montreal—Reay (Harmon)................. 8:17
Montreal—Richard (O'Connor)............. 9:46
THIRD PERIOD
Montreal—Allen (Bouchard)............... 5:40
Montreal—Reay (Allen, Bouchard)..........11:04
Montreal—Chamberlain (Quilty, Peters)......18:28

SECOND GAME (April 10, at Montreal)
Maple Leafs 4, Canadiens 0

FIRST PERIOD
Toronto—Kennedy (Lynn, Barilko)......... 1:12
Toronto—Lynn (Kennedy)................. 1:36
SECOND PERIOD
Toronto—Stewart (D. Metz, Barilko)......... 6:37
THIRD PERIOD
Toronto—Watson (Mortson)...............11:55

THIRD GAME (April 12, at Toronto)
Maple Leafs 4, Canadiens 2

FIRST PERIOD
Toronto—Mortson....................... 9:44
SECOND PERIOD
Toronto—Poile (Stewart, D. Metz)........... 4:48
Toronto—Lynn (Meeker).................12:23
Montreal—Gravelle (O'Connor)............12:34
Montreal—O'Connor (Blake)...............18:31
THIRD PERIOD
Toronto—Kennedy.......................19:14

FOURTH GAME (April 15, at Toronto)
Maple Leafs 2, Canadiens 1

FIRST PERIOD
Montreal—Harmon (Blake)................ 4:38
Toronto—Watson (Apps).................. 6:13
SECOND PERIOD
No scoring
THIRD PERIOD
Toronto—Apps (Watson)..................16:36

FIFTH GAME (April 17, at Montreal)
Canadiens 3, Maple Leafs 1

FIRST PERIOD
Montreal—Richard (Blake, Bouchard)........ 1:23
Montreal—Gravelle (Leger)................ 8:29
SECOND PERIOD
Montreal—Richard (O'Connor, Blake).......19:32
THIRD PERIOD
Toronto—Poile (Stewart).................. 8:37

SIXTH GAME (April 19, at Toronto)
Maple Leafs 2, Canadiens 1

FIRST PERIOD
Montreal—O'Connor...................... 0:25
SECOND PERIOD
Toronto—Lynn (Kennedy, Meeker)......... 5:34
THIRD PERIOD
Toronto—Kennedy (Meeker)...............14:39

109

DETROIT RED WINGS
TORONTO MAPLE LEAFS
1948

Amid a Nightclub's Glow,
a Toast to "the Greatest"

To win a second straight Cup and stiffen with maturity his young Maple Leafs, manager Conn Smythe decided on a gamble. He traded away five highly rated young players, including Gus Bodnar and Gaye Stewart, to obtain the veteran Black Hawk high scorer, Max Bentley. Around the league some people sneered that Smythe had given away too much for too little. But after convincing the veteran Syl Apps not to retire, Smythe could put on ice three lines that were anchored by three of the smartest and fastest-shooting centers in the league: Bentley, Apps, and Ted Kennedy. In 33 of the 50 games during the season, the Leafs rallied to come from behind and win. With Walter ("Turk") Broda again winning the Vezina Trophy as the league's most effective goalie, the Maple Leafs finished first, Detroit second, Boston third, New York fourth. The Canadiens were fifth and out of the playoffs for the first time since 1939.

Detroit finished second in the league in scoring (last-place Chicago led), the Red Wings' Production Line of Sid Abel, Ted Lindsay, and Gordie Howe getting most of the goals and glory. But a knife-slim backliner, Leonard ("Red") Kelly, a 21-year-old rookie, was also putting in goals when they counted. In the semifinal series against the Rangers, with the series tied at two games apiece, Kelly scored three goals in 3-1 and

4-2 victories that catapulted the Red Wings into their first final since 1945.

Toronto beat the third-place Boston Bruins in five games to meet in the finals a Red Wing team it had licked in the last two games of the season. The Red Wings had beaten the Maple Leafs only twice all season and were given little chance of wresting the Cup from Conn Smythe's crew.

The Maple Leafs won the first game convincingly, taking a 5-1 lead and coasting to a 5-3 victory. In the second game the Leafs jumped to an early 3-0 lead. Fights began to break out between the frustrated Red Wings and some of the Maple Leafs, who were beginning to swagger. Gordie Howe and Howie Meeker tangled, and at the end of the game, won by the Leafs, the crowd saw a hockey rarity—the two goalkeepers, Harry Lumley and Turk Broda, were trading roundhouse swings at each other's padded bodies.

In the third and fourth games the Maple Leafs backchecked so well that they shut out the Red Wings' Production Line, which scored only one goal in the series. The Maple Leafs won, 2-0 and 7-2, to sweep the series and capture a second straight Cup and their seventh since 1917, topping the previous record of six, held by the Ottawa Senators.

At a party in a Detroit nightclub after the final game, Conn Smythe toasted his team as "the

Detroit goalkeeper Harry Lumley kicks at a shot by Toronto's Harry Watson, who is down on one knee, but the puck flew by Lumley for a goal during Toronto's triumph in the third game. A hockey rarity seen in this series was a fight between the goalkeepers.

112

Detroit's Sid Abel (No. 12 in dark shirt)
rises on the tip of his skate as he tries to
ram the puck by Toronto goalkeeper
Turk Broda, but Broda fields it in his
glove. On the left in the foreground is
Toronto's Bill Barilko. Behind him
are teammates Joe Klukay (l.)
and Garth Boesch.

113

greatest hockey club in history." And he added his own evidence: "I never have to give them a pep talk."

Syl Apps:
For auld lang syne

Toronto's high-scoring center of the 1940s, Syl Apps recalled the last goal of his career.

In that final game we were ahead 3-0, and then Detroit scored a goal. That always gives the other team a bit of impetus, they start coming at you. What you need is a quick goal right away. It cools them down. About a minute or so later, our Jimmy Thomson went into the corner and dug out the puck. He threw it out into the center. I was on a breakaway when I caught the puck on my stick. I split between the two defensemen and I was sort of home free, only the goaltender to beat. I beat him for a goal that made the score 4-1, and after that we had an easy time, winning 7-2, I believe. I was 33 years old and I had played ten years and enjoyed every minute of it, but I thought it was time to call it quits and that was it ... the last goal I scored in the National Hockey League.

FIRST GAME (April 7, at Toronto)
Maple Leafs 5, Red Wings 3
FIRST PERIOD
Detroit—McFadden (Horeck).............. 7:20
Toronto—Watson (Apps)................... 8:21
Toronto—Klukay (Bentley, Costello)........ 9:03
Toronto—Apps (Mortson)................18:25
SECOND PERIOD
Toronto—Mortson (Bentley)............14:31
Toronto—Meeker (Stanowski, Kennedy)......19:22
THIRD PERIOD
Detroit—Conacher (Quackenbush, Lindsay)... 4:28
Detroit—Lindsay........................ 5:26

SECOND GAME (April 10, at Toronto)
Maple Leafs 4, Red Wings 2
FIRST PERIOD
Toronto—Bentley (Samis)...................13:31
SECOND PERIOD
Toronto—Ezinicki (Apps, Watson)......... 3:35
Toronto—Bentley (Costello, Klukay)........17:16
Detroit—Horeck (Abel)..................18:18
Toronto—Watson........................18:49
THIRD PERIOD
Detroit—Gauthier (McFadden).............17:19

THIRD GAME (April 11, at Detroit)
Maple Leafs 2, Red Wings 0
FIRST PERIOD
No scoring
SECOND PERIOD
Toronto—Watson (Ezinicki).................19:42
THIRD PERIOD
Toronto—Lynn (Kennedy)..................15:16

FOURTH GAME (April 14, at Detroit)
Maple Leafs 7, Red Wings 2
FIRST PERIOD
Toronto—Kennedy (Bentley)............... 2:51
Toronto—Boesch........................ 5:03
Toronto—Watson........................11:13
SECOND PERIOD
Detroit—Reise (Pavelich, Horeck)........... 2:41
Toronto—Apps (Thomson)................ 4:26
Toronto—Kennedy (Lynn)................. 9:42
Toronto—Watson........................11:38
THIRD PERIOD
Toronto—Costello (Bentley)................14:37
Detroit—Horeck (Fogolin)................18:48

Syl Apps: "What you need is a quick goal right away. It cools them down... I beat him for a goal...and after that we had an easy time."

DETROIT RED WINGS
TORONTO MAPLE LEAFS
1949

Lose the First at Home
and Kiss the Cup Good-bye

Who's Sid Smith?

—Detroit's Gordie Howe
after the second game of the final

Seeking a third straight Cup, achieved only by the Ottawa Silver Seven of 1903–05 and never by an NHL team, the Maple Leafs slumped during the season and finished in fourth place. Detroit's Red Wings raced home first, the Production Line of Sid Abel, Gordie Howe, and Ted Lindsay banging in 66 goals in 50 games. Red Wing coach Tommy Ivan counseled his players against overconfidence as they faced the third-place Canadiens: "Nothing is permanent in this business until you have the Stanley Cup perched on the trophy shelf."

The Red Wings were well-advised. They had to battle the Canadiens down to seven games, needing eight goals from Gordie Howe to win and go into the final. In the other semifinal, second-place Boston took on fourth-place Toronto. Bruin coach Aubrey ("Dit") Clapper advised his charges to forget about the Leafs' sorry fourth-place finish and remember they would come to the playoffs thirsting for a drink from that third successive Cup.

The Leafs won the first two games, then lost the third in overtime. Toronto coach Clarence ("Hap") Day brought up a winger, bald-headed Sid Smith, from Pittsburgh, then a minor league team, and Smith scored twice as the Leafs won the fourth game, 3-1, to lead three games to one. During the fifth game, at Boston Garden, Bruin fans tossed bottles at referee Francis ("King") Clancy in anger over one of his decisions. The fans went home sullen after Max Bentley slugged in the deciding goal in a 3-2 victory that won the series and left the Maple Leafs only four victories away from that third straight Cup.

The Red Wings had beaten the Maple Leafs seven times in 12 games during the season, two of the games ending in ties. Not one Maple Leaf was picked to the league All-Star team, while Detroit's Sid Abel won the Hart Trophy as the league's Most Valuable Player. But Hap Day, his fingers bandaged—raw from too much nail biting—reminded his players that he had never coached a losing team in a Stanley Cup final series.

With the score tied, 2-2, in the first game, at Detroit's Olympia Stadium, Toronto's Joe Klukay slammed a backhander, the puck whizzing under Harry Lumley's arm for a 3-2 Maple Leaf victory in overtime. Someone made the Red Wings feel worse by reminding them that only once in 22 years—in 1942—had a team lost the first game of the final on its home ice and gone on to win the Cup.

In the second game Sid Smith whacked three pucks by Lumley, accounting for all his team's goals in a 3-1 Toronto victory. After the game Gordie Howe, looking honestly puzzled, asked a reporter: "Who's Sid Smith?"

The Maple Leafs won the third game, also by a 3-1 score. In the fourth game the Maple Leafs were seeking a record nine straight victories in Cup finals, having won in four straight a year earlier plus the final game of the 1947 playoffs. Detroit's Production Line finally scored its first goal of the series in the first period, but Toronto's Ray Timgren batted in a rebound to tie the game, 1-1, in the second period. Cal Gardner and Max Bentley won the game for the Leafs, 3-1, with goals in the second and third periods. Toronto had won its third straight Cup, an NHL record, and, also a league record, its eighth since 1917. And by coming all the way from fourth place, these 1949 Leafs became the lowest-placed NHL team ever to win the Cup, before or since.

Detroit goaltender Harry Lumley skids forward on his skates to block a shot by Toronto's Jimmy Thomson in the first game, but Thomson nudged the puck under Lumley and into the cage. Closing his eyes didn't help Harry.

117

Detroit goaltender Harry Lumley and
defenseman Leonard ("Red") Kelly (No. 4)
watch a shot by Toronto skitter to the
side during the final game. Kelly is
checking Toronto's Bill Ezinicki. To
Ezinicki's right is teammate Cal Gardner.
No. 15 is Detroit's Nelson Podolsky.
In winning the Cup three straight years,
the Maple Leafs won 24 of 29
playoff games.

Gordie Howe:
When a watch was almost as good as a Cup

After having been lured out of retirement to play with the Houston Aeros of the World Hockey Association, Gordie Howe at 45 was a millionaire or close to it. He looked back to a Stanley Cup time when he wasn't near as rich.

I scored six goals against the Canadiens in the first five or six games of the semifinal. Mr. Jim Norris [the Detroit owner] promised me a watch if I got a seventh goal in the series. It wasn't a cheap watch either. It was an Omega, costing around $150 or $200. I was 21 years old at the time, I was making only about $6,000 a year, and I thought a watch like that looked like the crown jewels. I scored the seventh goal and an eighth, and we beat the Canadiens in seven games. Then we lost to Toronto in the finals ... but going home with that watch on my wrist, I didn't feel so bad. I don't think I've ever felt so rich.

Gordie Howe: "I was 21 years old at the
time, I was making only about $6,000
a year, and I thought a watch like that
looked like the crown jewels."

FIRST GAME (April 8, at Detroit)
Maple Leafs 3, Red Wings 2

FIRST PERIOD
Detroit—Gee (Lindsay, Howe)............. 4:15
Toronto—Bentley (Timgren, Klukay)........13:15
SECOND PERIOD
Toronto—Thomson (Bentley)................16:02
THIRD PERIOD
Detroit—Quackenbush (Lindsay, Gee).......15:56
OVERTIME
Toronto—Klukay (Thomson, Timgren).......17:31

SECOND GAME (April 10, at Detroit)
Maple Leafs 3, Red Wings 1

FIRST PERIOD
Toronto—Smith (Boesch)................... 8:50
Toronto—Smith (Barilko, Kennedy)......... 9:56
SECOND PERIOD
Toronto—Smith (Kennedy, Mackell).........17:58
THIRD PERIOD
Detroit—Horeck (Stewart, McFadden)....... 5:50

THIRD GAME (April 13, at Toronto)
Maple Leafs 3, Red Wings 1

FIRST PERIOD
Detroit—Stewart (Horeck)................. 4:57
SECOND PERIOD
Toronto—Ezinicki (Gardner, Watson).......11:02
Toronto—Kennedy (Smith, Mackell)........12:40
Toronto—Mortson (Thomson, Klukay).......16:15
THIRD PERIOD
No scoring

FOURTH GAME (April 16, at Toronto)
Maple Leafs 3, Red Wings 1

FIRST PERIOD
Detroit—Lindsay (Gee, Howe)............. 2:59
SECOND PERIOD
Toronto—Timgren (Bentley)................10:10
Toronto—Gardner (Thomson, Ezinicki)......19:45
THIRD PERIOD
Toronto—Bentley (Timgren)................15:10

DETROIT RED WINGS
NEW YORK RANGERS
1950

For the First Time,
All the Way to Sudden Death

To the Detroit Red Wings of the previous two years, Waterloo had been a place called Toronto. Twice the Red Wings had soared as high as the final—and twice Toronto's Maple Leafs had wiped them out in the final. After finishing first (for the second straight season), the Red Wings took on the third-place Maple Leafs in the semifinals; after five games the Red Wings were down three games to two, within one defeat of being wiped out by the Maple Leafs for a third straight year.

Then, rising to the challenge, Red Wing goalkeeper Harry Lumley was standing in front of the cage like King Kong, snatching down all the rubber flung at him. He shut out the Leafs, 4-0 and 1-0, and the Red Wings entered the final for a third straight year.

This time they faced the New York Rangers, whipped dogs of the league for most of the 1940s, who had wiped out the Canadiens in a five-game semifinal. Even as recently as December 4 of the season the Rangers had been looking up from last place. They had vaulted to fourth—and a playoff position—on the skills, someone said, "of Don Raleigh's pitching and Chuck Rayner's catching." The skinny "Bones" Raleigh centered a high-scoring line, and goalie Chuck Rayner, lean and hawk-faced, caught pucks with the quick hands of a pickpocket.

Rayner's hands figured to be busy against the Red Wings. Detroit's Production Line—Ted Lindsay, Sid Abel, and Gordie Howe—had finished one, two, three in league scoring. But Gordie Howe, his skull fractured by a stick during the

semifinal, would miss the final, and Lindsay was limping on an injured knee. Nevertheless, the Red Wings were 12-to-5 favorites, one reason being that "home ice" for the Rangers would be Toronto's Maple Leaf Gardens. The circus had pushed the Rangers out of Madison Square Garden. The Rangers could hardly view Toronto ice as neutral. They hadn't won in Toronto since December, 1947.

But after losing the first game in Detroit, the Rangers surprised and delighted a sellout crowd of Toronto fans by winning the second game, 3-1. The crowd booed the Red Wings, who had defeated their Maple Leafs in the semifinal. "You had to feel the crowd wanted to cheer for the Rangers," said a Maple Leaf fan after the Rangers went ahead 3-1 in the third period. "But you had to wait until the Rangers gave them something to cheer about."

The Red Wings won the third game, also in Toronto, and the two teams went back to Detroit to complete the series. At Olympia Stadium the Rangers won two games, both in overtime, to lead three games to two. "The Wings are a tired bunch after their seven-game semifinal," said an ebullient Ranger coach, Lynn Patrick. "Now they got to play two games in two nights. Maybe they can win one, but two victories should be too much for them from a physical standpoint alone."

He seemed correct as the Rangers jumped out to a 3-1 lead in the sixth game. But the Red Wings rallied to win, 5-4, tying the series at three games apiece.

The seventh game may well have been the most

Detroit's Production Line skidding for a puck (l. to r.): Gordie Howe, Sid Abel, and Ted Lindsay. All good lines have a "policeman," and this one had the stick-swinging Lindsay, who instilled more than a drop of fear into the opposition.

Two overtime game-winning goals in the
final by the Rangers' Don Raleigh:
In the fourth game (above), he is
sprawled on the ice, stick upright, after
wristing a weak shot, the slow-moving
puck sliding by a straining Harry Lumley,
who cannot move over in time; in the
fifth game (opposite page), Raleigh flips
the puck over the stick of Lumley to
put New York ahead, three games to two.
Watching from behind Lumley is Sid Abel.

exciting ever played at Detroit's Olympia. After three periods the teams were tied, 3-3. They battled through a 20-minute overtime, Rayner and Lumley kicking away pucks, the roars of some 13,000 fans assaulting the walls. The hour was past midnight as the teams swerved into a second overtime. Like Indians circling a covered wagon, the Red Wings swarmed around Rayner. George Gee collected the puck behind the cage and passed it out to Pete Babando. From 25 feet away, Babando swatted a liner that buzzed through a maze of elbows. Rayner saw the puck only as it blurred by him for the goal that won the game and the Stanley Cup.

This was the first Stanley Cup ever won in sudden-death overtime of a seventh game. The unhappy Rangers, seeing the Cup, which they could have won with one shot, carted away, complained that Detroit manager Jack Adams had hyped up his players with Benzedrine. Not so, Adams said. "All they took," he insisted, "was brandy-soaked sugar."

Ted Lindsay:
A few words from Jack

Fiery Ted Lindsay, as he was best known to newspaper readers of the day, teamed with Sid Abel and Gordie Howe to make up one of the highest-scoring lines of all time. He is now a commentator on NBC-TV's weekly hockey telecasts.

It's funny about some Stanley Cup playoffs. One team might not even belong on the same rink with another as far as talent is concerned, yet the weaker team can stretch out the series to seven games. That's what the Rangers did to us without having the talent we had. But they played a positional style of hockey that our system didn't go too well against—they threw the puck around a lot—and maybe we took them too much for granted. They were always tough for us.

Anyway, after we'd lost the fourth or fifth game, we were going back in our bus to Toledo where we stayed at a hotel. Jack Stewart stood up. He was near the end of his line and maybe figured this was the last time he'd be on a team that won the Cup. Jack said that if some of our guys didn't get going, he'd start body checking his own teammates, if that's what it took to get them going. Then he named the guys he thought had to get going, and three of the names were Lindsay, Howe, and Abel. We hadn't done that much. Jack told us that we had the better team and we just had to begin to put in the effort. Well, we were down three games to two, but we came back to win the sixth game and then we won the seventh on Babando's goal and Jack retired without having to hit anybody.

FIRST GAME (April 11, at Detroit)
Red Wings 4, Rangers 1

FIRST PERIOD
    New York—O'Connor (Gordon, Mickoski)... 5:58
SECOND PERIOD
    Detroit—Carveth (Gee, Babando)............ 4:43
    Detroit—Gee (J. Wilson).................... 9:33
    Detroit—McFadden (Couture)...............10:06
    Detroit—Couture (Pronovost, McFadden)....13:56
THIRD PERIOD
    No scoring

SECOND GAME (April 13, at Toronto)
Rangers 3, Detroit 1

FIRST PERIOD
    No scoring
SECOND PERIOD
    Detroit—Couture (Pavelich)................ 3:05
    New York—Egan...........................10:39
THIRD PERIOD
    New York—Laprade (Stanley)............... 3:04
    New York—Laprade.......................11:20

THIRD GAME (April 15, at Toronto)
Red Wings 4, Rangers 0

FIRST PERIOD
    Detroit—Couture (Kelly)..................14:13
    Detroit—Gee (Dewsbury)..................19:08
SECOND PERIOD
    Detroit—Abel............................19:16
THIRD PERIOD
    Detroit—Pavelich (Kelly).................16:55

FOURTH GAME (April 18, at Detroit)
Rangers 4, Red Wings 3

FIRST PERIOD
    Detroit—Lindsay (Stewart)................. 6:31
    Detroit—Abel (Lindsay)...................16:48
SECOND PERIOD
    New York—O'Connor (Kaleta, Mickoski)....19:59
THIRD PERIOD
    Detroit—Pavelich (Peters, Stewart).......... 3:32
    New York—Laprade (Fisher, Leswick)....... 8:09
    New York—Kyle (Kaleta).................16:26
OVERTIME
    New York—Raleigh (Slowinski)............ 8:34

FIFTH GAME (April 20, at Detroit)
Rangers 2, Red Wings 1

FIRST PERIOD
    No scoring
SECOND PERIOD
    New York—Fisher (Leswick)............... 7:44
THIRD PERIOD
    Detroit—Lindsay (Carveth, Abel)...........18:10
OVERTIME
    New York—Raleigh (Lund, Slowinski)....... 1:38

SIXTH GAME (April 22, at Detroit)
Red Wings 5, Rangers 4

FIRST PERIOD
    New York—Stanley (Mickoski, Kaleta)...... 3:45
    New York—Fisher (Laprade, Leswick)....... 7:35
    Detroit—Lindsay (Stewart)................19:18
SECOND PERIOD
    New York—Lund (Egan, Slowinski)......... 3:18
    Detroit—Abel (Lindsay, Carveth)........... 5:28
    Detroit—Couture (Babando, Gee)...........16:07
THIRD PERIOD
    New York—Leswick (Laprade, Fisher)....... 1:54
    Detroit—Lindsay (Abel)................... 4:13
    Detroit—Abel (Carveth, Dewsbury).........10:34

SEVENTH GAME (April 23, at Detroit)
Red Wings 4, Rangers 3

FIRST PERIOD
    New York—Stanley (Leswick)...............11:14
    New York—Leswick (Laprade, O'Connor)....12:18
SECOND PERIOD
    Detroit—Babando (Kelly, Couture).......... 5:00
    Detroit—Abel (Dewsbury)................. 5:30
    New York—O'Connor (Mickoski)...........11:42
    Detroit—McFadden (Peters)................15:57
THIRD PERIOD
    No scoring
FIRST OVERTIME
    No scoring
SECOND OVERTIME
    Detroit—Babando (Gee)................... 8:31

Opposite page, on the right, is Pete
Babando, who scored the Cup-winning
goal for the Red Wings. At left is
Ted Lindsay: "We won...and Jack
retired without having to hit anybody."

127

MONTREAL CANADIENS
TORONTO MAPLE LEAFS
1951

Sudden Death for the Fifth Time . . .
Then Back to Lugging Beer Barrels

Who could doubt that the Red Wings were on their way to a second straight Stanley Cup triumph? The Detroit club had finished first for the third straight year, amassing 101 points, a new record. "With 101 points and only 13 losses all season," crowed Detroit manager Jack Adams, "we set records that might never be broken."

Adams' powerhouse Red Wings towered over hockey the way Casey Stengel's Yankees loomed over baseball at the time. Gordie Howe led the league in scoring, breaking Herbie Cain's record set in 1943–44. Four Red Wings—goalkeeper Terry Sawchuk, defenseman Leonard ("Red") Kelly, and forwards Howe and Ted Lindsay—were named to the six-man All-Star team. In the semifinals they met a young Montreal Canadien team loaded with ten fresh-faced rookies, including Bernie ("Boom-Boom") Geoffrion. The young Canadiens seemed not to have read the Detroit clippings. They vanquished the Red Wings in six games.

In the other semifinal the second-place Maple Leafs overcame Boston, also in six games. This was a Leaf team with enormous depth. Tod Sloan, Ted Kennedy, and Sid Smith roamed on one line; Max Bentley, Danny Lewicki, and Joe Klukay whacked in goals on a second line; and Harry Watson, Howie Meeker, and Cal Gardner made up probably the best third line in the business. In goal were veteran Walter ("Turk") Broda and young Al Rollins, the winner of the 1951 Vezina Trophy as the league's top goalie.

As usual, the Canadiens would be led into battle by Maurice ("Rocket") Richard, who had finished second behind Howe in scoring. The two had been neck and neck in scoring until the explosive Rocket socked a referee in a New York hotel lobby, was fined $500, and seemed to sulk

the rest of the season. But with cash up for grabs in the semifinal, the Rocket had snapped in two goals in overtime to help defeat the Wings. In the final he would score his 64th career playoff point (42 goals and 22 assists), a new Stanley Cup record.

Sid Smith, a comical fellow often called the team's Groucho Marx, won the first game for Toronto with a backhand shot in overtime. The second game also went into sudden death, Rocket Richard winning it when he lured the veteran Broda out of the cage and whipped the puck by him for a 3-2 Canadien victory that tied the series at a victory apiece.

Leaf coach Joe Primeau replaced Broda for the rest of the series with Al Rollins. The third game also went into overtime. It ended when Kennedy jerked in the puck from the face-off circle for a 2-1 Toronto victory.

The fourth game was knotted in overtime, 2-2, when Toronto's Harry Watson leaped off the bench, seized the puck, slid it around defenseman Doug Harvey, then walloped it past goalkeeper Gerry McNeil for a 3-2 Maple Leaf victory. The Leafs now led three games to one. For the first time in Stanley Cup history, the first four games of a playoff had been decided in overtime.

In the fifth game the Canadiens led, 2-1, with less than a minute to play. Primeau threw six skaters onto the ice, and with 37 seconds remaining Tod Sloan pushed in a rebound to tie the game, 2-2. For the fifth time—another record—the teams went into sudden death.

Early in the overtime, Toronto's Howie Meeker snatched the puck from behind the net and saw teammate Bill Barilko charging toward goalkeeper McNeil. Meeker flipped the puck toward Barilko, who slapped it over McNeil's shoulder for the

Toronto coach Joe Primeau leans next to the Cup, goaltender Turk Broda's hand on his shoulder. Next to Broda, on the far left, is Bill Barilko, the hero of the final, who would die a few weeks later when a small plane, carrying him on a fishing trip, crashed.

The winning puck flies over the shoulder
of Montreal goaltender Gerry McNeil
in overtime of the final game. The man who
walloped it, Toronto's Bill Barilko (No. 5),
watches it even as he topples. Battling
on the left are Toronto's Howie Meeker (in
white) and Montreal's Tom Johnson,
later coach of the Bruins. Looking over
Barilko's shoulder is teammate Cal
Gardner, while Emile ("Butch") Bouchard,
the Montreal captain, observes the
worst as it is happening.

winning goal and the Stanley Cup. It was Toronto's fourth in the past five years and its ninth since 1917—extending its own record.

That slap shot made Barilko the winner of season-long arguments with Joe Primeau, who had claimed the slap shot was a fad. "I told you it was a deadly shot," the curly-haired Barilko roared at Primeau in the dressing room. "We wanted to get rid of Barilko," said general manager Conn Smythe. "At times he was such a problem I wanted to send him down to Pittsburgh, but thank God we kept him." A few weeks after the biggest goal of his life, Barilko was dead, killed in a plane crash.

After pocketing his Stanley Cup winnings, Toronto's Fern Flaman went back to lugging beer barrels, his off-season job in Boston—an indication of how little the professional hockey players of the time were paid.

Gerry McNeil: Hell on the nerves

Now a sales executive in Montreal, Gerry McNeil, the Canadien goalkeeper, recalled Barilko's Cup-winning goal.

I always look back on that 1951 series, even though we lost. I got as much of a thrill out of that series as I got out of winning the Stanley Cup. We were only a third-place club and not the strong Canadien team of a few years later. In the semifinals we beat Detroit and they had won the Cup the year before. In that series we won two overtime games in a row and then we went into the final against Toronto and it seemed hard to believe: In game after game after game we were playing another overtime.

I don't think it's ever happened before or since. It had to play hell with the nerves, especially for the goalkeepers. There was no leeway at all in any of the games. It was either a tie game or you were behind by one goal or ahead by one goal. The other players can take some of their tension out by slamming some guy into the boards but in the net you just stand there and hope the next shot doesn't hit the post and bounce in.

Barilko let go a slap shot. At that time most of the shooters were using the wrist shot. The

slap shot is not difficult for the goalkeeper because it is telegraphed ahead of time, and if the goalkeeper plays his angle he should stop it. But that one got by me. I didn't know it was Barilko. Half the time I never knew who scored. I didn't give a damn who it was; it was a goal. When the shot went in, the Maple Leafs were jumping all over the ice and we were down on the ice. But now I am proud of what we achieved. I mean that was something: knocking out the Cup champion in the semifinals and then five straight overtime games in the finals. We achieved something.

FIRST GAME (April 11, at Toronto)
Maple Leafs 3, Canadiens 2

FIRST PERIOD
Toronto—Smith (Kennedy, Sloan) 0:15
Montreal—Richard 15:27
Toronto—Sloan (Mortson) 15:42
SECOND PERIOD
Montreal—Masnick (Reay) 4:02
THIRD PERIOD
No scoring
OVERTIME
Toronto—Smith (Sloan) 5:51

SECOND GAME (April 14, at Toronto)
Canadiens 3, Maple Leafs 2

FIRST PERIOD
Montreal—Masnick (Meger) 3:44
SECOND PERIOD
Montreal—Reay (Richard, Olmstead) 9:24
Toronto—Smith (Bentley, Kennedy) 15:31
THIRD PERIOD
Toronto—Kennedy (Sloan) 8:16
OVERTIME
Montreal—Richard (Harvey) 2:55

THIRD GAME (April 17, at Montreal)
Maple Leafs 2, Canadiens 1

FIRST PERIOD
Montreal—Richard (Olmstead) 2:18
SECOND PERIOD
Toronto—Smith (Bentley) 5:58
THIRD PERIOD
No scoring
OVERTIME
Toronto—Kennedy (Sloan) 4:47

FOURTH GAME (April 19, at Montreal)
Maple Leafs 3, Canadiens 2

FIRST PERIOD
Toronto—Smith (Kennedy) 0:38
Montreal—Richard (Reay, Harvey) 14:41
SECOND PERIOD
Toronto—Meeker (Watson) 1:27
THIRD PERIOD
Montreal—Lach (Richard, Bouchard) 13:49
OVERTIME
Toronto—Watson (Bentley) 5:15

FIFTH GAME (April 21, at Toronto)
Maple Leafs 3, Canadiens 2

FIRST PERIOD
No scoring
SECOND PERIOD
Montreal—Richard (MacPherson) 8:56
Toronto—Sloan (Kennedy) 12:00
THIRD PERIOD
Montreal—Meger (Harvey) 4:47
Toronto—Sloan (Smith, Bentley) 19:23
OVERTIME
Toronto—Barilko (Meeker, Watson) 2:53

Opposite page, Bill Barilko: "I told you it was a deadly shot." Left, Gerry McNeil: "When the shot went in, the Maple Leafs were jumping all over the ice . . . but now I am proud of what we achieved."

133

DETROIT RED WINGS
MONTREAL CANADIENS
1952

Winning Took Only Eight Games
—and Some 60 Extra Seconds

The Red Wings stormed into first place for the fourth consecutive year, finishing 22 points ahead of second-place Montreal. And this year, unlike the previous year, the Red Wings survived the semifinals, brushing by the Maple Leafs in four straight games. Again four Red Wings were among the league's six All-Stars: Terry Sawchuk, winner of the Vezina Trophy as the league's most effective goaltender; forwards Gordie Howe and Ted Lindsay, the league's No. 1 and No. 2 scorers; and defenseman Leonard ("Red") Kelly. The Red Wings guarded their net zealously, yielding an average of fewer than two goals a game, the league's lowest. On offense no line in the league cranked out more goals than the Production Line of Lindsay, Howe, and Sid Abel. Young Alex Delvecchio centered a free-shooting line with Metro Prystai and Johnny Wilson on the wings. Behind them was a scooter line of Glen Skov, Tony Leswick, and Marty Pavelich, three of the league's quickest skaters. Red Wing fans loudly proclaimed this to be the No. 1 team of all time.

In the other semifinal, Montreal came down to a seventh game against the fourth-place Bruins. That game produced one of the most memorable moments of Stanley Cup play. In the second period Boston's Leo Labine bowled over Maurice Richard, who gashed his head on the ice. Late in the game, with blood seeping from the bandaged wound, the still-woozy Richard took the puck, weaved around four Bruins, and jerked the puck past goaltender "Sugar Jim" Henry. Montreal fans poured down a four-minute ovation. Later, Boston coach Lynn Patrick said, "A truck couldn't have stopped Richard on that play." Montreal won the game and went into the final against Detroit.

Detroit won the first game, 3-1, Tony Leswick

winging in two goals. This game is famous for being probably the first—and, hopefully, the last—61-minute Stanley Cup game. At the end of the regulation 60 minutes the siren failed to go off, and the teams played an extra 60 seconds before it suddenly burst alive. "I don't know what I would have done," said the official timer, "if a goal had been scored in the last minute."

Late in the first period of the second game, Montreal's Elmer Lach punched the puck by Sawchuk to tie the game, 1-1. It would be the last goal of the season for the Canadiens. Early in the second period Ted Lindsay lofted a shot past Canadien goalie Gerry McNeil, and that was the winning goal in a 2-1 Detroit triumph. "Two more and we go to Florida," the Red Wings were shouting in their dressing room.

His Red Wings were leading 1-0 in the third game when, from 65 feet away, Lindsay blooped a shot that hopped in front of McNeil and bounced crazily into the cage. Delighted Red Wing fans called it The Detroit Bounce after the Red Wings went on to win, 3-0.

In the fourth and final game Sawchuk again shut out the Canadiens, 3-0. It was his fourth shutout of the playoffs, tying a record. The Red Wings, victors in the final for the second time in three years, were the first team to go through the playoffs without a loss.

Alex Delvecchio:
The goals were an added feature

Perhaps the most underrated center of all time after having played so many years at Detroit in the shadow of Gordie Howe, Alex Delvecchio ended more than two decades of playing in 1973

In a scene that might have been painted by an imaginative artist if it hadn't actually happened and been photographed, a bloodied Rocket Richard shakes hands with a black-eyed Sugar Jim Henry. Richard's Canadiens had just eliminated Sugar Jim's Bruins in a best-of-seven semifinal.

The puck, hit by an
unidentified Red Wing
(l.), ricochets off the
partition to the right of
the Montreal cage during
the final game. Hanging
at the cage is Montreal's
Billy Reay (No. 14), now
the Chicago coach.

136

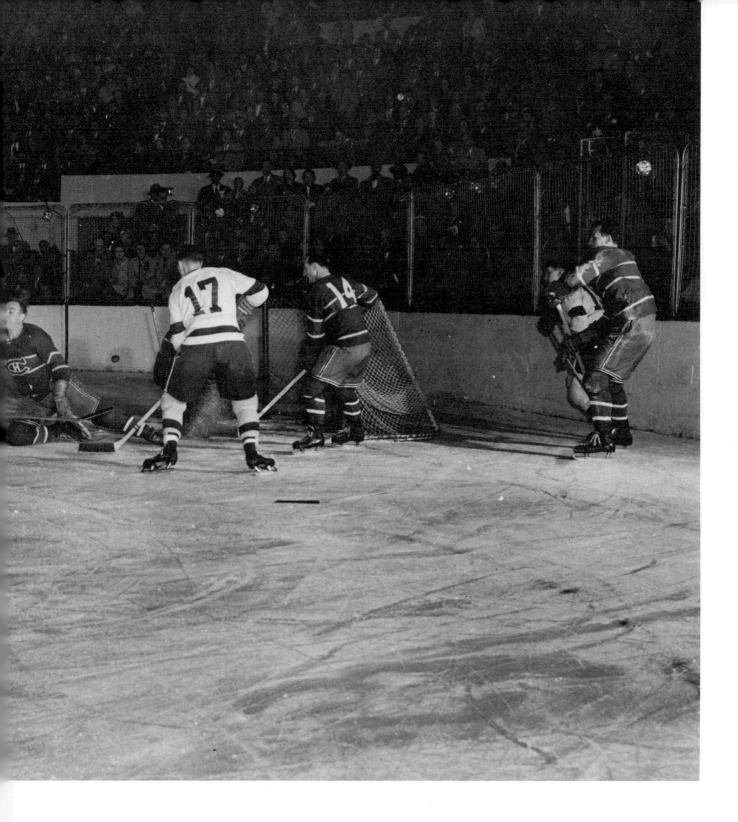

Above: Terry Sawchuk, in the middle, rubs the heads of Tony Leswick (l.) and Ted Lindsay after the Red Wings won the first game of the final, Leswick scoring twice. This was the 11th final for the Red Wings since 1934. Up to this year they had won only four of them. Opposite page: Maurice Richard (in white) is sandwiched among three Red Wings, including Gordie Howe (No. 9) and goaltender Terry Sawchuk, during a scramble for the puck in the first game.

to become coach of the Red Wings—and in 1974 general manager as well. At Madison Square Garden for a game with the Rangers, he talked about his first Stanley Cup final.

We had a very defensive team. You could argue all night about the best team of the 1950s—us or the Canadiens, who won five straight Cups. But I think we might have been better defensively. I think that year when we won eight straight playoff games, Sawchuk had four shutouts.

We were the third line—myself, Prystai, and Johnny Wilson. When we went out, we didn't want to get scored on. That's what we concentrated on—don't let them score on us. Let the big line of Abel, Howe, and Lindsay do the scoring. So when our line got the three goals that won the last game, it was like an added feature.

138

FIRST GAME (April 10, at Montreal)
Red Wings 3, Canadiens 1

FIRST PERIOD
No scoring
SECOND PERIOD
Detroit—Leswick (Pavelich)................. 3:27
THIRD PERIOD
Detroit—Leswick (Skov)................... 7:51
Montreal—Johnson (Olmstead, Curry).......11:01
Detroit—Lindsay (Abel)...................18:44

SECOND GAME (April 12, at Montreal)
Red Wings 2, Canadiens 1

FIRST PERIOD
Detroit—Pavelich (Leswick, Skov)...........16:09
Montreal—Lach (Geoffrion)................18:37
SECOND PERIOD
Detroit—Lindsay......................... 0:43
THIRD PERIOD
No scoring

THIRD GAME (April 13, at Detroit)
Red Wings 3, Canadiens 0

FIRST PERIOD
Detroit—Howe (Stasiuk)................... 4:31
SECOND PERIOD
Detroit—Lindsay (Howe)................... 9:13
THIRD PERIOD
Detroit—Howe (Pavelich).................. 6:54

FOURTH GAME (April 15, at Detroit)
Red Wings 3, Canadiens 0

FIRST PERIOD
Detroit—Prystai (Delvecchio, Wilson)....... 6:50
SECOND PERIOD
Detroit—Skov (Prystai)...................19:39
THIRD PERIOD
Detroit—Prystai.......................... 7:35

BOSTON BRUINS
MONTREAL CANADIENS 1953

The Bruins Make a Coach a Happy Liar

How cruel it is, the Detroit Red Wings might have said of the playoff system in particular and life in general. The Red Wings won the Prince of Wales Trophy for the fifth straight year, running away from the rest of the league. Red Wing goaltender Terry Sawchuk, leading the league in allowing the fewest goals, had won his second straight Vezina Trophy. Winger Gordie Howe had won the league scoring title for the third year in a row, rapping in 49 goals, only one shy of Maurice ("Rocket") Richard's record of 50. How could the Red Wings fail to win a second straight Cup?

The Boston Bruins supplied the answer. While 36-year-old Bruin veteran Woody Dumart clamped handcuffs on Howe, guarding him so closely that Gordie scored only two goals, Boston goaltender "Sugar Jim" Henry dipsy-doodled in and out of the cage to stop pucks. Boston won in six games.

A second upset seemed likely in the other semi-final as the second-place Canadiens trailed the fourth-place Chicago Black Hawks, three games to two. His nerves frayed by the pressure, Montreal goalkeeper Gerry McNeil asked to be replaced "for the good of the team." Young Jacques Plante stepped in, and Montreal won the next two games. The Canadiens skated into their third final in three years, searching for a Cup they hadn't won since 1946.

"Boston has the best defense in hockey," moaned Montreal's silver-haired coach Dick Irvin. "If they can stop a high-scoring team like the Red Wings, what chance have we got? I predict Boston will win in four."

With the inexperienced Plante in the net opposite Boston's dependable Sugar Jim Henry, Montreal indeed seemed the underdog. But the spearhead of the Boston attack, Milt Schmidt, sat out the first game with an injury and Montreal won,

4-2. With Schmidt back on ice and leading the Boston snipers, the Bruins won the second game, 4-1, but during the game Sugar Jim sprained an ankle.

He was replaced in goal for the third game by Gordon ("Red") Henry, not related by either blood or ability. The Canadiens replaced Plante with the refreshed McNeil. In the third game McNeil kicked away 34 shots while Red Henry missed 3 of 18, and the Canadiens won, 3-0, to lead the series two games to one.

In the fourth game Red Henry appeared flustered as the Canadiens winged pucks by him. Rocket Richard whacked in three, the Canadiens winning 7-3. They were within one game of winning their first Stanley Cup in seven years.

The Bruins crossed their fingers and sent a limping Sugar Jim Henry into the cage for the fifth game. He fended off shot after shot over the first three periods, but Gerry McNeil was equally effective, shunting aside all of Boston's shots. The 0-0 game went into sudden-death overtime.

Early in the overtime, Montreal's Elmer Lach, still a thunderball at 35, flew across the blue line and flashed a shot at Henry. The puck hit Henry's stick and bounded away. Richard pounced on it, thrust it backward into Lach's path as Elmer steamed toward Henry. Lach smacked the puck on a low line past Henry's right elbow for a 1-0 Montreal victory.

"I never saw it go in . . . I never saw it go in," Lach kept yelling, jumping up and down, as teammates pounded him and several hundred fans poured onto the Forum ice. Emile ("Butch") Bouchard weaved among them, hoisting high the Cup.

"I never saw it either," Sugar Jim said in the clubhouse. "He really wound up on that one."

Montreal coach Dick Irvin was asked about his

Montreal's Bernie Geoffrion grimaces as Boston goaltender Sugar Jim Henry stops his shot during the first game. Looking to clear the puck is Boston defenseman Bill Quackenbush. This was the first of three finals for the Bruins in the 1950s.

Rocket Richard slips the
puck by Red Henry,
one of three goals scored
by Richard in the fourth
game. It was the fourth
time in playoff competition
that the Rocket had
scored three goals in a
game. He holds the
record for the most games
scoring three or more
goals: seven.

143

prediction that Boston would win in four. "They sure made a liar out of me," he said.

Butch Bouchard and Elmer Lach: Memories of blood and desire

Both Butch Bouchard, a stalwart of defense for Montreal for more than a decade, and Elmer Lach, who teamed with Hector ("Toe") Blake and Rocket Richard on the Montreal Punch Line, discussed Lach's Cup-winning goal.

Bouchard: *The Rocket got clipped in the face during the overtime. He went into the room for repairs and was gone for maybe five minutes. The doctor tried to do a thorough job but Rocket told him to put a patch on his face, he wanted to get right out. When he came out his face was smeared with blood. He jumped onto the ice and ran around like a crazy man. He made a rush, passed to Lach, Lach shot, and that was that. I remember seeing him and Lach jumping high off the ice, they were so happy . . .*

Lach: *When I got the puck from Richard I was in the corner and I slapped it at the net. I didn't think I could shoot a puck that fast. I never did see it go in.*

The playoffs, the way I look at them, they are like a student who goes to school all year and then takes a final exam on what he knows. The playoffs are the final exams. The student, he is crammed with all that information, now he has to produce it. That is why the clubs that have been taught the most and have the best discipline . . . the ones that have great direction . . . they win. I think the thing that is lacking today is that players have no discipline, no direction, no desire. There's too much money. Richard had only one object: to put the puck in the net. It's difficult to pick people and say this one has great heart and desire but you can probably see it in young Bobby Clarke at Philadelphia. I think he has it.

144

FIRST GAME (April 9, at Montreal)
Canadiens 4, Bruins 2
FIRST PERIOD
Boston—Armstrong (Mackell, Laycoe) 2:08
Montreal—Moore 13:42
SECOND PERIOD
Montreal—Mosdell (Mazur) 2:37
Montreal—Curry (MacKay, St. Laurent) 16:05
THIRD PERIOD
Boston—Pierson (Mackell, Sandford) 10:11
Montreal—Richard (Mosdell) 11:12

SECOND GAME (April 11, at Montreal)
Bruins 4, Canadiens 1
FIRST PERIOD
Boston—Labine (Quackenbush) 3:30
Boston—Sandford (Klukay, Chevrefils) 18:20
SECOND PERIOD
Montreal—Olmstead (Curry, Harvey) 1:20
Boston—Sandford (Mackell) 7:30
THIRD PERIOD
Boston—Schmidt (Dumart) 15:16

THIRD GAME (April 12, at Boston)
Canadiens 3, Bruins 0
FIRST PERIOD
Montreal—Johnson (Mosdell) 12:53
SECOND PERIOD
Montreal—Masnick 6:30
THIRD PERIOD
Montreal—Mosdell (Bouchard) 11:27

FOURTH GAME (April 14, at Boston)
Canadiens 7, Bruins 3
FIRST PERIOD
Montreal—Davis (MacKay, St. Laurent) 3:23
Montreal—Richard (Harvey) 10:56
Montreal—Moore 16:40
Boston—Creighton (Dumart) 18:22
SECOND PERIOD
Montreal—Geoffrion 18:58
THIRD PERIOD
Montreal—Richard 5:33
Boston—Schmidt (Labine) 7:23
Boston—McIntyre (Creighton) 16:25
Montreal—MacKay 17:59
Montreal—Richard (Lach, Olmstead) 18:27

FIFTH GAME (April 16, at Montreal)
Canadiens 1, Bruins 0
FIRST PERIOD
No scoring
SECOND PERIOD
No scoring
THIRD PERIOD
No scoring
OVERTIME
Montreal—Lach (Richard) 1:22

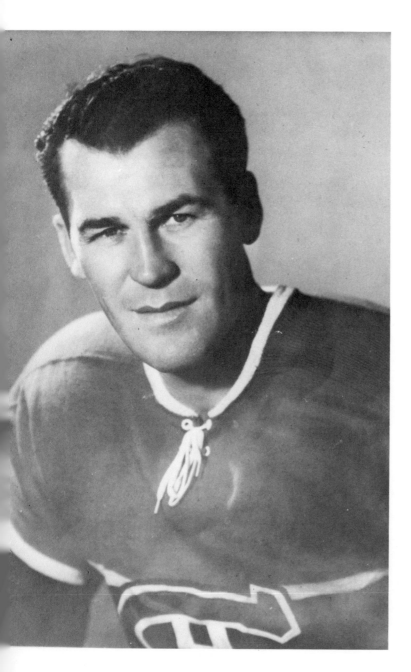

Left, Butch Bouchard:
"The Rocket...like a
crazy man." Above, Elmer
Lach: "Young Bobby
Clarke...I think he
has it."

145

DETROIT RED WINGS
MONTREAL CANADIENS 1954

A Gamble Is Lost
As a Finger Gets in the Way

For years people had been saying that the Canadiens needed only strength at center to be a great hockey team. That time of greatness seemed to have arrived in Montreal in the fall of 1953 with the coming of Jean Beliveau, a rangy center who left the amateurs for the most money ever given up to that time to an NHL rookie. "I just opened the vault," said Canadien general manager Frank Selke, "and told Jean to take what he liked."

Big Jean centered a "dream line," flanked by two rugged, high-scoring wingers—Bernie ("Boom-Boom") Geoffrion and Dickie Moore. In 1953–54 the Canadiens finished second, some leaky goaltending by Gerry McNeil keeping the Canadiens from edging the Red Wings out of first. Late in the season McNeil lost his job to young Jacques Plante; in the semifinal against Boston, Plante twice shut out the Bruins, the Canadiens winning in four games.

For the sixth successive year Detroit finished first, an achievement never accomplished before in any big league sport. On defense, goaltender Terry Sawchuk and defenseman Leonard ("Red") Kelly were still sweeping the Detroit zone clean of pucks. On offense, Gordie Howe led the league in scoring for the fourth consecutive year. The Red Wings crushed Toronto in five games and were 2-to-1 favorites to recapture the Cup they had owned in 1952 and relinquished in 1953.

The Red Wings split the first two games in Detroit and then won the next two in Montreal. In the train on the way back to Detroit, Montreal coach Dick Irvin mulled over a gamble he had been considering ever since the train left Montreal. Plante had played well in the last game, a 2-0 loss. But Irvin wondered . . . should he replace Plante with McNeil? True, McNeil was

rusty, not having played in two months. But Irvin thought that the sight of their veteran goalkeeper in the cage might arouse the Canadiens. The next night when McNeil came into the dressing room, he saw his gear laid out. He was replacing Plante.

McNeil shut out the Red Wings for three periods. In the overtime Montreal's Ken ("Big Mo") Mosdell sailed down the full length of the ice, pivoted around a Detroit defenseman, and whisked a foot-high liner by Sawchuk. The Canadiens were 1-0 winners and still alive, now behind three games to two.

Back in Montreal, McNeil had an easier time, the Canadiens winning, 4-1, to tie the series at three victories apiece. "This is the comeback of the year," proclaimed Montreal journalists, predicting that the Canadiens would win a third straight game and the Cup.

True, the seventh game would be played in Detroit, and only two teams in the previous ten years had won the Cup on foreign ice. "Ah yes," said Montreal fans, "but both times it happened in Detroit." (In 1945 and 1948.)

Superstitious Montreal fans were gleeful when the Canadiens scored first in the seventh game; in every game of the series so far, the team that had scored first had gone on to win. Detroit scored early in the second period, tying the game, 1-1. For the remainder of the second period and all during the third, Olympia Stadium was filled with roars. McNeil twice stopped shots on breakaway drives by Detroit's Marc Pronovost, and Sawchuk batted away bullets from the horde of Montreal shooters.

Now it was overtime, the two teams swaying back and forth between the end lines, the arena a bedlam, one missed puck the difference between winning the Stanley Cup and losing it.

Detroit goalkeeper Terry Sawchuk gets some help in drinking from the Stanley Cup, which he is holding, after the seventh game. A gap of three days, instead of the usual two, between the sixth and seventh games helped the weary Red Wings, who were employing only three lines against Montreal's four.

Toronto goalkeeper
Harry Lumley looks
understandably horrified
as he sees the puck
drilling toward him during
the semifinal series
against Detroit. The
Detroit player in
the middle is Leonard
("Red") Kelly, who holds
the record for the most
years in playoffs (19).

Detroit slammed the puck into the Montreal zone. Glen Skov, elbows flying, hustled the puck off the boards near the Montreal cage and shot it across ice to Tony Leswick. Little Tony was standing in the face-off circle, some 30 feet from the cage.

Tony swatted at the puck, and Montreal defenseman Doug Harvey saw it rising over his shoulder. He stabbed at the puck with one gloved hand. The puck ticked off a finger of the glove and angled downward—over Gerry McNeil's shoulder and into the Montreal cage.

That deflected shot won the game, 2-1, and the Cup, Detroit's second in three years and third in the past five. Detroit players mobbed Leswick. The Canadiens skated quickly off the ice without congratulating the Red Wings. They dressed hastily and fled into the night. Later, at a Detroit victory party, the Canadiens' Gaye Stewart, a former Red Wing, said: "The players wanted to come out on ice and shake hands, but were restrained from higher up."

"If I had shaken hands," muttered Montreal coach Dick Irvin, "I wouldn't have meant it, and I refuse to be hypocritical."

Butch Bouchard:
To lose on a fluke, unforgettable...

Emile ("Butch") Bouchard played on his first Cup-winning team in 1944 and was the captain of Canadien Cup winners of the 1950s. But at his home in Montreal, the big former defenseman recalled the seventh game of a Cup final the Canadiens lost.

A few minutes before Leswick scored on that fluke shot, we had a breakaway. One of our players—it was Howard Riopelle—came in alone on Sawchuk, and he just missed the corner of the net. I think it hit the corner and bounced out. There was only a minute to play in the third period and if that puck had gone in, we would have won the Cup.

But it went into the overtime. And their goal was such a fluke. Leswick let this high shot go from the blue line. Leswick wanted only to clear it from his own end to make a change of players. After he let it go—it was like what you call an

infield pop fly in baseball—he started for the bench. I was sitting on our bench. I saw the puck going up and I remember thinking, "There is no danger there." Harvey went to grab it with his hand and it tipped the end of his finger. If Gerry McNeil had been taller, say 6-foot-2, it would have ticked his shoulder, maybe, but he was about 5-foot-7 and he couldn't see it—his view was obstructed by Harvey. The puck dropped over his shoulder and into the goal. Even Leswick was surprised. He heard the crowd yell and turned. He just wanted to get rid of the thing. We didn't say anything to Harvey. It could happen to any fellow. But to come so close to winning the Cup when Riopelle was free on that breakaway and then to lose on a fluke shot like Leswick's, that's still hard to take.

Of all the Cups we won, I still remember best that Cup we lost on a fluke.

FIRST GAME (April 4, at Detroit)
Red Wings 3, Canadiens 1
FIRST PERIOD
Detroit—Lindsay (Reibel, Delvecchio).......13:44
SECOND PERIOD
Montreal—Geoffrion (Harvey, Masnick)......12:16
THIRD PERIOD
Detroit—Reibel (Lindsay, Howe)........... 2:52
Detroit—Kelly (Pavelich, Leswick).......... 7:13

SECOND GAME (April 6, at Detroit)
Canadiens 3, Red Wings 1
FIRST PERIOD
Montreal—Moore (Geoffrion, Beliveau).......15:03
Montreal—Richard (Moore)................15:30
Montreal—Richard (Moore)................15:59
SECOND PERIOD
Detroit—Delvecchio....................... 6:37
THIRD PERIOD
No scoring

THIRD GAME (April 8, at Montreal)
Red Wings 5, Canadiens 2
FIRST PERIOD
Detroit—Delvecchio (Howe)................ 0:42
Detroit—Lindsay (Kelly)...................17:06
SECOND PERIOD
Detroit—Wilson (Prystai).................. 4:57
THIRD PERIOD
Montreal—Johnson....................... 7:19
Detroit—Prystai (Delvecchio)............... 7:59
Detroit—Howe (Delvecchio, Woit)..........11:32
Montreal—St. Laurent (MacKay)...........15:02

150

FOURTH GAME (April 10, at Montreal)
  Red Wings 2, Canadiens 0
FIRST PERIOD
  No scoring
SECOND PERIOD
  Detroit—Wilson (Prystai) 2:09
THIRD PERIOD
  Detroit—Kelly 19:53

FIFTH GAME (April 11, at Detroit)
  Canadiens 1, Red Wings 0
FIRST PERIOD
  No scoring
SECOND PERIOD
  No scoring
THIRD PERIOD
  No scoring
OVERTIME
  Montreal—Mosdell 5:45

SIXTH GAME (April 13, at Montreal)
  Canadiens 4, Red Wings 1
FIRST PERIOD
  No scoring
SECOND PERIOD
  Montreal—Geoffrion (Beliveau) 12:07
  Montreal—Curry (Olmstead, Masnick) 13:07
  Montreal—Curry (Lach, Mazur) 14:25
THIRD PERIOD
  Detroit—Prystai 5:11
  Montreal—Richard (Lach) 10:05

SEVENTH GAME (April 16, at Detroit)
  Red Wings 2, Canadiens 1
FIRST PERIOD
  Montreal—Curry (Masnick) 9:17
SECOND PERIOD
  Detroit—Kelly (Delvecchio, Lindsay) 1:17
THIRD PERIOD
  No scoring
OVERTIME
  Detroit—Leswick (Skov) 4:29

Butch Bouchard: "I saw the puck going
up and I thought, 'No danger there'...To
come so close to winning the Cup...
that's still hard to take."

151

DETROIT RED WINGS
MONTREAL CANADIENS
1955

Drink Hearty, Boys, Because You'll Not Drink Again from This Cup

It was a wild, wild finish. In third place during the closing weeks of the season, the Red Wings won seven straight victories to edge within a point of the first-place Canadiens with only a few days remaining in the season. In a game at Boston, the Canadiens and Bruins began to swing sticks at one another. A linesman got in the way and Maurice ("Rocket") Richard, an elemental man if anything, punched him. League president Clarence Campbell suspended the Rocket for the remainder of the season and the playoffs.

Apoplectic Montreal fans threatened to kill Campbell if he showed his face at the Forum. The night after the suspension, the Red Wings were playing the Canadiens at the Forum, first place at stake. Into that cauldron of simmering passions marched Campbell. At first the fans only booed him, but when the Canadiens, without Richard, fell hopelessly behind, 4-1, the fans began to hurl peanuts and garbage onto the ice. A tear gas bomb exploded. A spectator slugged Campbell. Fistfights erupted. Police surged into the arena. Campbell forfeited the game to the Red Wings, and that night howling Canadien fans burned and looted in the streets around the Forum.

The forfeit vaulted the Red Wings into first place. They won the next day—their ninth victory in a row—to clinch first place, winning their seventh straight Prince of Wales Trophy.

These were the same old Wings, nicely balanced on offense and defense. On the Production Line this year was Earl ("Dutch") Reibel at center with Gordie Howe and Ted Lindsay on the wings. On defense, Leonard ("Red") Kelly jammed up attacking lines and goalkeeper Terry Sawchuk, although not personally liked by some of his teammates because of his swaggering manner, could be an iron door in front of the net.

Despite the absence of the suspended Rocket, Montreal breezed by Boston in five games. The Canadiens' Bernie ("Boom-Boom") Geoffrion had led the league in scoring and Jean Beliveau, in the words of Boston's Milt Schmidt, was "the greatest. There just isn't a better player in the game." In goal was young Jacques Plante, considered by many the superior to Sawchuk, who had won the Vezina Trophy for his stinginess in the cage.

The Red Wings stretched their winning streak to 13 straight by knocking Toronto out of their semifinal in four consecutive games. Detroit then won its 14th and 15th straight, setting an NHL record, by winning the first two games of the final against the Canadiens, both games being played at Detroit's Olympia Stadium.

In the friendlier Forum, the Canadiens won the next two games, snapping the Detroit streak and tying the series at two games apiece. The Red Wings left Montreal muttering to themselves. In both defeats they had outshot the Canadiens, 37 to 26 and 40 to 30.

The teams continued to win on their home ice —Detroit winning the fifth game, 5-1, in Detroit, the Canadiens winning the sixth game, 6-3, in Montreal to square the series at three victories apiece.

The seventh game would be played on Detroit ice because the Red Wings had finished first, helped by that forfeit that was still a raw wound in Montreal memories. What made the wound even more painful was the knowledge that Detroit had not lost in their last 23 games on home ice.

This was the second straight year the Red Wings had skated onto the ice at the Olympia for the seventh game of a final; they had won the previous year on Tony Leswick's goal in overtime.

Detroit owner Marguerite Norris loses a hand to Ted Lindsay's grip but keeps a victor's smile as she awaits a kiss after the winning of the Cup.

Montreal defenseman Tom Johnson plops on the ice after failing to stop a goal scored by Detroit's Ted Lindsay, in the center facing the camera. Kneeling above Johnson is Canadien goaltender Jacques Plante. At the far left is Detroit's Gordie Howe. The goal was one of four scored by Lindsay in this second game.

This time they didn't keep their fans in suspense that long. Their 23-year-old center, Alex Delvecchio, scored early in the second period for a 1-0 lead. Later in the period, Howe deflected a puck past Plante for a 2-0 lead. The goal was Howe's 20th point of the playoffs and 12th of the final, both records; his 12 points for the final are still a record.

Detroit won, 3-1, the Red Wings sipping champagne from the Cup for the fourth time in six years. "There was money at stake," said Delvecchio. "There was only $500 if we lost, $1,000 if we won."

Around the league some fans were borrowing baseball's cry, "Break up the Yankees," calling for the breaking up of the Red Wings. Most of the Red Wings were young, the alarmists were warning, and most of hockey's promising young talent was growing up on Red Wing farm teams. Yet as bright as the future seemed for the Red Wings, never again would Gordie Howe or any of his teammates drink from the Cup as winning Red Wing players.

Bob Goldham:
Making one big save after another

The former bulwark on defense for the Red Wings during their championship years, Bob Goldham now lives in Toronto and is associated with Hockey Night in Canada.

That [1955] was the last year of our dynasty. In 1956 the Canadien dynasty began. They were two well-balanced teams—the Wings and the Canadiens—and it was a life-and-death struggle to beat them. You could tell how closely matched we were: we went down to seven games two years in a row. The key guy for us was Sawchuk. We called him Ukey—he was a Ukrainian boy. I played against all the great ones . . . Bill Durnan, Frankie Brimsek, Charlie Rayner . . . and Ukey was the greatest goaltender who ever lived. We could always count on him to come up with the big save. When I look back on those Stanley Cup series, what I remember is Ukey making one big save after another.

I roomed with him. He was a tough guy to live

with. Like all great athletes, his concentration on his job was so great that he ignored a lot of the other things. All he ever wanted was to be the greatest goaltender there ever was. He had a bad arm. They used to take bone chips out every year, and he used to put them in a bottle and save them.

His whole life was being a Red Wing, when you get right down to it. We had this tremendous pride in our organization in those days. All of us wanted to end up our careers as Wings. It counted for a lot. Tommy Ivan used to say that he could send our guys out on the road without a coach and never have to worry. The boys would show up at the games ready to play. Which is a compliment, when you think about it. It's something you have, I guess, the pride, and I guess the guys today have it. I don't know. But we sure as hell had it.

FIRST GAME (April 3, at Detroit)
Red Wings 4, Canadiens 2

FIRST PERIOD
No scoring
SECOND PERIOD
Montreal—Curry (MacKay, Mosdell)........ 5:09
Detroit—Delvecchio (Lindsay, Howe)........14:00
THIRD PERIOD
Montreal—Curry (MacKay, Mosdell)........ 8:57
Detroit—Stasiuk (Howe, Lindsay)...........13:05
Detroit—Pavelich...........................17:07
Detroit—Lindsay (Howe)....................19:42

SECOND GAME (April 5, at Detroit)
Red Wings 7, Canadiens 1

FIRST PERIOD
Detroit—Pronovost (Goldham)............. 2:15
Detroit—Lindsay (Howe, Reibel)........... 9:57
Detroit—Delvecchio (Stasiuk, Goldham)......16:00
Detroit—Howe (Reibel)....................17:11
SECOND PERIOD
Detroit—Lindsay (Howe, Reibel)........... 8:10
Detroit—Lindsay (Delvecchio)..............15:48
Detroit—Lindsay (Reibel, Howe)...........19:37
THIRD PERIOD
Montreal—Mosdell (St. Laurent, Curry)......12:32

THIRD GAME (April 7, at Montreal)
Canadiens 4, Red Wings 2

FIRST PERIOD
Montreal—Geoffrion (Beliveau, Olmstead).... 8:30
Montreal—Geoffrion....................... 8:42
Detroit—Kelly (Stasiuk)...................18:12

SECOND PERIOD
Montreal—Geoffrion (Beliveau)..............14:23
Detroit—Stasiuk (Pavelich, Delvecchio).......16:16
THIRD PERIOD
Montreal—Leclair (Moore)................. 7:50

FOURTH GAME (April 9, at Montreal)
Canadiens 5, Red Wings 3

FIRST PERIOD
Montreal—MacKay (Mosdell, Harvey)....... 0:40
Detroit—Reibel (Kelly)....................12:38
SECOND PERIOD
Montreal—Geoffrion..................... 3:40
Montreal—Beliveau..................... 8:25
Montreal—Johnson..................... 9:07
THIRD PERIOD
Montreal—Curry (MacKay)................ 2:33
Detroit—Reibel (Lindsay, Howe)............ 3:40
Detroit—Hay (Reibel).....................12:00

FIFTH GAME (April 10, at Detroit)
Red Wings 5, Canadiens 1

FIRST PERIOD
Montreal—Beliveau (Harvey, Moore)........ 8:01
Detroit—Skov...........................12:59
Detroit—Howe...........................18:29
SECOND PERIOD
Detroit—Howe (Delvecchio, Lindsay).......12:29
Detroit—Howe (Lindsay, Kelly)............16:20
THIRD PERIOD
Detroit—Stasiuk (Delvecchio, Bonin)........ 2:09

SIXTH GAME (April 12, at Montreal)
Canadiens 6, Red Wings 3

FIRST PERIOD
Montreal—Beliveau (Harvey)............... 7:30
Detroit—Delvecchio (Stasiuk)..............13:36
SECOND PERIOD
Montreal—Leclair (Geoffrion, Harvey)....... 3:45
Montreal—Geoffrion (Beliveau, Harvey)..... 5:21
Detroit—Delvecchio (Lindsay, Pronovost).....15:54
Montreal—Geoffrion (Beliveau, Bouchard)....18:18
THIRD PERIOD
Montreal—Curry (MacKay, Mosdell)........ 0:19
Detroit—Kelly (Leswick, Pavelich)..........16:23
Montreal—MacKay (Olmstead)..............18:55

SEVENTH GAME (April 14, at Detroit)
Red Wings 3, Canadiens 1

FIRST PERIOD
No scoring
SECOND PERIOD
Detroit—Delvecchio (Kelly)................ 7:12
Detroit—Howe (Pronovost)................19:49
THIRD PERIOD
Detroit—Delvecchio....................... 2:59
Montreal—Curry (Geoffrion, Beliveau).......14:35

Bob Goldham: "It's something you have,
I guess, the pride, and I guess the
guys today have it. I don't know. But
we sure as hell had it."

157

DETROIT RED WINGS
MONTREAL CANADIENS 1956

Beliveau and the Rocket Take On the Champions . . . and Their Fans

Tick off the great teams in sport—the Yankees of the twenties, Notre Dame of the thirties and forties, the Boston Celtics of the fifties and sixties, the UCLA basketball team of the sixties and seventies—and you have to include the Montreal Canadiens of the Beliveau years. In 1955–56 the team sprang to greatness. It won 45 games, lost only 15, and tied 10, becoming the first team in NHL history to win 45 games in a 70-game schedule. Its 6-foot-3 mountain on skates, Jean Beliveau, captured the league's scoring title with 47 goals and 88 points, both new records for a center. Four Canadiens—forwards Beliveau and Maurice ("Rocket") Richard, defenseman Doug Harvey, and goalkeeper Jacques Plante—dominated the six-man All-Star team. Defenseman Tom Johnson and winger Bert Olmstead were on the All-Star second team. Beliveau won the Hart Trophy as the league's Most Valuable Player; Harvey, the Norris Trophy as the league's best defenseman; Plante, the Vezina Trophy as the best goalie; and freshman coach Hector ("Toe") Blake was picked Coach of the Year.

Richard and Beliveau, the team's two superstars, were contrasting personalities—the fiery Rocket Richard, at 34 still capable of thumping a skull with his stick, so fast he seemed to leap over the ice, unleashing shots that caused some goalkeepers to duck their heads; the cool Jean Beliveau, precise and long-striding, long arms holding the puck away, his rubbery wrists flipping the puck into the net from impossible angles. Richard and Beliveau: fire and ice.

The Canadiens marched by the Rangers in five games. The second-place Red Wings moved as decisively by the Maple Leafs, also winning in five, and the Canadiens and Red Wings clashed in the final for the third year in a row.

Detroit's often-sulky Terry Sawchuk was gone, replaced in goal by rookie Glenn Hall. Leonard ("Red") Kelly's carrot top still scooted all over the ice, repelling attackers; and the same collection of puck-slingers—Gordie Howe, Ted Lindsay, Alex Delvecchio, Earl ("Dutch") Reibel, and the rest—were primed to win a third straight Cup. Only the Maple Leafs of the late 1940s, the Ottawa Silver Seven of 1903–05, and the Montreal Victorias of 1896–98 had won three Cups in a row.

In the first game, at Montreal, the Red Wings led 4-2 in the third period. Then, in characteristic fashion, the Canadiens fired off a machine-gun burst of goals—four in five and a half minutes—and won, 6-4. In the second game the Red Wings still seemed to be in a state of shock after that burst, the Canadiens winning easily, 5-1.

In Detroit's Olympia Stadium the Red Wings continued their mastery of the Canadiens at home, winning 3-1. All three Red Wing goals were scored while Doug Harvey, Montreal's All-Star defenseman, was supposed to be guarding the Canadiens' goal. Detroit fans near the Montreal bench heckled Harvey. He and other Canadiens stood up, brandishing their sticks at the hecklers. Later, Detroit manager Jack Adams said gleefully: "You know the Canadiens are choking when they start fighting our fans."

Adams' grin faded when the Canadiens won the fourth game, 3-0. The shutout by Jacques Plante stopped talk among Detroit writers that he was effete because he wore a mask in practice and talked about wearing one during a game. (In the 1959–60 season Plante became the first goalie to wear a mask regularly. By the early 1960s masks were in general use.) Montreal now led, three games to one.

In the semifinal round, Montreal's Dickie Moore (No. 12) seems to be swinging his stick at a whistle-blowing official, but is actually trying to dodge him. Ranger Harry Howell (No. 3) looks for puck smothered by New York goaltender Lorne ("Gump") Worsley and a teammate.

Detroit's Glenn Hall
(No. 1) turns his head to
see the puck billow the
rear of the net (near top)
for a goal by Montreal's
Jean Beliveau. The goal
helped to win the fifth
game, 3-1, and the
Stanley Cup.

161

Back in the Forum, Montreal took the fifth game, 3-1, winning its second Cup in four years. As the siren blew, veteran Canadien Emile ("Butch") Bouchard, who was playing his last game, scooped the Cup off its perch and skated around the rink, pursued by one of the Cup guardians, who slipped on the ice as he tried to collar Butch. Beliveau had scored 12 goals in the playoffs, tying a record set by Richard in 1944. After three seasons, in which he competed in three final series, he could say: "I have realized my ambition—to be on a Cup-winning team. I hope to be on a few more others." He would, he would, he would, he would . . . .

Dickie Moore:
You never said more than hello

Dickie Moore led the league in scoring for two straight years—1958 and 1959. He played on six Canadien teams that won the Cup, but the win in 1956 gave him his greatest satisfaction.

There was a tremendous rivalry between Montreal and Detroit. The rivalry between Montreal and Boston was more a physical one—the Big Bad Bruins, they were rougher. Detroit was a better skating team. They had been the champions for two straight years. They were always beating us, while we could always beat Toronto and Boston. They had the big guns—Howe and Lindsay. And they had been lucky two years earlier when Tony Leswick's shot went over Harvey's arm.

We had a lot of stars—Beliveau, the Rocket, Harvey, Johnson, Henri Richard—they're all in the Hall of Fame or will be. But when you come down to the finals of the Stanley Cup, hockey is a team game. You got to work together. We did, and I think that 1956 team was the best team I ever played on. And beating Detroit, the team that had embarrassed us so often, it was a big moment for us.

It might be hard for people to imagine how big the rivalry was in those days between teams. Like I'm from Montreal, most of our players were, and even those who were not from Montreal, they lived there during the off-season. We had this closeness—we were the Montreal team. If you met a player from another team on the street, you would never say more than hello. We would never, NEVER have a conversation.

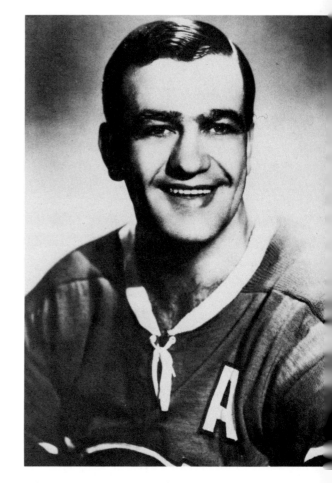

Bernie ("Boom-Boom") Geoffrion: In 14 playoff years with Montreal he scored 14 game-winning goals. Only Maurice Richard, with 18, scored more. Gordie Howe is third, with 11.

The 1956 Canadiens. Top row (l. to r.): Henri Richard, Claude Provost, Jackie Leclair, Bud MacPherson, Floyd Curry, Doug Harvey, Tom Johnson, Jean-Guy Talbot. Middle row: Don Marshall, Dickie Moore, Dick Gamble, Ken Mosdell, Butch Bouchard, Jean Beliveau, Bert Olmstead, Dollard St. Laurent. Seated: Trainer Hector Dubois, Bernie Geoffrion, Jacques Plante, coach Toe Blake, Gerry McNeil, Maurice Richard, assistant trainer Gaston Bettez.

FIRST GAME (March 31, at Montreal)
Canadiens 6, Red Wings 4

FIRST PERIOD
Detroit—Delvecchio (Reibel, Howe)......... 8:17
SECOND PERIOD
Montreal—Beliveau (Olmstead)............. 3:00
Detroit—Dineen (Bucyk, Ullman)........... 3:45
Montreal—H. Richard (Moore, M. Richard).. 6:40
Detroit—Lindsay (Howe)................. 8:11
Detroit—Delvecchio (Howe, Ferguson)......11:20
THIRD PERIOD
Montreal—Leclair (Curry, Harvey).......... 5:20
Montreal—Geoffrion (Talbot).............. 6:20
Montreal—Beliveau (Geoffrion, Olmstead).... 7:31
Montreal—Provost (Leclair, Curry).........10:49

SECOND GAME (April 3, at Montreal)
Canadiens 5, Red Wings 1

FIRST PERIOD
Montreal—Marshall (Olmstead)............ 7:23
SECOND PERIOD
Montreal—H. Richard (Moore).............11:37
Montreal—Geoffrion (Olmstead, Beliveau)....14:38
THIRD PERIOD
Detroit—Ullman (Lindsay, Howe)........... 0:31
Montreal—Beliveau (Olmstead, M. Richard).. 2:48
Montreal—M. Richard (Moore, H. Richard)..19:21

THIRD GAME (April 5, at Detroit)
Red Wings 3, Canadiens 1

FIRST PERIOD
Detroit—Kelly (Howe)....................14:27
Montreal—Beliveau (Provost)..............19:20
SECOND PERIOD
No scoring
THIRD PERIOD
Detroit—Lindsay (Pavelich, Arbour)........11:36
Detroit—Howe (Lindsay, Delvecchio).......18:12

FOURTH GAME (April 8, at Detroit)
Canadiens 3, Red Wings 0

FIRST PERIOD
Montreal—Beliveau (Olmstead, Harvey)......15:32
SECOND PERIOD
Montreal—Beliveau (Olmstead, Geoffrion)....11:39
THIRD PERIOD
Montreal—Curry (Provost, Mosdell)........11:34

FIFTH GAME (April 10, at Montreal)
Canadiens 3, Red Wings 1

FIRST PERIOD
No scoring
SECOND PERIOD
Montreal—Beliveau (Curry, Harvey)........14:16
Montreal—M. Richard (Geoffrion, Beliveau)..15:06
THIRD PERIOD
Montreal—Geoffrion (Beliveau, Olmstead).... 0:13
Detroit—Delvecchio (Lindsay).............. 0:35

BOSTON BRUINS
MONTREAL CANADIENS —1957

The Canadiens Have a Brother Act
—But Could This Be Boston's Year?

Detroit's Red Wings flashed home first, and the rest of the league could be excused for posing the cliché question: What else is new? This was the Red Wings' eighth first-place finish in nine years (the other year they finished second). Close behind were the Stanley Cup champions, Les Canadiens. Montreal, with its fistful of shooters, led the league in scoring. The Canadien power play—Bernie ("Boom-Boom") Geoffrion and Doug Harvey on the points at the blue line, with Maurice ("Rocket") Richard, Jean Beliveau, and Dickie Moore circling the cage—was sometimes scoring two and three goals during the two minutes the other team had a man in the penalty box.

The third-place Bruins surprised the Red Wings by winning their semifinal in five games. The upset prompted Detroit manager Jack Adams to predict: "This is Boston's year."

In the other semifinal, the Canadiens teamed Rocket Richard on the same line with his younger brother, Henri ("Pocket") Richard. With goalie Jacques Plante springing far out of the crease to confuse shooters, the Canadiens overwhelmed the fourth-place Rangers in five games.

Boston had licked Montreal seven times and tied three times in 14 meetings, but the array of Montreal shooters marshalled against journeyman Boston goalie Don Simmons convinced oddsmakers that Montreal should be a 12-to-5 favorite.

Boston fans disagreed, arguing that the 35-year-old Rocket was slowing up. He had scored only two goals against Boston all season long. But in the first game he whizzed around the ice like the Rocket of yesteryear, banging home four goals, three in the second period, leading the Canadiens to a 5-1 victory.

The Canadiens won the second game, 1-0, on Beliveau's late goal, a backhand shot that flew over the kneeling Simmons. "I started in," Jean later explained in his impassive way, "and I was going to shoot but Simmons moved out to meet me and then moved back again. I knew I had him beat. He moved to my right and I put the puck in on his right."

Montreal won the third game, played on Boston ice, 4-2. "There was no turning point in the game," said the glum Bruin coach, Milt Schmidt. "We were never in it."

Boston won the fourth game, 2-0, scoring its second goal when Montreal took out goalkeeper Jacques Plante near the end of the game and put six skaters on ice. Rocket Richard tried to stop the puck, swatted at it, but missed. "Somebody's finally found Rocket's weakness," said a humorist in the press box. "He can't play goal."

The fifth game, played in Montreal, was punctuated by bloody fistfights, 17 penalties being called in the game, 10 in the first period. A power-

Merry Canadiens celebrate a victory during the playoffs (l. to r.): Maurice Richard, Jean Beliveau, Boom-Boom Geoffrion. Speaking of the whirlwind Montreal attack, Boston coach Milt Schmidt said: "The Canadiens kill you with those long passes ahead, with fellows like Boom-Boom getting them on their sticks for breakaways."

165

With a stab of his glove, Bruin goaltender
Don Simmons pockets a puck blasted
by Montreal's Rocket Richard from under
Simmons' nose during the fifth game.
The Rocket's four goals in the first game
were only one shy of his record of five,
set in 1944. This was the fourth Cup final
between Boston and Montreal. The
Canadiens had won the previous three,
won this one, and have yet to be beaten by
the Bruins in a Cup final.

play goal by Dickie Moore put Montreal ahead 2-0 and after that the Bruins seemed content to let the clock run out, the Canadiens winning 5-1. As the Rocket skated around the Forum ice, embracing the Cup, a crowd of 15,286—largest ever in Montreal—stood and cheered. For the second straight year, the Cup resided in Montreal.

Phil Goyette:
Keeping up with the Rocket

A rookie with the Cup champions of 1957, Phil Goyette sat in his office in Montreal and talked about what it was like to be young and a Canadien.

Someone got hurt and they brought me up from the farm club for the last portion of the season. I got a five-game tryout and I stayed with the club. To stay with the team they had in those days was quite a thrill. In the playoffs I got more ice time than I did during the season. They used to put me on and I did well, production-wise and defensively, and everything went so well, they didn't take me off. I always had good playoff years. What helped me was playing with the Rocket. He was quiet, didn't say much, but you could feel the tension inside him. You always had the feeling he would score the big goal for us. But we didn't rely on him. Often you yourself would get the big goal, or someone else would. That was because you were working twice as hard just to keep up with the Rocket. I think that's one reason why I got so many big goals for us in playoffs. It was because of the Rocket.

FIRST GAME (April 6, at Montreal)
Canadiens 5, Bruins 1

FIRST PERIOD
No scoring
SECOND PERIOD
Boston—Mackell (Mohns, Regan)............ 7:37
Montreal—M. Richard (Moore, Johnson).....10:39
Montreal—M. Richard (Harvey).............13:29
Montreal—Geoffrion (Harvey)..............15:35
Montreal—M. Richard (H. Richard, Harvey)..17:00
THIRD PERIOD
Montreal—M. Richard (H. Richard)........18:17

SECOND GAME (April 9, at Montreal)
Canadiens 1, Bruins 0

FIRST PERIOD
No scoring
SECOND PERIOD
No scoring
THIRD PERIOD
Montreal—Beliveau (Geoffrion, St. Laurent)... 2:27

THIRD GAME (April 11, at Boston)
Canadiens 4, Bruins 2

FIRST PERIOD
Montreal—Geoffrion (Olmstead, Harvey)..... 1:30
Montreal—Curry (Goyette)................14:39
Montreal—Geoffrion (Beliveau).............19:54
SECOND PERIOD
Boston—McKenney (Armstrong)............ 6:16
THIRD PERIOD
Montreal—Goyette (Marshall, Curry)........ 7:31
Boston—Mackell (Flaman)................19:16

FOURTH GAME (April 14, at Boston)
Bruins 2, Canadiens 0

FIRST PERIOD
Boston—Mackell (Toppazzini, Regan)....... 2:56
SECOND PERIOD
No scoring
THIRD PERIOD
Boston—Mackell (Labine, McKenney).......19:40

FIFTH GAME (April 16, at Montreal)
Canadiens 5, Bruins 1

FIRST PERIOD
Montreal—Pronovost (Marshall, Provost).....18:11
SECOND PERIOD
Montreal—Moore (Geoffrion, Harvey)....... 0:14
Montreal—Geoffrion (Olmstead, Johnson)....15:12
THIRD PERIOD
Boston—Labine (Bonin)..................13:43
Montreal—Marshall (Moore, Curry)........17:38
Montreal—Curry (Moore, Broden)..........18:31

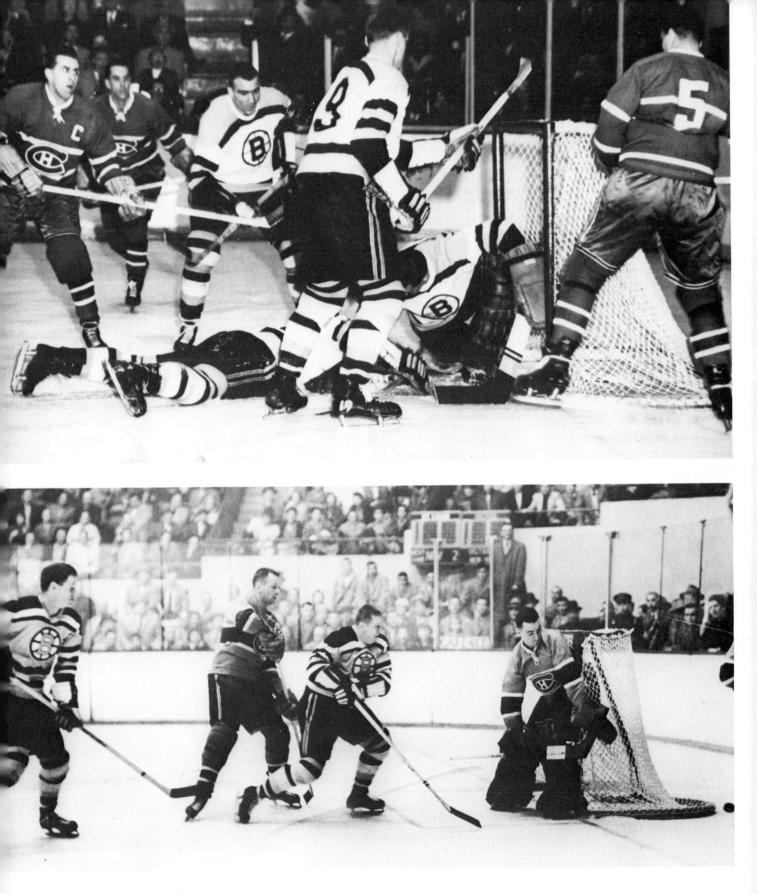

Top: In action around the Boston cage,
Bruin goaltender Don Simmons and a
teammate crawl on the ice looking
to smother a missing puck. Canadien
observers include Boom-Boom Geoffrion
(No. 5), Rocket Richard (far l.) and,
behind the Rocket, Bert Olmstead.
Bottom: In action at the other end, the
puck skids by Jacques Plante and
the Montreal net after a shot by Boston's
Cal Gardner (far l.). Between Gardner
and another Bruin is Canadien
defenseman Doug Harvey.

169

BOSTON BRUINS

MONTREAL CANADIENS
1958

Play Nicely, Milt Told the Bruins, It's the Only Way to Win

Montreal and Boston crossed sticks in the final for the second straight year. The Canadiens had finished first, scoring more goals—250—than any other team in National Hockey League history. Montreal's Dickie Moore led in individual scoring, even though he had played the last part of the season with one wrist in a cast.

Two of the Canadien top guns seemed likely to watch the playoffs from the stands. In a practice session mishap earlier in the season, a stick had ruptured Bernie ("Boom-Boom") Geoffrion's bowel and for days he was close to death, receiving the last rites. His wife and parents pleaded with him to retire. A skate had partially severed the Achilles tendon of 36-year-old Maurice ("Rocket") Richard, and he had missed most of the last half of the season, scoring only a handful of goals. But when the semifinal began—Montreal against the third-place Red Wings—out skated Geoffrion and Richard, swathed in bandages, taking their turns on ice. In four games Richard whipped in seven goals, the Canadiens sweeping the Red Wings to enter their eighth straight final.

The Bruins had finished fourth. In the semifinal they upset the second-place Rangers in six games. The Bruins' most potent scoring threat—some said their only threat—was the line of Flem Mackell, Jerry Toppazzini, and Don McKenney, which registered 17 goals against the Rangers' Gump Worsley (he yielded 28 in the six games). Guarding goal for Boston was Don Simmons, who had been banished to the minor leagues earlier in the season when too many pucks got by him. Several other Bruins were also recent minor leaguers, giving the team a Cinderella quality that made it a sentimental favorite.

Simmons played gallantly in the first game, peppered by 44 shots compared to only 29 thrown at Jacques Plante. But Montreal used its power

play to tally twice when Boston was shorthanded and won, 2-1.

In that game Boston's Leo Labine rapped his stick across the face of Claude Provost, fracturing his nose and shaking loose a half-dozen teeth. "They'd rather play rough than play hockey," grumbled Montreal coach Hector ("Toe") Blake.

Surprisingly, Bruin general manager Lynn Patrick pleaded guilty as charged. "We can't play unless we're hitting," he said. "Take Leo Labine. He's useless unless he's in there hitting somebody." Labine's reaction to that testimonial to his hockey playing went unrecorded.

The teams split the next two games. Before the fourth game Bruin coach Milt Schmidt counseled his warriors to play nicely and avoid penalties. If there were no Bruins in the penalty box, Milt reasoned, there could be no Montreal power plays. "If Milt can quiet down that bunch," someone said of the bellicose Bruins, "he can get a job as a peacemaker at the UN."

The Bruins, however, did play nicely in the fourth game, incurring only three penalties. They won, 3-1, to even the series at two games apiece.

In the fifth game, with the score tied 2-2 in overtime, Rocket Richard skirted over the blue line, lined up Boston defenseman Allan Stanley between himself and Simmons, then let fly a 35-foot blur. The puck flew by the screened Simmons, clanging against the iron at the bottom of the cage, making the Canadiens 3-2 winners. It was the Rocket's 18th game-winning goal in Stanley Cup play.

That other invalid, Boom-Boom Geoffrion, rapped in two goals in the sixth game, the Canadiens building a 4-1 lead. Facing extinction if they lost this game, the Bruins stormed back to score two goals in the third period, the packed crowd in Boston Garden urging them on. Plante

Boston's Johnny Bucyk (No. 9) crashes
on top of Montreal's Doug Harvey during
the fourth game. Poking his stick at
the puck—and Harvey's tummy—is Boston's
Bronco Horvath. Behind Horvath,
ready to do battle with his stick, is
Montreal's Jean Guy Talbot.

171

Montreal's young Jacques Plante shuts
both eyes but he fends off a Bruin shot.
In his NHL career, Plante appeared in
109 playoff games, only six shy of the
record for goaltenders held by Glenn Hall.
Plante holds the record for most shutouts
in the playoffs: 14. Walter ("Turk")
Broda had 13, Terry Sawchuk 12.

juggled one Bruin shot, fell on top of another inches from the line. Boston sent six skaters flying at Plante. But Montreal's Doug Harvey intercepted a pass and raced toward the open Boston net, pursued by Larry Regan. Harvey shot the puck. Regan dived and knocked it away. Harvey retrieved the puck and knocked it by the helpless Regan. A minute later the game ended, the Canadiens a 5-3 winner. Montreal had captured its NHL third straight Stanley Cup and the ninth in its history, sharing with Toronto the modern records for consecutive Cups and total number of Cups.

Gump Worsley: What makes a superstar

The former goaltender for the Rangers and Canadiens, Gump Worsley, whose playing career spanned two decades, joined the Minnesota North Stars in the 1969–70 season.

Home ice is an advantage in the playoffs, no doubt about it. Four of the seven games are going to be played on your ice—that's a real advantage. It really helps in the playoffs. People say, "No, you should be able to play as good away as you do at home." That's bull. Some guys do. But if you take the majority, you look at any hockey club, most of them always play better at home. I'm talking about the average hockey player. Which you have a lot of on hockey clubs. But superstars, they play good all over the place. You can go see a Bobby Orr in Philadelphia or Chicago, he plays just as well as in Boston. But then you see another guy who plays well at home, you see him a couple of games on the road, he's just a so-so hockey player. He loses that category of superstar because he doesn't play as well on the road. Whether that guy just gets livened up by his own home crowd and he needs that for a push, or what, I just don't know. But that is the difference between an average player and a superstar—playing the same way all around the league. Why? That's a good question. But I'll say this: I read where [Edward] Snider, who owns the Philadelphia club, said that Rick MacLeish plays better at home than on the road. Why would you make

a statement like that about your own hockey player? It doesn't do anything for a hockey player. You should boost him up. But I'll tell you this: If I could find a solution for why most guys don't play as good on the road, I'd be coaching probably. Or I'd just tell them what to do and take the million-dollar check.

FIRST GAME (April 8, at Montreal)
  Canadiens 2, Bruins 1
FIRST PERIOD
  Montreal—Geoffrion (Marshall, Harvey)......12:24
SECOND PERIOD
  Boston—Stanley (Mackell, McKenney)....... 5:54
  Montreal—Moore (Beliveau, M. Richard).....13:52
THIRD PERIOD
  No scoring

SECOND GAME (April 10, at Montreal)
  Bruins 5, Canadiens 2
FIRST PERIOD
  Boston—Johnson (Regan, Labine).......... 0:20
  Montreal—Geoffrion (Harvey, Moore)....... 3:42
  Boston—McKenney (Regan, Mackell)........ 6:06
  Boston—Horvath (Boone)..................17:23
SECOND PERIOD
  Boston—Regan (Stanley)................. 5:10
  Montreal—Harvey (Moore)................ 7:00
THIRD PERIOD
  Boston—Horvath (Stasiuk, Mohns).........16:52

THIRD GAME (April 13, at Boston)
  Canadiens 3, Bruins 0
FIRST PERIOD
  Montreal—M. Richard (Geoffrion, Harvey)...18:30
SECOND PERIOD
  No scoring
THIRD PERIOD
  Montreal—H. Richard (Harvey)............ 3:00
  Montreal—M. Richard (H. Richard, Moore)..15:06

FOURTH GAME (April 15, at Boston)
  Bruins 3, Canadiens 1
FIRST PERIOD
  Boston—McKenney (Mackell, Regan)....... 5:35
SECOND PERIOD
  Boston—McKenney (Stasiuk, Horvath)...... 3:30
THIRD PERIOD
  Boston—Toppazzini (Mackell).............. 2:30
  Montreal—Provost (Beliveau, Bonin)........12:57

FIFTH GAME (April 17, at Montreal)
  Canadiens 3, Bruins 2
FIRST PERIOD
  Boston—Mackell (Stanley, Toppazzini)......18:43

174

Two one-time Canadiens, shown here in Ranger uniforms, who helped Montreal to Cup victories: Gump Worsley (top) in the 1960s, Doug Harvey in the 1950s. Harvey played on six Cup-winning Canadien teams, Worsley on four.

SECOND PERIOD
Montreal—Geoffrion (Beliveau). 2:20
Montreal—Beliveau (Geoffrion). 3:02
THIRD PERIOD
Boston—Horvath (Stasiuk, Boone). 10:35
OVERTIME
Montreal—M. Richard (H. Richard, Moore). . 5:45

SIXTH GAME (April 20, at Boston)
Canadiens 5, Bruins 3
FIRST PERIOD
Montreal—Geoffrion (Beliveau, Olmstead). . . . 0:46
Montreal—M. Richard (Moore). 1:54
Boston—McKenney (Mohns). 18:35
SECOND PERIOD
Montreal—Beliveau (Geoffrion, Harvey). 6:42
Montreal—Geoffrion. 19:26
THIRD PERIOD
Boston—Johnson (Regan). 5:20
Boston—Regan (Flaman). 13:21
Montreal—Harvey. 19:00

MONTREAL CANADIENS
TORONTO MAPLE LEAFS
1959

The Rocket and Jean Are Hurt
—and Punch Looks for an Upset

We're going to beat them in six games. A good fighting club with balance will beat a club that has superstars on it every time.

—Punch Imlach

I guess everything is all settled then. I don't see any reason for playing the finals unless perhaps for the money.

—Toe Blake

We'll outmuscle the Canadiens.

—Punch Imlach

Punch talks pretty tough as long as he is safe behind the bench.

—Toe Blake

That sort of serio-comic dialogue flowed between Hector ("Toe") Blake, the Canadien coach, and George ("Punch") Imlach, the Maple Leaf coach, as the Canadiens sought a record fourth straight Stanley Cup. Few took Imlach seriously when he predicted a Maple Leaf triumph. The Leafs had been the ragged urchins of the league most of the season, in last place 17 days before season's end. Powered by the scoring of their big winger, Frank Mahovlich, they had won their last five games and sneaked into fourth. In the semifinal they lost the first two games to the Bruins, tied the series at three games apiece, were losing 2-1 in the seventh game before coming back with two late goals, then held off the raging Bruins. It had, obviously, not been a laugher of a year. But the breezy Punch, the Leo Durocher of hockey, lipped confidence as he prepared his team for Montreal. "We have more good scorers than Montreal," he proclaimed.

What he really meant was that the Maple Leafs might steal the Cup because Montreal's two big men, Maurice ("Rocket") Richard and Jean

Beliveau, were likely to miss the final. Beliveau had been put into a hospital bed by a Glen Skov body check during the semifinal with the Black Hawks, won by Montreal in six games. Jean would miss the entire final and Richard played only briefly.

But the Canadiens met Toronto well armed. There was Dickie Moore, who had won a second straight scoring title with 41 goals and 55 assists for 96 points, breaking by one point the league record set in 1953 by Gordie Howe. Rookie Ralph Backstrom and youngsters Claude Provost and Henri ("Pocket") Richard figured to contribute firepower, and goalie Jacques Plante had won the Vezina award for the fourth straight year.

The Canadiens won the first two games, lost the third in overtime on a goal by forward Dick Duff, then won the fourth by powering three goals past Maple Leaf goalie Johnny Bower in the third period. Ahead three games to one, they needed only one more victory for that record fourth straight Cup.

A few minutes after that fourth game a reporter asked Toe Blake one of those fatuous questions that are so often asked in dressing rooms: "Can you wrap it up Saturday night in Montreal, Toe?"

Toe gave the question the answer it deserved. "If I knew the answer to that," he said solemnly, "I'd bet $10,000 on the game and retire from coaching."

In the fifth game Backstrom scored one goal and assisted on three more as the Canadiens built a 5-1 lead. Canadien fans implored Rocket Richard, sitting on the bench, to enter the game. (Except for his disciplinary suspension during the 1955 playoffs, Richard had appeared in every

The two antagonists of the final: Toronto's Punch Imlach (top), shown during what was, for him, an unusual moment—he is listening instead of talking; and Montreal's Toe Blake, who talked, someone once said, "as though he were getting ready to punch you in the mouth."

Toronto's Ron Stewart (No. 12) backhands the puck toward Montreal's Jacques Plante, the pursuit by Bernie ("Boom-Boom") Geoffrion (No. 5) arriving too late. Bert Olmstead slapped in the rebound to put the Maple Leafs ahead, 2-1, in the third game, which they won in overtime, 3-2. In this series Rocket Richard replaced Ted Lindsay as the player appearing in the most playoff games—125.

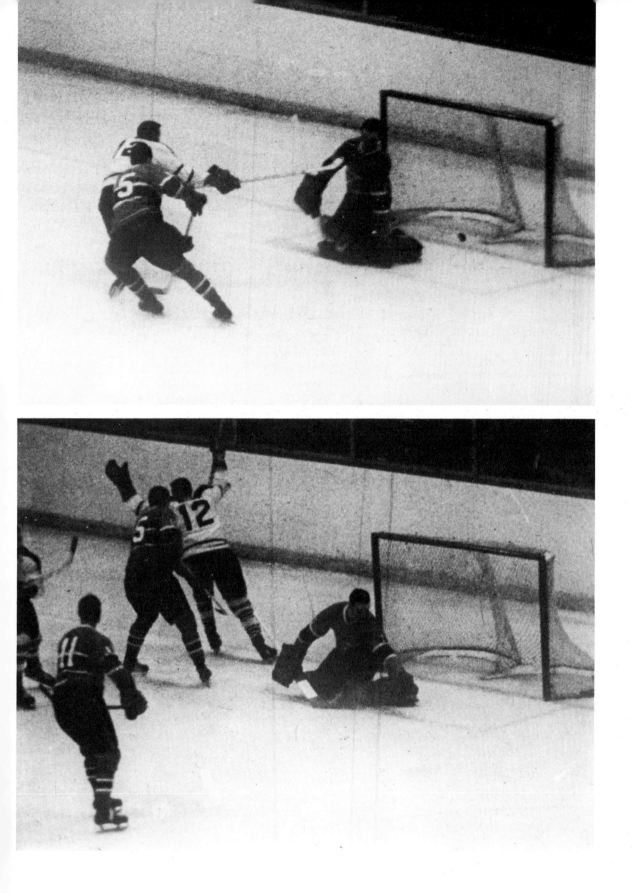

game in every final series since 1951.) But Rocket refused. "Those guys were winning the game," he said later, pointing to the young Canadiens. His young 'uns won it, 5-3, drinking from their fourth Stanley Cup in a row and the tenth Cup since 1917—both records.

"They say we're getting old," Toe Blake said in the dressing room, holding the Cup he had held as a player with the Montreal Maroons back in 1935. "But we won this one without Beliveau most of the way and with Richard very little of the way. They'll be back next season and so will we. I don't see why we can't win a fifth in a row."

Jacques Plante:
The thrill wasn't gone

Jacques Plante signed with the Edmonton Oilers of the World Hockey Association in 1974, attempting a comeback as a goaltender at the age of 45.

I was very fortunate. I was on six championship teams. But each time it was a different thrill. You never got tired of winning the Cup. Each time I would have paid money to win that Cup. I remember one year—in 1960—when we were trying to win for the fifth straight time. We were ahead of Toronto three games to none. And in the fourth game we were ahead 3-0 in the third period. I kept thinking: Hey, they could score three goals, they could tie us and beat us in overtime. Then they could beat us back in Montreal and they could beat us in Toronto—they are always strong at home—and we're down to a seventh game. Until the bell rings you are never sure you have won the Cup. When I was young Sylvio Mantha, an old defenseman for the Canadiens, told me: "I was on three championship teams and each time it was a different thrill." I found out that was exactly so.

FIRST GAME (April 9, at Montreal)
Canadiens 5, Maple Leafs 3
FIRST PERIOD
Montreal—H. Richard (Moore, Talbot)...... 0:36
Toronto—Duff.......................... 4:53
Toronto—Harris (Horton)................. 6:24
Montreal—Backstrom (Provost)............15:41

SECOND PERIOD
Montreal—Pronovost (Goyette, Provost)......16:28
Toronto—Stewart (Brewer, Olmstead).......18:26
THIRD PERIOD
Montreal—Bonin (H. Richard, Harvey)......11:50
Montreal—Moore (Bonin, H. Richard).......15:42

SECOND GAME (April 11, at Montreal)
Canadiens 3, Maple Leafs 1
FIRST PERIOD
Montreal—Johnson (H. Richard, Moore)..... 5:12
SECOND PERIOD
Toronto—Stewart (Olmstead, Pulford).......11:41
THIRD PERIOD
Montreal—Provost (Harvey)............... 5:02
Montreal—Provost (Goyette, Harvey).......18:33

THIRD GAME (April 14, at Toronto)
Maple Leafs 3, Canadiens 2
FIRST PERIOD
Toronto—Harris (Mahovlich, Stanley).......16:29
Montreal—Bonin (Geoffrion, Harvey).......17:31
SECOND PERIOD
Toronto—Olmstead (Stewart, Pulford).......17:11
THIRD PERIOD
Montreal—Moore (Turner, Marshall)........ 1:30
OVERTIME
Toronto—Duff (Armstrong)................10:06

FOURTH GAME (April 16, at Toronto)
Canadiens 3, Maple Leafs 2
FIRST PERIOD
No scoring
SECOND PERIOD
No scoring
THIRD PERIOD
Toronto—Harris (Ehman, Duff)............ 3:45
Montreal—McDonald (Backstrom,
   Geoffrion)............................ 9:54
Montreal—Backstrom (McDonald,
   Geoffrion)...........................13:01
Montreal—Geoffrion (H. Richard, Bonin).....15:56
Toronto—Mahovlich (Ehman)..............18:36

FIFTH GAME (April 18, at Montreal)
Canadiens 5, Maple Leafs 3
FIRST PERIOD
Montreal—Backstrom (Geoffrion, Moore).... 4:13
Montreal—Geoffrion (Backstrom, Harvey)....13:42
Montreal—Johnson (Backstrom).............16:26
SECOND PERIOD
Toronto—Pulford (Armstrong, Brewer)...... 4:27
Montreal—Bonin (H. Richard, Harvey)...... 9:55
Montreal—Geoffrion (Backstrom, Johnson)...19:25
THIRD PERIOD
Toronto—Mahovlich (Harris, Ehman).......12:07
Toronto—Olmstead (Ehman)...............16:19

180

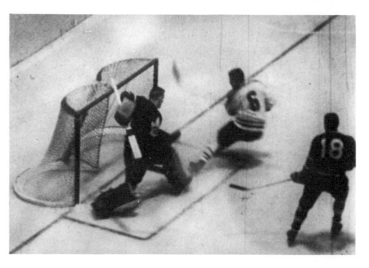

Montreal's Ralph
Backstrom (No. 6) flies
into the crease—the
rectangle in front
of the goalkeeper—and
slams the puck by Johnny
Bower's left side. It was
the second of three
goals scored by Montreal
in the third period of
the fourth game.

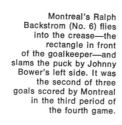

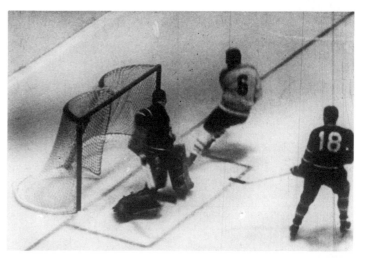

MONTREAL CANADIENS
TORONTO MAPLE LEAFS 1960

The Rocket Blasts His 82nd Goal— a Record That Would Stand

We would beat those guys if we could only hypnotize ourselves into believing we were playing some ordinary team like Chicago or New York instead of Montreal.

> —Toronto forward Gerry James
> during the 1960 playoffs

The Canadiens finished first for a third straight year. "This is the greatest hockey team ever assembled," boasted Montreal general manager Frank Selke. Around the league, fans were measuring this team against two other great teams: the Red Wings of the early fifties and the Maple Leafs of the late forties. Many people were rating the Canadiens first. This season three Canadien forwards—Jean Beliveau, Henri ("Pocket") Richard, and Bernie ("Boom-Boom") Geoffrion—had scored 30 or more goals, the equivalent at the time of a baseball team with three .350 hitters in the lineup. Jacques Plante, now wearing his mask in games, refuted the belief that a mask would obscure a goalkeeper's vision: he led the league in allowing the fewest goals, winning his fifth straight Vezina Trophy. Doug Harvey won the Norris Trophy as the league's best defenseman for the fifth time in six years (teammate Tom Johnson won it the other year). "One-third of the players on this team are superstars," said a Toronto writer after the Canadiens skated over Bobby Hull and his Black Hawks in the semifinal, winning with a four-game sweep.

George ("Punch") Imlach's Maple Leafs, after finishing second, met the Red Wings in the other semifinal. Before the first game the canny Punch stacked $1,250 in dollar bills in the center of the dressing room. On the blackboard he scrawled, "This represents the difference between winning and losing." The Maple Leafs won in six games,

going into the final to meet the Canadiens for a second straight year.

"We got a better defense and more depth than last year," Punch said, ever optimistic. "If we can win one of the two games in Montreal, we'll spring an upset." An upset was thought unlikely, the Canadiens 16-to-5 favorites to win a fifth straight Cup.

The Canadiens jumped out to an early 3-0 lead in the first game and won, 4-2. Dickie Moore and Jean Beliveau scored in the first period of the second game, and the Canadiens won it, 2-1. "I'd like to play those guys starting even just once," grumbled the Leafs' Larry Regan, commenting on the Leafs having to play catch-up. But, wrote one observer, "the belief lurks that should Montreal need an extra goal, they can get it. The Canadiens always seem to play well enough to win without embarrassing an opponent with a lot of goals."

"The Leafs are playing well," agreed a reporter, "but the Canadiens never seem worried."

Montreal won the third game, 5-2. Maurice ("Rocket") Richard seemed 10 years younger than 38 as late in the game he flashed around behind the cage, picked up a loose puck, and backhanded it past goalie Johnny Bower. The goal was the Rocket's 82nd in Stanley Cup play— and his last, Richard retiring a few weeks later. Richard's 82 playoff goals are still a Stanley Cup record.

In the fourth game the Canadiens jumped out to another early lead, the team's superstars pooling goals and assists as though joining together for one last collective effort. They buried the Leafs, 4-0. For Plante this was one of 14 playoff shutouts he would turn in during 15 playoff years, a record that no active goalkeeper is even close to (Tony Esposito, for example, has only five).

Three Maple Leafs in a row—goaltender Johnny Bower, a gap-toothed Allan Stanley, and Tim Horton (No. 7)—reach for, swing at, and eye a puck that escapes all three. Said Toronto official King Clancy: "The Canadiens are the best clutch and grabbers in the league." Said Montreal's Hector ("Toe") Blake: "The Leafs do more clutch and grabbing than anyone in the league . . ."

The puck rolls between
Toronto goalkeeper
Johnny Bower and
a Toronto defenseman
while Montreal's
Boom-Boom Geoffrion
(No. 5) raises a stick to
abscond with it. Toronto
officials were angered at
the faraway seats given
them in the Montreal
Forum, calling them
"nosebleed seats."

185

Richard skated off the ice at Maple Leaf Gardens—and out of hockey—with Montreal's fifth consecutive Stanley Cup held high. This was only the second time the Cup had been won in eight playoff games (the Red Wings of 1952 were the first to do it). The Canadiens were calm. "When you win 4-0 in four games and after four Cup titles," said Doug Harvey, "you don't get too excited."

Was this the greatest team ever? Said Clarence ("Hap") Day, a former Maple Leaf coach, "They are certainly the greatest of the era. . . ."

Henri Richard: Lucky to be a Canadien

The name Henri Richard is written on the Stanley Cup more often than that of any other man. At his home in Montreal he talked about the team he considered the best of the 11 Canadien teams that have won the Cup with Henri Richard as player or captain.

That 1960 team was the best I ever played on. We had a well-balanced team—Plante in goal, Doug Harvey and Tom Johnson on defense, Geoffrion, my brother, Beliveau, Backstrom. We won in eight straight games and that was the last time it was ever done or ever will be done, now that a team has to play in three series.

Geoffrion, Beliveau, and Olmstead were the scoring line. I played on the third line with Moore and my brother. As the center I was looking a little too much for Maurice, too much. Now I am always still looking for someone and that's why they say I don't shoot enough. Maurice was 15 years older than me . . . he never told me anything, never helped me . . . I was just playing with him.

When I see my name on the Cup, I think of all those great players I had with me. I wouldn't have my name there if I didn't have all those big stars that played with the Canadiens over these years. The first five years I was in the league, we won five Stanley Cups. Obviously, that's not a personal record, it's a team record, a team I was just lucky enough to be on.

FIRST GAME (April 7, at Montreal)
Canadiens 4, Maple Leafs 2
FIRST PERIOD
Montreal—Moore (H. Richard, Geoffrion). . . . 2:27
Montreal—Harvey (H. Richard). 8:55
Montreal—Beliveau (Geoffrion, H. Richard). . .16:56
SECOND PERIOD
Toronto—Baun (Armstrong, Regan). 5:23
Toronto—Olmstead (Horton, Kelly). 17:38
THIRD PERIOD
Montreal—H. Richard (Moore, Geoffrion). . . . 1:30

SECOND GAME (April 9, at Montreal)
Canadiens 2, Maple Leafs 1
FIRST PERIOD
Montreal—Moore (H. Richard, M. Richard). . 1:26
Montreal—Beliveau (Bonin, Talbot). 5:56
Toronto—Regan (Armstrong, Duff). 19:32
SECOND PERIOD
No scoring
THIRD PERIOD
No scoring

THIRD GAME (April 12, at Toronto)
Canadiens 5, Maple Leafs 2
FIRST PERIOD
Montreal—Goyette (Provost, Pronovost). 13:54
SECOND PERIOD
Montreal—Goyette (Provost, Pronovost). 0:21
Montreal—H. Richard. 15:27
Toronto—Wilson (Brewer, Harris). 16:19
THIRD PERIOD
Montreal—Goyette. 8:57
Montreal—M. Richard (H. Richard, Moore). .11:07
Toronto—Olmstead (Kelly, Edmundson). 19:47

FOURTH GAME (April 14, at Toronto)
Canadiens 4, Maple Leafs 0
FIRST PERIOD
Montreal—Beliveau (Geoffrion, Langlois). 8:17
Montreal—Harvey (Geoffrion, Langlois). 8:45
SECOND PERIOD
Montreal—H. Richard (M. Richard, Moore). .16:40
THIRD PERIOD
Montreal—Beliveau (Bonin, Geoffrion). 1:26

Henri Richard: "We won in eight straight games and that was the last time it was ever done or ever will be done, now that a team has to play in three series... I was just lucky."

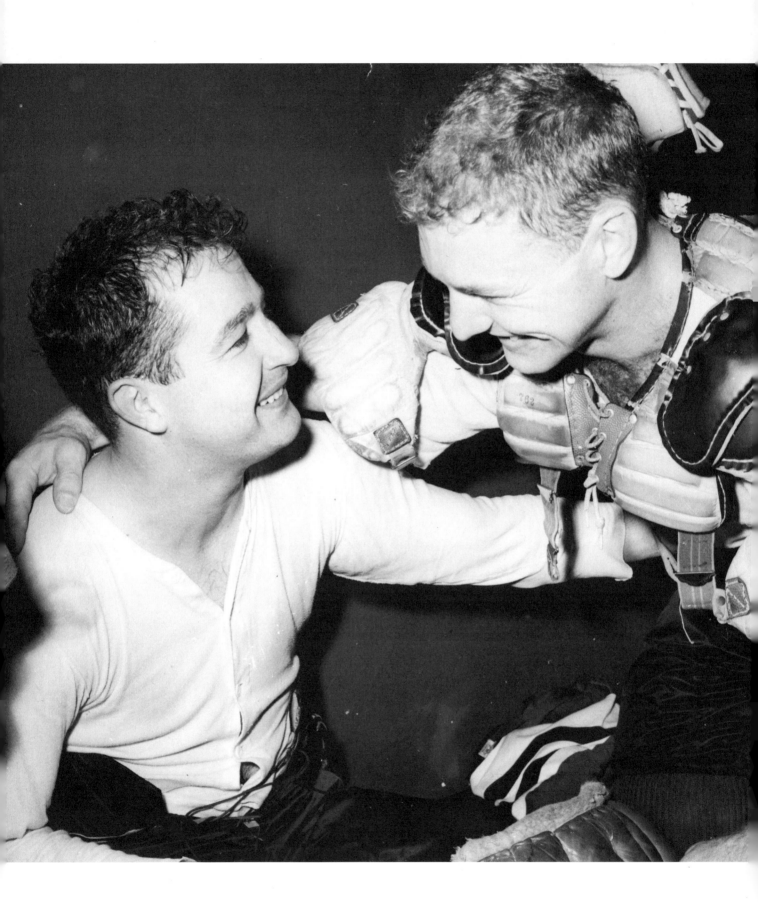

CHICAGO BLACK HAWKS
DETROIT RED WINGS
1961

From Beer in the Cellar
to Champagne in the Penthouse

While these Stanley Cup playoffs were going on, Russia's Yuri Gagarin became the first man in space, sailing above earth in a rocket ship for almost two hours.

Badly in need of a new "Rocket" were Montreal's Canadiens. Even without the retired Maurice ("Rocket") Richard, the Canadiens had managed to finish first; but it was a tired, battered bunch of Canadiens who sought a sixth straight Cup in the semifinal against a young, eager Chicago Black Hawk team. Montreal's Bernie Geoffrion had led the league in scoring, but now his leg was in a cast. With the Canadiens down three games to two, "Boom-Boom" stripped off the cast, ordered the leg deadened with novocaine, and tried to play. He got off one shot, then hobbled to the bench. The Black Hawks won and roared their derision at the defeated Stanley Cup champions. "Those guys," said goalkeeper Glenn Hall, pointing toward the Montreal dressing room, "have laughed at us long enough."

The Black Hawks had been a league joke for two decades. The team had last won the Stanley Cup in 1938 and had missed the playoffs 14 of the intervening 22 years. Then Chicago owner Jim Norris took out his wallet. He spent what was said to have been over a million dollars to buy players from other teams, notably Detroit, which was owned by Norris' brother and sister. Of the 18 Black Hawks on the 1960–61 roster, 13 had been bought from other teams. Not surprisingly, some in the league suspected that the Detroit Norrises were shipping excess talent to brother Jim in Chicago. "There's a revolving door between those teams," one writer claimed.

Chicago's star, however, had come up from the Black Hawk farm system, arriving in 1958. "A young blond Adonis," wrote one reporter. Built

like a baby bull, he ripped off slap shots that goalkeepers called the fastest and hardest in hockey. This was Bobby Hull, the "Golden Jet," whose ferocious charges scattered defenses, leaving goalkeepers wide open for those bullet drives.

"I've never been afraid of what I do," said Detroit goalkeeper Hank Bassen. "But when Bobby blasts one, he puts the fear of God in you. You see that thing coming at you like a bullet and your life flashes before your eyes. No one else ever shot so hard and so heavy. If he hits a man with it, the man's skull could split open."

On the line with the 22-year-old Hull were Murray Balfour and Bill ("Red") Hay. In tribute to Jim Norris' way with a buck, it was called the Million Dollar Line. On a second line was bony-hard Stan Mikita, a flashy center and stick-handler. The Hawks, the heaviest club in the league, threw their weight around to wear down opponents. "We can't skate with most teams," said coach Rudy Pilous. "We got to knock them down."

Detroit's Red Wings had finished fourth, then upset the second-place Toronto Maple Leafs in the other semifinal in five games. During the regular season Toronto's Frank Mahovlich had narrowly missed beating out Geoffrion for the league scoring title, but he and his teammates were stymied in the semifinal by the acrobatics in goal of Detroit's Terry Sawchuk, who had been traded back to the club he had starred for in the early 1950s. "What pitching is in a short series in baseball," said Detroit general manager Jack Adams, "goalkeeping is in the Stanley Cup playoffs."

But to win you also have to score, and Detroit had the scorer: forward Gordie Howe, at 33 a 15-year NHL veteran, who would become in 1962 the second player (Maurice Richard was the first)

On the eve of the final series against Detroit, Chicago's Glenn Hall (l.) and a young Golden Jet, Bobby Hull, congratulate each other after the Black Hawks eliminated Montreal in the semifinal round.

Opposite page: His bald spot showing,
Detroit's Gerry Odrowski seems closest to
the flying puck. On the ice is Terry
Sawchuk, above him teammate Warren
Godfrey. Detroit's Howie Glover (No. 15)
imprisons a Black Hawk with his stick.
Detroit won this fourth game, 2-1. Above:
In the same game, Chicago goalie
Glenn Hall lunges for the puck that the
stick of teammate Jack Evans (No. 5)
misses. Hovering on the other side is No. 6,
Chicago's Reg Fleming. Red Wings are
Al Johnson (No. 17) and Parker MacDonald.

191

to score more than 500 career goals. Mean with a stick and tricky on skates ("Like a cobra," someone wrote), Howe was avoided by many defensemen, who gave him the room and time to swat line drives at the near and far corners.

Fans looked forward to the clash between Hull and Howe. In the first game Hull scored two goals in a 3-2 Black Hawk victory. Hull was stopped in the second game by Hank Bassen, who replaced the injured Sawchuk, and Detroit won, 3-1, Howe getting two assists on goals by Alex Delvecchio.

The teams split the next two games, evening the series at two victories apiece. Each had been able to win only at home. That held true for the fifth game, played in Chicago and won, 6-3, by the Black Hawks, to the joy of a beer-drinking crowd packed wall to wall in Chicago Stadium and estimated unofficially at more than 20,000.

In Detroit for the sixth game, the Red Wings, behind three games to two, had to win to stay alive. They took an early 1-0 lead and, with a Black Hawk in the penalty box, they swarmed around Chicago goalkeeper Glenn Hall, looking to fatten their lead. Alex Delvecchio saw Howe cutting and slapped the puck toward him. But Chicago's Reg Fleming intercepted and sped on a breakaway straight at Bassen in the Detroit net, a shocked hush suddenly falling over the Olympia.

Fleming came at Bassen from the side, flying across the goal mouth, puck in tow. Bassen shifted to guard the far side and, as he did, Fleming tucked the puck into the space Bassen had opened on the near side. That goal, scored while Chicago was shorthanded, seemed to flatten the Red Wings, and they wilted under the bruising Black Hawk attack. "We just ran out of gas," Jack Adams said later.

The Black Hawks won, 5-1, then carried the Stanley Cup off the Olympia ice through a spatter of applause. "The Black Hawks," a reporter wrote, "have come in four years from drinking beer in the cellar to drinking champagne in the penthouse."

Stan Mikita:
Better to sip than shake

Still weaving through defenses some 15 years after he first joined the Black Hawks with his boyhood buddy, Bobby Hull, Stan Mikita has won the Art Ross Trophy four times as the league's leading scorer and twice the Hart Trophy as the league's Most Valuable Player.

It has always bothered me to shake hands with opposing players after losing a Stanley Cup series. I think it bothers most players, and they would rather not do it—at least not the minute after you've lost. You want to cool down. But you're expected to shake hands with a guy who is dipping his hand into your pocket to take your money. I can't be ready to break a stick over a man's head one minute and then shake his hand the next. My wife is always after me about good sportsmanship, to shake hands, but I'm not that way. I remember, after we beat Detroit, Gordie Howe came into our clubhouse and drank champagne with us. I thought that was a real good way of congratulating the opposing team, and that's the way I have done it since.

FIRST GAME (April 6, at Chicago)
Black Hawks 3, Red Wings 2

FIRST PERIOD
Chicago—Hull (M. Balfour, Mikita) 9:39
Chicago—Wharram (McDonald, Mikita) 10:10
Chicago—Hull (Pilote, M. Balfour) 13:15
SECOND PERIOD
Detroit—Lunde (Howe) 16:14
THIRD PERIOD
Detroit—Johnson (Howe, Ullman) 19:18

SECOND GAME (April 8, at Detroit)
Red Wings 3, Black Hawks 1

FIRST PERIOD
Detroit—Young (Stasiuk, Delvecchio) 8:10
Detroit—Delvecchio (Howe, Johnson) 17:39
SECOND PERIOD
Chicago—Pilote 0:41
THIRD PERIOD
Detroit—Delvecchio (Stasiuk, Howe) 19:22

THIRD GAME (April 10, at Chicago)
Black Hawks 3, Red Wings 1

FIRST PERIOD
No scoring
SECOND PERIOD
Chicago—Mikita (Pilote, Hull) 11:56
Chicago—Murphy (Pilote, Litzenberger) 14:19
Chicago—M. Balfour (Hull, Hay) 18:17
THIRD PERIOD
Detroit—Howe (Delvecchio, Young) 9:28

FOURTH GAME (April 12, at Detroit)
Red Wings 2, Black Hawks 1

FIRST PERIOD
No scoring
SECOND PERIOD
Chicago—Hay (M. Balfour, Hull)............ 7:34
Detroit—Delvecchio (MacGregor, Howe)..... 8:48
THIRD PERIOD
Detroit—MacGregor (Fonteyne, Godfrey)....13:10

FIFTH GAME (April 14, at Chicago)
Black Hawks 6, Red Wings 3

FIRST PERIOD
Detroit—Labine (Johnson, Ullman).......... 2:14
Chicago—M. Balfour (Hay, Hull)............ 9:36
Chicago—Murphy (Nesterenko, St. Laurent)..10:04
Detroit—Glover (MacGregor, Fonteyne)......15:35
SECOND PERIOD
Chicago—M. Balfour (Pilote, Hay)..........16:25
Detroit—Stasiuk (Howe, Pronovost).........18:49
THIRD PERIOD
Chicago—Mikita (Vasko, Pilote)............ 2:51
Chicago—Pilote (Wharram, Mikita)......... 7:12
Chicago—Mikita (Murphy)................13:27

SIXTH GAME (April 16, at Detroit)
Black Hawks 5, Red Wings 1

FIRST PERIOD
Detroit—MacDonald (Howe, Delvecchio).....15:26
SECOND PERIOD
Chicago—Fleming....................... 6:45
Chicago—McDonald (Mikita, Hull).........18:47
THIRD PERIOD
Chicago—Nesterenko (Sloan, Pilote)........ 0:57
Chicago—Evans......................... 6:27
Chicago—Wharram......................18:00

Stan Mikita: "You're expected to shake
hands with a guy who is dipping his hand
into your pocket to take your money.
I can't...break a stick over a man's head
one minute and then shake his
hand the next."

CHICAGO BLACK HAWKS
TORONTO MAPLE LEAFS
1962

A Cup Victory Calls for a Parade—and the Twist

"The National Hockey League," wrote Los Angeles columnist Jim Murray during the 1962 playoffs, "makes a mockery of its title by restricting its franchises to six teams, waging a kind of private little tournament of 70 games just to eliminate two teams. Other big money sports are expanding, but hockey likes it there in the back of the cave."

Though expansion talk began clouding the air, the NHL through the mid-sixties continued to be what one writer called "the world's most exclusive skating club." The 1961–62 season ended with Montreal flying home first for the fifth straight year. Toronto came in second, the Black Hawks third, the Rangers fourth, New York entering the playoffs for only the fourth time in 12 years.

The Maple Leafs ousted the Rangers after six games, despite Horatio-at-the-gate goaltending by the Rangers' Lorne ("Gump") Worsley. The Canadiens, looking to win their first Cup without Maurice Richard, pasted two straight losses on the Black Hawks. But sparked by the scoring of 165-pound Stan Mikita and his lightweight mates on the Scooter Line, Ab McDonald and Kenny Wharram, the Black Hawks ran off with four straight victories to go into the finals and defend the Cup they had won a year earlier.

With seven former Cup-winning Canadiens on the squad, the Black Hawks could outslick you with the Scooter Line or bowl you over with the Million Dollar Line of Bobby Hull, Bill ("Red") Hay, and Murray Balfour. Hull had slammed in 50 goals that season, tying Maurice Richard's record. The beefy Black Hawks had the reputation of being the league bully-boys, flinging around their weight to wear down opponents.

Under the direction of brash George ("Punch") Imlach, a former minor league manager, the Maple Leafs had risen from last place in 1958 to play in two finals during the past three years. With the exception of Frank Mahovlich, a Hull-type high-scoring winger, and a few others, most of Punch's players were veterans, castoffs from other teams. Goalkeeper Johnny Bower and forwards Bert Olmstead and Leonard ("Red") Kelly were typical of the hungry, hustling, smart Punch Imlach kind of player. Other sharpshooters included little center Dave Keon (winner of the Lady Byng sportsmanship award), Dick Duff, George ("Chief") Armstrong, and Bob Pulford, who was playing despite torn shoulder ligaments, the shoulder numbed by drugs to reduce the pain.

Punch's Senior Citizens won the first game, 4-1, surprising the Black Hawks with the fierceness of their body checks. "The Leafs took us by surprise," admitted Black Hawk coach Rudy Pilous. "Usually they don't try to hurt anybody. They never ran at us like they did tonight." In the second game the Leafs were checking just as brutally, one collision sending Murray Balfour to the hospital with a concussion. The Leafs won again, 3-2.

"We've been down two games before," growled Pilous. But he had to concede: "It's not nice to be two down."

In friendly Chicago Stadium, the Black Hawks took the cloaks off their brawn, dealing four board-shaking checks within the first two minutes of the third game. They won the third and fourth games, 3-0 and 4-1, tying the series at two victories apiece. In the fourth game Johnny Bower was injured and seemed likely to miss the rest of the playoffs. Replacing him in goal was Don Simmons, the former Bruin. With Bower out, the Hawks were sudden favorites to win the Cup.

Back in Toronto, however, the Maple Leafs, losing 3-2, rapped five straight shots past Glenn

Out of a tussle near the Chicago cage during the second game, the puck comes to Toronto's George Armstrong, who backhands it by Glenn Hall. Armstrong and a teammate hoist high their hands—and with reason: the goal turned out to be the game-winner in a 3-2 Toronto victory.

Toronto's Frank Mahovlich
(No. 27) hangs at the
goal mouth, where the
Black Hawks shouldn't let
him stand. Chicago
goaltender Glenn Hall is
drawn out by a shot
that connects onto
Mahovlich's stick in the
crease, and he puts
the puck into the net
despite a last-second dive
by a Black Hawk. Later
Frank (l.) talks of the
goal, which helped
the Maple Leafs win the
fifth game, 8-4; he sports
a smile and the haircut
of the times.

197

Hall. That made the breathing easier for Don Simmons and the Maple Leafs, who coasted to an 8-4 victory. Bob Pulford, despite that stiff shoulder, scored three of the goals.

Ahead three games to two, the Maple Leafs came to Chicago for the sixth game trying to win the Cup in the notably unfriendly-to-strangers Stadium. In the third period of a scoreless tie, Bobby Hull drilled a low whistler by Simmons' shoulder to put Chicago ahead, 1-0. Chicago fans went hog-wild, hurling layers of garbage onto the ice. For ten minutes attendants were clearing away the litter.

The delay may have cooled down the Hawks; they did not score again. Some 90 seconds later Toronto's Bob Nevin slipped the puck by Glenn Hall to tie the game, 1-1. A little later Toronto's Tim Horton sucked the puck to his stick near his own cage, sped across the blue line, passed off, took the puck back, and fed it to Dick Duff near the Chicago cage. Duff jerked the puck by Hall to put Toronto ahead, 2-1, in a suddenly hushed Stadium. The Leafs protected that lead for the next five minutes and skated off the ice under sullen stares with their first Cup since 1951.

The team flew to Toronto for "the greatest reception ever tendered by the city," according to the mayor. A sea of faces filled the square around City Hall, the sidewalks packed from buildings to curbs with a crowd estimated at more than 50,000. The players rode in open cars up Bay Street. The bouncy Eddie Shack climbed on a seat and did one of the new dances. It was called the Twist.

Rod Gilbert:
A goal to build a dream on

Rod Gilbert is the Rangers' leading scorer of all time. Of all his goals and assists, he remembers best two goals and an assist he collected in his first Stanley Cup playoff game.

In 1962 the Rangers were playing Toronto in the semifinal round, and I joined them from the minor leagues for the playoffs. Doug Harvey was coaching our team. In the first period I came on ice for the first shift, and on my first shot I scored a goal. It was against Johnny Bower. Then with a minute left in the period, I took another shot and got another goal. Muzz [Murray] Patrick

was the manager then, and when we came into the room after the period I said to him, "Mr. Patrick, give me a pinch to see if I'm awake or dreaming." Later I got an assist and we won, 4-2. We didn't win the series, but I don't know . . . even if I'm on a team that wins the Cup, I'll never forget that game.

FIRST GAME (April 10, at Toronto)
Maple Leafs 4, Black Hawks 1
FIRST PERIOD
Chicago—Hull (Pilote, Mikita) 3:36
SECOND PERIOD
Toronto—Keon (Duff, Armstrong) 1:32
Toronto—Mahovlich (Stewart, Kelly) 13:54
THIRD PERIOD
Toronto—Armstrong (Duff) 6:02
Toronto—Horton (Armstrong, Keon) 14:32

SECOND GAME (April 12, at Toronto)
Maple Leafs 3, Black Hawks 2
FIRST PERIOD
Toronto—Harris (Horton, Stewart) 2:35
SECOND PERIOD
No scoring
THIRD PERIOD
Chicago—Mikita (Wharram, McDonald) 8:47
Toronto—Mahovlich (Stewart, Kelly) 9:47
Toronto—Armstrong (Duff, Stanley) 16:08
Chicago—Mikita (Pilote, Hull) 18:27

THIRD GAME (April 15, at Chicago)
Black Hawks 3, Maple Leafs 0
FIRST PERIOD
No scoring
SECOND PERIOD
Chicago—Mikita (Pilote, McDonald) 4:35
Chicago—McDonald (Pilote, Hay) 8:33
THIRD PERIOD
Chicago—Horvath (Nesterenko) 19:21

FOURTH GAME (April 17, at Chicago)
Black Hawks 4, Maple Leafs 1
FIRST PERIOD
Chicago—Hull (Mikita) 10:35
Chicago—Fleming (Nesterenko) 15:41
Toronto—Kelly (Armstrong, Duff) 18:05
SECOND PERIOD
Chicago—Hull (Hay, Mikita) 0:46
Chicago—Fleming (Nesterenko, Horvath) 7:31
THIRD PERIOD
No scoring

FIFTH GAME (April 19, at Toronto)
Maple Leafs 8, Black Hawks 4

FIRST PERIOD
Toronto—Pulford (Olmstead, Nevin)........ 0:17
Toronto—Pulford........................17:45
Chicago—Balfour (Hay, Hull)............18:05

SECOND PERIOD
Chicago—McDonald (Mikita, St. Laurent).... 0:50
Chicago—McDonald (Hull, Mikita)......... 3:07
Toronto—Harris (Mahovlich, Horton)....... 8:31
Toronto—Keon (Mahovlich, Horton)....... 9:50
Toronto—Mahovlich (Kelly, Stewart).......14:24

THIRD PERIOD
Toronto—Armstrong (Brewer, Baun)........ 4:41
Toronto—Mahovlich (Stewart, Baun)........ 6:31
Chicago—Turner (Nesterenko, St. Laurent)...10:31
Toronto—Pulford (Harris, Horton).........13:51

SIXTH GAME (April 22, at Chicago)
Maple Leafs 2, Black Hawks 1

FIRST PERIOD
No scoring
SECOND PERIOD
No scoring
THIRD PERIOD
Chicago—Hull (Hay, Balfour).............. 8:58
Toronto—Nevin (Baun, Mahovlich).........10:29
Toronto—Duff (Horton, Armstrong)........14:14

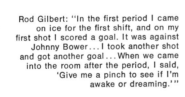

Rod Gilbert: "In the first period I came on ice for the first shift, and on my first shot I scored a goal. It was against Johnny Bower...I took another shot and got another goal...When we came into the room after the period, I said, 'Give me a pinch to see if I'm awake or dreaming.'"

DETROIT RED WINGS
TORONTO MAPLE LEAFS **1963**

Even the Egg Throwers from Windsor Couldn't Stop These Donkey Heads

During the season someone calculated that in the last 32 seasons 17 of the teams that had finished first had gone on to win the Cup. After finishing first, one point ahead of the Black Hawks, the Maple Leafs had probability on their side as they set out to win the Cup a second straight year.

The triumph by George ("Punch") Imlach's Senior Citizens in 1962 had been called a fluke in more than one NHL city. The Maple Leafs were an earlier version of the Washington Redskins' Over the Hill Gang. Imlach had picked up a slew of aged rejects: Leonard ("Red") Kelly from Detroit; Eddie Shack, Allan Stanley, and Johnny Bower from New York; Don Simmons from Boston and the minor leagues. In 1961 Ed Litzenberger was a slow skater with the Black Hawks when they won the Stanley Cup. Punch obtained him for the $20,000 waiver price. In 1962 Litzenberger was a slow-slow skater with the Maple Leafs, but he fitted in with Punch's other clever, hard-hitting veterans and for the second year in a row he was on a Cup winner.

"I got to say we have depth and we have balance," Punch said in 1963. "I can reach down the bench any time and get somebody who'll do the job. We have the best center in hockey in Dave Keon and we have the best old pro who ever played in Johnny Bower. There is nothing unusual in our success. We work harder and practice longer than any of the other clubs."

Keon certainly was the most polite center in the league, incurring only two minutes in penalties during the entire season, winning the Lady Byng award for sportsmanship for the second year in a row. As for goalkeeper Johnny Bower, a minor leaguer until he was 34, someone said of him, "He's 42 going on 46."

Imlach was one of the first NHL coaches to use the two-goalkeeper system, alternating Bower and Simmons from one game to the next. Once Bower complained about a sore leg. "Hey, where's Simmons?" Punch shouted. "I'm okay," Bower yelped, "I'm okay."

Of this group of hard-bitten veterans, Chicago coach Rudy Pilous said, "They're big and they're strong and they wear you down. After three periods against that kind of play, any other team gets tired and begins to make mistakes."

The Maple Leafs wore down the Canadiens in five games. Meanwhile, the fourth-place Red Wings lost the first two games of their semifinal to the Black Hawks, then won four straight to go into the final against Punch's Senior Citizens. Punch said he had rooted for Chicago. "They play our kind of hockey—rough."

Detroit's Gordie Howe had led the league in scoring; there was a question whether Punch had a skater quick enough to stay with Howe. In goal for the Red Wings was Terry Sawchuk, past his prime but still a redoubt at playoff time.

The Leafs' high scorer, Frank Mahovlich, was limping on strained knee ligaments. A year earlier, Chicago owner Jim Norris had signed a $1,000,000 certified check to buy "Big M." After agreeing to the deal, the Maple Leafs had later changed their minds. Filling in on some shifts for the $1,000,000 Mahovlich would be the $20,000 Litzenberger.

Last year's Toronto hero, Dick Duff, scored two goals in the first 68 seconds of the first game, won 4-2 by the Maple Leafs. They won the second by an identical score, Litzenberger moving like a barge, yet scoring one goal and assisting on two others, proving that occasionally a $20,000 player can be worth a million.

In Detroit the Red Wings won the third game, 3-2, but the Leafs won the fourth, again by a 4-2

Sprawled on the ice, Toronto goaltender Johnny Bower stops a puck hit by Detroit's Ed Joyal, but the puck bounces back onto the onrushing Joyal's stick and he tucks it into the corner as he flies by the cage. The goal put Detroit ahead, 2-1, in the fourth game, but Toronto rallied to win, 4-2.

Detroit goaltender Terry Sawchuk comes
out (opposite page) to meet Toronto's
Dave Keon (No. 14), but Keon flies over
Sawchuk and shoves the puck into the
cage before he can be collared by
Red Wing pursuers. Moments earlier Keon
had broken up a Detroit rush and stolen
the puck. This goal was Toronto's first
of the third game, which was won,
3-2, by the Red Wings.

score, to lead three games to one. Glum Detroit fans hurled eggs at the Maple Leafs. "The egg throwers must have been from Windsor, not Detroit," Red Wing coach Sid Abel said later, his face as solemn as he could make it.

Punch was not amused. As he left Olympia Stadium he yelled at the fans, "Go home, you bums, you've seen your last game of the year."

Punch was certain the series would not return to Detroit as the teams flew to Toronto for the fifth game. "If my players don't clinch this thing in the next game," he snapped, "they're a bunch of donkey heads."

Late in the third period of that fifth game, with the score tied 1-1, Toronto's Kent Douglas snapped a low drive. The puck ricocheted off the skate of a Detroit defenseman and onto the stick of Toronto's Eddie Shack. With some amazement, Shack watched the puck deflect off his stick, which he hadn't moved, and into the cage. Toronto led, 2-1.

"I was just trying to get the hell out of the way," Shack said later, "and it hit my stick and went in."

With time running out, Detroit pulled Sawchuk out of the cage. Dave Keon drilled the puck into the open cage, sealing a 3-1 Toronto victory. The Maple Leafs sailed off ice with the Stanley Cup in their grasp for the second straight year.

As the Maple Leafs sipped champagne from the Cup, an exhausted Gordie Howe sat in the Red Wing dressing room. "We tried," he said, "but it was like growling against thunder."

Frank Mahovlich:
One octopus, sunny-side up

The former Toronto high-scoring wingman, later a top scorer for the Red Wings and the Canadiens, recalled more of the antics of those "egg-throwers from Windsor" at his Montreal home.

They threw everything at you in Detroit. What I remember best was seeing an octopus come down. There was a chap who had a pet shop, I guess, and every year at the Stanley Cup it was a kind of tradition. He'd throw this little octopus, and it would be alive until it landed flat on the ice and then it was a big blah. They just swept it away, the poor thing . . .

204

FIRST GAME (April 9, at Toronto)
Maple Leafs 4, Red Wings 2

FIRST PERIOD
Toronto—Duff (Keon, Stanley) 0:49
Toronto—Duff (Stanley, Horton) 1:08
Toronto—Nevin 14:42
SECOND PERIOD
Detroit—Jeffrey (Ullman, Smith) 5:36
Detroit—Jeffrey (Howe, Ullman) 8:05
THIRD PERIOD
Toronto—Nevin (Pulford, Shack) 5:08

SECOND GAME (April 11, at Toronto)
Maple Leafs 4, Red Wings 2

FIRST PERIOD
Toronto—Litzenberger (Pulford, Horton) 5:31
Toronto—Stewart (Litzenberger, Kelly) 18:42
SECOND PERIOD
Toronto—Nevin (Stanley, Horton) 0:49
Detroit—Howe (Delvecchio, M. Pronovost) 1:32
Toronto—Stewart (Litzenberger, Harris) 8:55
THIRD PERIOD
Detroit—Howe (Jeffrey, Ullman) 2:03

THIRD GAME (April 14, at Detroit)
Red Wings 3, Maple Leafs 2

FIRST PERIOD
Detroit—Stasiuk (Ullman, Smith) 0:33
Toronto—Keon (Duff, Brewer) 14:56
SECOND PERIOD
Detroit—Faulkner (MacGregor, M.
Pronovost) 8:13
Toronto—Horton (Kelly) 13:06
Detroit—Faulkner (A. Pronovost, M.
Pronovost) 13:39
THIRD PERIOD
No scoring

FOURTH GAME (April 16, at Detroit)
Maple Leafs 4, Red Wings 2

FIRST PERIOD
Detroit—Howe (Delvecchio, P. MacDonald) . . . 2:54
SECOND PERIOD
Toronto—Armstrong (Keon) 1:17
Detroit—Joyal (Howe) 2:38
Toronto—Kelly (Mahovlich, Baun) 17:41
THIRD PERIOD
Toronto—Keon 9:42
Toronto—Kelly 17:45

FIFTH GAME (April 18, at Toronto)
Maple Leafs 3, Red Wings 1

FIRST PERIOD
Toronto—Keon (Armstrong) 17:44
SECOND PERIOD
Detroit—Delvecchio (Howe, M. Pronovost) . . . 0:49
THIRD PERIOD
Toronto—Shack (Douglas, Pulford) 13:28
Toronto—Keon (Armstrong, Stanley) 19:55

Toronto's Bob Nevin (No. 11) evades a falling Red Wing and swoops in on Terry Sawchuk, beating him with a sideways swipe. Note Detroit's No. 10 sliding helplessly on the ice along a route almost parallel with Nevin's.

DETROIT RED WINGS
TORONTO MAPLE LEAFS ──1964

Between Losers and Winners
a Swapping of Sticks, a Clicking of Glasses

Midway through the season the Boston Bruins swamped the defending champion Maple Leafs, 11-0, and George ("Punch") Imlach decided he wanted to see some new faces above the Maple Leaf. He traded away five young players, including 1962 playoff hero Dick Duff, to the Rangers for two former All-Star forwards, Don McKenney and Andy Bathgate, both now on the downslope of their careers. Punch hoped that Bathgate and McKenney, after spending years in the basement with weak teams, might skate with the fire of their youth just long enough for the Maple Leafs to win a third straight Stanley Cup.

Bathgate and McKenney played better than Punch dared dream. Bathgate led the league in assists with 58, tying a league record, and McKenney scored more goals in three weeks with Toronto than he had scored during the entire season in New York. Shifted from left wing to center, Frank Mahovlich skated and stick-handled with a new zest. Though nearly 40, Johnny Bower was bouncing in the cage like a boy on a trampoline. The Maple Leafs finished third and faced the first-place Canadiens. Down three games to two, the Maple Leafs won the sixth game and came from behind in the third period of the seventh game to go into their fifth final in the six-year reign of Punch Imlach.

The Chicago Black Hawks, after finishing second, made no secret of it: They thought they could erase the fourth-place Red Wings in four or five games. The Red Wings, for their part, were making no secret of their plans to become the first fourth-place finisher to win the Cup since the Maple Leafs did it in 1949.

"Everyone laughs at us when we talk about winning the Cup," said Detroit coach Sid Abel. "But the experts forget that we played with in-

juries all year long, that we had six regulars hurt at one time, that we were forced to use every goalkeeper in our minor league system. It's just lately that we've had all our varsity together."

The all-together Red Wings shocked the Black Hawks by winning the semifinal in seven games. "We've got some rampaging younger players, some good veterans—and Gordie Howe," said Red Wing veteran Alex Delvecchio on the eve of the final. "And Terry Sawchuk knows a thing or two about what it's like to play in a Stanley Cup final."

But the champion Maple Leafs were 3-to-1 favorites. "We have only one superstar, Frank Mahovlich," said a Toronto writer. "But we have balance. Anybody can score."

The first game was tied 2-2 with 10 seconds left and the Maple Leafs short a man. As Detroit worked the puck around the Toronto cage, the Maple Leafs' Bob Pulford intercepted a pass and sped across the blue line, juggling the puck in front of him. He feinted around Norm Ullman and looked down a lane at the crouched figure of Terry Sawchuk, Maple Leaf Gardens a sea of noise. As Pulford wound up to shoot, Howe sped up to him from behind, stick outstretched. Howe's stick flicked at the puck a split second too late, Pulford teeing off a low liner that whizzed over Sawchuk's left shoulder for a goal with only two seconds left in the game. The Maple Leafs were 3-2 winners.

The second game ended just as frantically. Tied 3-3, the teams went into overtime. Howe flew in on Toronto's Johnny Bower. Larry Jeffrey crept in on the side of the cage. Howe wound up to shoot, then whisked the puck to Jeffrey. The puck skipped off Jeffrey's stick and into the cage for a 4-3 Detroit victory that evened the series at a

Detroit's Floyd Smith (No. 17) stands at the entrance to an empty Toronto cage, set to score, but he is missing a vital ingredient for a goal: the puck. Flopped on top of the puck is Toronto's Tim Horton (No. 7); goalkeeper Johnny Bower, not looking where he is going, descends on him.

Toronto goaltender Johnny Bower drops his
glove to snare a puck coming at him.
Toronto's Bobby Baun (No. 21) is fending
off Detroit's Parker MacDonald. Toronto
won this sixth game, 4-3, when Baun scored
a goal in overtime. Note the jubilation
of the lady in white and her companions (r.).

In what looks like a stick-swinging brawl
—but is actually a pileup in front of the
Toronto net—Toronto's Bob Pulford (No. 20)
checks a Detroit player while Detroit's
Ed Joyal (No. 21) and Toronto netminder
Johnny Bower (r.) hunt for the puck.

game apiece. "I did not even have to move my stick," Jeffrey said later of Howe's perfect pass. "I just snapped my wrists and it was game ball. It happened so quick I think Bower was still watching Howe."

The third game was another crowd-howler. The Maple Leafs came back from a 3-0 deficit to tie the game, 3-3, with only 73 seconds left. With fewer than 20 seconds remaining, Howe stole the puck from Mahovlich and slipped it to Delvecchio standing alone on the open side of the cage. Delvecchio ticked the puck by Bower for a 4-3 Red Wing victory.

On their days off during the finals, Detroit players went to the racetrack. But Punch Imlach lashed his Toronto players through two-hour drills. Some of the Leafs complained. "There's a limit to an athlete's endurance," said Andy Bathgate.

Sipping milk to appease an ulcer, Punch retorted, "There's no limit to what you can do. Who says there's a limit? Only you! . . . If you're going to play a hockey game for an hour, you should be able to practice two hours. That's the way you build endurance."

The teams split the next two games, each winning on the other team's rink, and now the Red Wings led, three games to two. The sixth game was being played at Detroit's Olympia Stadium, Detroit only 60 minutes away from its first Cup since 1955.

The game was another close one, tied 3-3 late in the third period. A flying puck cracked the ankle of Toronto's Bob Baun. He collapsed. "My leg just turned to cream cheese," he said later. He was taken off the ice in a stretcher. In the dressing room a doctor told him a bone was broken. "Freeze it," Baun told the doctor.

He returned to the ice, the game now in overtime. He lashed a long shot from near the blue line that caromed off the stick of Detroit's Bill Gadsby and hopped high over Sawchuk's right shoulder and into the cage for a 4-3 Maple Leaf victory. "I got the stick out of the way too late," a weeping Gadsby said in the dressing room.

Doctors told Baun he had played with a hairline fracture of the fibula in the right leg. He insisted on playing in the seventh game. "You don't think I'm going to miss the last chapter because of this, do you?" he asked the doctors.

The last chapter ended happily for the Leafs,

who won the seventh game, 4-0, to capture their third Cup in a row, tying the Maple Leafs of 1947–49. The Leafs needed two more consecutive triumphs to match the record of the 1956–60 Canadiens, who had won five successive Cups.

After the game, Gordie Howe came into the Toronto dressing room to shake hands with the Leafs. He swapped sticks with Johnny Bower. "I should have taken your stick away seven years ago, Bower," Howe said, and then he clicked glasses of champagne with the Stanley Cup winners.

In the Detroit dressing room, Bill Gadsby slumped on a stool, still seeing that puck hop high off his stick in the sixth game. "Those Leafs must live right, the lucky bastards," he said. Despite almost 20 years of trying, Gadsby had yet to place his name on the Cup. This time he had come close—within one shot, one goal—and never again would he come as close.

Red Kelly:
A babe in the Cup

The former All-Star defenseman of the Red Wings and Maple Leafs, Leonard ("Red") Kelly served as a Member of Parliament while playing defense for Toronto. The coach of the Maple Leafs, he talked about winning the Cup for a third straight year.

I played in that seventh game with an injured knee. After the game they were pouring champagne in the clubhouse, but the pain killer on my knee had worn off and I was in all kinds of pain and I didn't feel like drinking any champagne. I passed out in the shower. They had to carry me to the hospital. They took me home the next day by ambulance.

I never got any champagne. The next day I had to go to Ottawa for a session. I remember sitting in my seat in the House of Commons with the leg stretched straight out in the aisle. I couldn't bend the leg.

Anyway the following day Mr. Ballard [the owner of the Maple Leafs] brought the Stanley Cup over to my house. I wasn't there, still being in Ottawa. But he brought along some champagne and he posed my wife for a picture, she standing behind the Cup with my youngest, Clancy—he was about a year old—sitting in the Cup.

210

Mr. Ballard knew I had missed all the celebrating. He didn't leave the Stanley Cup but he did leave the champagne, and I thought it was tremendously thoughtful of him.

FIRST GAME (April 11, at Toronto)
Maple Leafs 3, Red Wings 2

FIRST PERIOD
  Detroit—MacGregor (Barkley) 4:31
  Toronto—Armstrong (Stanley, McKenney) 4:44
  Detroit—Howe (MacDonald, Delvecchio) 10:25
SECOND PERIOD
  No scoring
THIRD PERIOD
  Toronto—Armstrong (Kelly, McKenney) 4:02
  Toronto—Pulford 19:58

SECOND GAME (April 14, at Toronto)
Red Wings 4, Maple Leafs 3

FIRST PERIOD
  Toronto—Stanley (Kelly, Mahovlich) 11:57
  Detroit—Ullman (Gadsby, Jeffrey) 12:43
SECOND PERIOD
  Detroit—Joyal (Barkley) 3:19
  Detroit—Smith (Howe) 16:15
THIRD PERIOD
  Toronto—Kelly (Baun, Mahovlich) 11:57
  Toronto—Ehman (Bathgate, Stewart) 19:17
OVERTIME
  Detroit—Jeffrey (Ullman, Howe) 7:52

THIRD GAME (April 16, at Detroit)
Red Wings 4, Maple Leafs 3

FIRST PERIOD
  Detroit—Smith 2:40
  Detroit—MacGregor (Barkley, Martin) 3:38
  Detroit—Smith (Ullman, Delvecchio) 14:47
SECOND PERIOD
  Toronto—Bathgate (Mahovlich, Kelly) 4:16
THIRD PERIOD
  Toronto—Keon (McKenney, Armstrong) 7:34
  Toronto—McKenney (Keon, Horton) 18:47
  Detroit—Delvecchio (Howe, A. Pronovost) 19:43

FOURTH GAME (April 18, at Detroit)
Maple Leafs 4, Red Wings 2

FIRST PERIOD
  Toronto—Keon (Horton, McKenney) 5:45
SECOND PERIOD
  Detroit—MacGregor (Joyal) 5:57
  Detroit—Howe (Ullman, Jeffrey) 13:05
  Toronto—Keon (McKenney, Armstrong) 16:09
THIRD PERIOD
  Toronto—Bathgate (Mahovlich, Kelly) 10:55
  Toronto—Mahovlich (Pulford, Stewart) 18:09

FIFTH GAME (April 21, at Toronto)
Red Wings 2, Maple Leafs 1

FIRST PERIOD
  Detroit—Howe (Delvecchio) 10:52
SECOND PERIOD
  No scoring
THIRD PERIOD
  Detroit—Joyal (A. Pronovost) 7:50
  Toronto—Armstrong (Mahovlich, Bathgate) . . . 14:57

SIXTH GAME (April 23, at Detroit)
Maple Leafs 4, Red Wings 3

FIRST PERIOD
  Toronto—Pulford (Stanley) 17:01
SECOND PERIOD
  Detroit—Henderson (Martin) 4:20
  Detroit—Martin (MacMillan, Howe) 10:56
  Toronto—Pulford (Stewart, Brewer) 14:36
  Detroit—Howe (Delvecchio, Gadsby) 15:56
  Toronto—Harris (Armstrong, Baun) 17:48
THIRD PERIOD
  No scoring
OVERTIME
  Toronto—Baun (Pulford) 3:07

SEVENTH GAME (April 25, at Toronto)
Maple Leafs 4, Red Wings 0

FIRST PERIOD
  Toronto—Bathgate 3:04
SECOND PERIOD
  No scoring
THIRD PERIOD
  Toronto—Keon (Harris) 4:26
  Toronto—Kelly (Mahovlich, Stanley) 5:53
  Toronto—Armstrong (Mahovlich) 15:26

CHICAGO BLACK HAWKS
MONTREAL CANADIENS
1965

Pete Meets Bobby, and the Band Plays "Me and My Shadow"

Hector ("Toe") Blake leaned forward, sitting on a chair in the dressing room of the Montreal Canadiens. He was speaking in low tones, almost a whisper, to his craggy-faced forward, Claude Provost, whom most everyone called Pete. "Crowd Hull," said the rotund Montreal coach, "lean on him, follow him around like a busted garter."

Other teams had assigned shadows to Bobby Hull, usually without success. In the semifinal against Chicago, the first-place Detroit Red Wings had told several forwards at various times to glue themselves to Bobby. But the "Golden Jet" had broken free to score eight goals and add five assists as the third-place Hawks ousted the Red Wings in seven games. The Red Wings were the fourth Prince of Wales winner in five years to be kicked out of the playoffs in the opening round.

Now Toe Blake was sending Provost on the difficult mission of checking Hull. For most of the season Pete's goals had kept the Canadiens winning, especially during the first half when Jean Beliveau slumped, seeming to have lost his confidence, and then, having regained it, was hobbled by a knee injury. Pete, guarding Hull, wouldn't score at his usual pace. Toe was gambling that the other Canadien shooters would make up for the goals Pete wouldn't score. The Black Hawks

came to the final acclaimed as the best overall team in hockey despite their third-place finish. Coach Billy Reay boasted a skirmish line of shooters: Bobby Hull and his brother Dennis, who was said to hit a harder shot than Bobby; plus Stan Mikita, Kenny Wharram, Ronald ("Chico") Maki, and a young dock-walloper of a center, Phil Esposito, who fed Hull so cleverly that the Golden Jet called Espo "My good right arm." In goal was the veteran Glenn Hall, so nervous before games that he usually retched, but quick and poised when the shooting started.

Facing all those Black Hawk fusiliers was a watery Montreal defense. Toe Blake's best defenseman, Jacques Laperriere, would miss the final, his ankle broken. The two Montreal goalkeepers, Charlie Hodge and Lorne ("Gump") Worsley, ranked only fourth in the six-team league in goals allowed. Montreal had finished second by bulging opposing nets with rubber, the offense inspired by three fine centers: Beliveau, Henri ("Pocket") Richard, and Ralph Backstrom.

In the first game Pete Provost stuck close enough to Hull to read the brand name on his underwear. The Golden Jet unleashed only one shot on goal. The teams were tied, 2-2, in the third period when Yvan Cournoyer, the newest

After shutting out the Black Hawks in the seventh game, Gump Worsley (in pads at top) is mobbed by his teammates. Asked how he felt about being replaced by Worsley for the seventh game, Charlie Hodge replied: "I don't like it." The Canadiens were underdogs in this series for one of the few times in their history.

The Golden Jet, Chicago's Bobby Hull, flashes by a Montreal defenseman, ducks under his stick, and slams the puck by Charlie Hodge for one of the two goals he scored in the third period of the fourth game. Growled Montreal general manager Sam Pollock later: "A blind man can see that Hull is getting away with murder. Hull is great, but why are the officials so careful with him? He's no Lady Byng player, you know."

high-scoring Montreal forward, winged a puck by Glenn Hall. That was the game-winner, Montreal the 3-2 victor.

Despite a spread-out skating style that looked labored, Provost continued to hang close to Bobby in the second game. The Golden Jet got off only two shots on goal, neither for a score, as Worsley shut out Chicago, 2-0. It was Worsley's second shutout of the season.

Someone asked Hull how he felt about being shadowed by Provost. "He is very determined," said the Golden Jet, obviously trying to cover up his frustration with politeness.

Provost seemed eager to placate Hull before the Golden Jet tried to slice off his head. "You can't blame him for feeling frustrated," Pete said. "I know it's tough on him having a guy shadowing him all the time. But that's my job."

In Chicago for the third game, the Black Hawks hit more aggressively and they won, 3-1. For the fourth game Charlie Hodge replaced the injured Worsley in goal for the Canadiens and Charlie looked helpless at times as the Hawks won, 5-1, tying the series at two victories apiece. Hull scored two of the goals, but both times Provost was off-ice.

So far the home team had won every game. That pattern continued: Montreal won in the Forum, 6-0, Hodge suddenly impregnable before the home folks; Chicago won the sixth game at Chicago Stadium.

Why were the home teams winning? "They make the ice slower in Chicago," explained Montreal's J. C. Tremblay. "We lose our speed, which is our big edge against any team."

"It's tough for us in Montreal's Forum," said Chicago's Pierre Pilote. "Their corners are deep. Once they get you in their corners, you just can't get out."

Fortunately for the Canadiens, the seventh game would be played in the Forum. Toe Blake brought back Gump Worsley to play goal even though Hodge had allowed only two goals in two games. "I thought Gump would be less nervous than Charlie in a seventh game," Blake explained.

"How in hell," retorted the ever-candid Gump, "can you *not* be nervous?"

Big Jean Beliveau immediately made Gump less nervous by slapping in a goal at the 14-second mark. The Montreal siege guns—Duff, Cour-

noyer, Richard—wheeled up to whiz three more pucks past Glenn Hall before the first period had ended. The Gumper needed only the first one, the Canadiens winning 4-0. At the siren, Beliveau picked up the Cup and skated around the Forum, hugging the 12th Cup won by the Canadiens. Only Toronto had won as many.

For the first time, a Conn Smythe Trophy was awarded to the player judged to be the most valuable in the playoffs. The winner was Beliveau, but some thought the award should have gone to Provost, who had tailed Hull so closely that the Golden Jet had failed to score while Provost was on-ice. Hull gave Provost an award of his own. "I've never been checked like that in my life," Hull said.

Bobby Hull and Phil Esposito: Changing times

Two of the high-scoring stars for the Black Hawks of 1965 were gone far away by 1974—Bobby Hull to the Winnipeg Jets of the World Hockey Association and Phil Esposito to the Boston Bruins. Hull compared the difference between a Maurice Richard, who once helped win a Cup with blood streaking down his face, and today's hockey players. Esposito talked about the ultimate Stanley Cup playoff.

Bobby Hull: *Why should a guy with a half-million dollar contract want to have blood dripping down his face, or sweat, or play with bruises? Hell, they won't even play with bruised feelings now.*

Phil Esposito: *Playing in that first Stanley Cup final was a thrill, even though I didn't get much ice time that year. I never really played well for Chicago in the playoffs, and I guess that was one of the reasons why Billy Reay traded me to Boston. The first Cup we won [after Phil joined the Bruins] here in Boston, in 1970, that was a big thrill. Even though we were ahead three games to nothing, I didn't feel we had it won until I was jumping over the boards after Orr socked in that goal in overtime of the fourth game. But I think an even bigger thrill than winning the Cup—well, it's damn close, anyway—was beating the Russians for Team Canada in Moscow. You had to be there to feel how it was. Some day I guess we will play the Russians for the Stanley Cup. We should play them with an All-Star team, because that's what the Russians have—an All-Star team. It could happen. It should happen.*

FIRST GAME (April 17, at Montreal)
Canadiens 3, Black Hawks 2

FIRST PERIOD
No scoring
SECOND PERIOD
Montreal—Richard (Berenson) 2:39
Chicago—Henry (R. Hull) 4:47
Montreal—Ferguson 5:26
THIRD PERIOD
Chicago—Ravlich (Maki, Mikita) 2:38
Montreal—Cournoyer (Harris, Beliveau) 8:59

SECOND GAME (April 20, at Montreal)
Canadiens 2, Black Hawks 0

FIRST PERIOD
No scoring
SECOND PERIOD
Montreal—Beliveau (Picard, Provost) 2:55
THIRD PERIOD
Montreal—Duff (Beliveau, Tremblay) 8:07

THIRD GAME (April 22, at Chicago)
Black Hawks 3, Canadiens 1

FIRST PERIOD
No scoring
SECOND PERIOD
Montreal—Ferguson (Tremblay, Backstrom) . . 4:16
Chicago—Esposito (Maki, Pilote) 5:03
THIRD PERIOD
Chicago—Wharram (Mikita) 2:00
Chicago—Maki (R. Hull, Esposito) 19:24

FOURTH GAME (April 25, at Chicago)
Black Hawks 5, Canadiens 1

FIRST PERIOD
Chicago—Stanfield 2:57
SECOND PERIOD
Montreal—Beliveau (Duff, Tremblay) 6:29
THIRD PERIOD
Chicago—R. Hull (Pilote) 0:26
Chicago—Hay (Stanfield) 16:17
Chicago—R. Hull (Maki) 18:48
Chicago—Jarrett 19:57

FIFTH GAME (April 27, at Montreal)
Canadiens 6, Black Hawks 0

FIRST PERIOD
Montreal—Beliveau (Rousseau, Duff) 7:14
Montreal—Duff (Beliveau, Rousseau) 16:36
SECOND PERIOD
Montreal—Rousseau (Beliveau, Tremblay) 4:29
THIRD PERIOD
Montreal—Beliveau (Duff, Tremblay) 4:29
Montreal—Richard (Provost) 6:46
Montreal—Tremblay 19:55

SIXTH GAME (April 29, at Chicago)
Black Hawks 2, Canadiens 1

FIRST PERIOD
No scoring
SECOND PERIOD
Montreal—Backstrom (Harris, Ferguson) 16:57
THIRD PERIOD
Chicago—Vasko (Mohns, Ravlich) 6:06
Chicago—Mohns (Mikita, Ravlich) 8:15

SEVENTH GAME (May 1, at Montreal)
Canadiens 4, Black Hawks 0

FIRST PERIOD
Montreal—Beliveau (Duff, Rousseau) 0:14
Montreal—Duff (Beliveau, Rousseau) 5:03
Montreal—Cournoyer (Duff, Rousseau) 16:27
Montreal—Richard (Harris) 18:45
SECOND PERIOD
No scoring
THIRD PERIOD
No scoring

Phil Esposito (shown here as a Bruin):
"Some day I guess we will play the
Russians for the Stanley Cup. We should
play them with an All-Star team . . . It
could happen. It should happen."

DETROIT RED WINGS
MONTREAL CANADIENS
1966

Gump Speaks Out,
and Toe Turns Purple

Worsley wasn't even tested. His underwear can't even be wet.

> —Detroit's Bill Gadsby,
> after Montreal's 5-1 victory

What most people don't know is that my underwear is wet before the game even starts.

> —Worsley

Les Canadiens finished first for the second time in three years—and for the eighth season of the past eleven. This team had the style and character if not the skill of Canadien teams of the previous ten years. It was spearheaded by the skating and scoring of its three premier centers: Jean Beliveau, Ralph Backstrom, and Henri ("Pocket") Richard. It was saved quite often by the clutch goaltending of balloon-shaped Lorne ("Gump") Worsley. And, as always, it was flogged toward perfection by its nervous martinet of a coach, Hector ("Toe") Blake.

Toe Blake's Canadiens rolled over George ("Punch") Imlach's Maple Leafs in four straight games. In the other semifinal the fourth-place Red Wings took on Chicago's Black Hawks, led by Bobby Hull, who had set NHL scoring records during the season with 54 goals and 97 points. But Detroit's "Superpest," Bryan Watson, hung all over Bobby, and Detroit beat the Black Hawks in six games.

The Red Wings were a mixed bag. They included castoffs like ex-Ranger and ex-Maple Leaf Andy Bathgate, aging veterans like 38-year-old Gordie Howe and 35-year-old Alex Delvecchio, and a sprinkling of youngsters, notably 24-year-old goalkeeper Roger Crozier. The slight, clerkish-looking Crozier was afflicted with a pancreas ailment; he had left a hospital bed only a few weeks before the playoffs. Crozier, a left-hander,

held the stick in his left hand, confusing some shooters accustomed to right-handed goalkeepers, who held the stick in their right hands. When the puck was driven at Crozier's right side, his glove was waiting to snare the shot.

This was the fourth final for the Red Wings in the past six years; they had lost each of those finals. But hopes soared high this year in Cadillac Square when the Red Wings won the first two games, both played on Montreal ice, Crozier tumbling and sprawling to make one miracle save after another.

On the way to Detroit for the third game, Red Wing defenseman Bill Gadsby, who had yet to be on a Cup winner in 20 years of trying, told a friend: "So close. We need to win only two more games, and we play the next two in our building." In that building, Detroit's Olympia Stadium, the Canadiens had won only twice in the past two years.

Muttering that his Canadiens were "just plain lousy," Toe Blake formed a new line, combining Pocket Richard with Leon Rochefort, whom he hastily recalled from a minor league team, and Dave Balon. In the first period of the third game, Detroit leading 1-0 and Red Wing fans thinking they were seeing a sweep, Balon tied the game, 1-1. Late in the period Beliveau stole the puck from Delvecchio, swung around Leo Boivin, and rode in alone on Crozier. Beliveau made a sweeping motion with his stick, faking Crozier onto the ice, then crossed in front of the cage and angled the puck into the right corner. "Everyone has been trying to go to Crozier's left, to his stick side," Beliveau said later. "I decided to try him the other way."

The Canadiens won, 4-2, appearing to skate faster than they had in Montreal. In the fourth

Detroit's Norm Ullman (in dark uniform) flies after puck, cranks up, and powders it by Montreal's Gump Worsley in the fourth game, won 2-1 by Montreal. Later Worsley complained he had trouble seeing the puck because of the bright lights and blue-tinted ice needed for color telecasts. "It's like flashbulbs always going off in your eyes," he said.

Montreal's Jean Beliveau
(No. 4) drills the puck
at Detroit goaltender
Roger Crozier, who tips
the puck upward with
his glove, then catches
it—note his footwork
—sandwiching it between
stick and glove.

220

game Crozier wrenched a knee and was replaced in goal by Hank Bassen, who had played fewer than a dozen games all season. The loss of Crozier seemed to numb the Red Wings, who didn't get off a shot at Worsley for the next 13 minutes. Meanwhile, Beliveau and Backstrom slung pucks by Bassen for a 2-1 Montreal victory that tied the series at two wins apiece.

As the teams journeyed to Montreal, the Red Wings were loose and laughing. "They're like a bunch of guys at a country club," remarked one reporter. By contrast, under Toe Blake's regimen, the Canadiens acted like a platoon of legionnaires.

Playing now in their customary swift style, the Canadiens swept over the Red Wings in the fifth game, 5-1. "We left our skates in Detroit," moaned Red Wing coach Sid Abel, "and the Canadiens were going at 90 miles an hour."

"Detroit has simply lost its speed," said the outspoken Gump Worsley. "Howe is the greatest player I've ever faced. But Gordie doesn't have the steam he once did. Age has taken its toll."

Toe Blake's round face turned purplish when he read what his goalkeeper had said. "What are you trying to do?" he screamed at Gump. "Steam them up? They won't be cold tonight. They'll come out of that chute like kids."

And indeed they did, even though Olympia Stadium was a steambath on a day when the temperature soared to 88° in Detroit. The Red Wings tied the game, 2-2, midway through the third period and fought into overtime, Crozier back in goal and again superb. Early in the overtime, Montreal's Balon dug the puck out of the corner and slid it across the front of the net, where Pocket Richard was crashing through a tangle of bodies. The puck hit Richard's knee or hip (accounts differed), bounced onto the ice, and trickled by Crozier into the cage for the goal that won the game, 3-2, and the Stanley Cup.

Crozier screamed to the referee that Richard had carried the puck into the cage with his hand. The referee said no; moments later Beliveau was raising the Cup, Montreal's 13th, to the scowls and patter of applause of wet-washed Detroit fans.

In the Red Wing clubhouse Bill Gadsby soaked a broken toe in a pail of water and growled, "If Richard had rifled the bastard into the net, you don't mind. But you hate to lose like that."

He stared at the toe, perhaps also seeing in the bucket of water the Stanley Cup that would never bear his name. "Well, what the hell," he said, "it's not the end of the world."

The Canadiens boarded a chartered train for the trip home, $5,750 richer (the Red Wings pocketed $2,750). "Me," said the Gumper, "I'm going to get drunk."

Jean Beliveau:
Of 79 goals, one to remember

The former Canadien superstar is now the team's vice-president, director of corporate relations. In his office at the Forum, he looked back on a career in which he played in 13 Stanley Cup finals in an 18-year career and was on the winning side 10 of those years. Only Maurice Richard, with 82 goals, has scored more goals in Stanley Cup play.

It is always a pleasure to win the Cup. I was very fortunate to be with good teams for years and win it on so many different occasions. I joined the Canadiens in 1953 and we lost the Cup to the Wings in the finals my first two years. Then we won five straight Cups. What I remember best about those years was an overtime goal that knocked Boston out of a semifinal. I don't remember the year but I think it was my only overtime goal of the 79 I scored in Stanley Cup play.

In 1966 we lost the first two games to Detroit in Montreal. But we were not discouraged. We knew that even if we had won one of the games in Montreal, we would have to win one of the games in Detroit. So we won that third game in Detroit and felt better. We built up a kind of momentum after that and we won four straight games.

I can still see that goal by Henri Richard that won the final game. A Detroit defenseman tripped him. He was sliding toward the net and the pass from Balon came from the corner. He just had time to swat at the puck. It went up his body but he didn't carry it in, there was nothing intentional about it.

That was quite a series—to lose the first two games at home, then win the next four in a row. How can you explain it? That's what makes sports. You never know what's going to happen, eh?

FIRST GAME (April 24, at Montreal)
Red Wings 3, Canadiens 2

FIRST PERIOD
    Detroit—Smith (Bathgate) 13:25
SECOND PERIOD
    Montreal—Backstrom (J. C. Tremblay) 4:23
    Detroit—Gadsby (McDonald) 5:14
THIRD PERIOD
    Detroit—Henderson (Marshall) 2:14
    Montreal—Harper (Rousseau) 2:36

SECOND GAME (April 26, at Montreal)
Red Wings 5, Canadiens 2

FIRST PERIOD
    Montreal—J. C. Tremblay
        (Beliveau, Cournoyer) 6:55
    Detroit—Bathgate (Prentice, Ullman) 18:39
SECOND PERIOD
    No scoring
THIRD PERIOD
    Detroit—MacGregor (Henderson, Ullman) 1:55
    Detroit—McDonald (Gadsby, Smith) 2:45
    Montreal—Cournoyer (Harper, Price) 12:00
    Detroit—Smith (Bathgate) 12:28
    Detroit—Prentice (Delvecchio) 16:25

THIRD GAME (April 28, at Detroit)
Canadiens 4, Red Wings 2

FIRST PERIOD
    Detroit—Ullman 4:20
    Montreal—Balon (Harper, Richard) 15:40
    Montreal—Beliveau 19:12
SECOND PERIOD
    No scoring
THIRD PERIOD
    Montreal—G. Tremblay (Beliveau) 1:45
    Montreal—G. Tremblay (J. C. Tremblay,
        Rousseau) 3:21
    Detroit—Howe (Marshall, Delvecchio) 19:59

FOURTH GAME (May 1, at Detroit)
Canadiens 2, Red Wings 1

FIRST PERIOD
    No scoring
SECOND PERIOD
    Detroit—Ullman (MacGregor, Henderson) 11:24
    Montreal—Beliveau (J. C. Tremblay, Duff) 19:51
THIRD PERIOD
    Montreal—Backstrom (Duff, Roberts) 13:37

FIFTH GAME (May 3, at Montreal)
Canadiens 5, Red Wings 1

FIRST PERIOD
    Montreal—Provost (Backstrom,
        J. C. Tremblay) 1:06
    Montreal—Cournoyer (J. C. Tremblay,
        G. Tremblay) 19:21
SECOND PERIOD
    Montreal—Balon (Rochefort, Richard) 1:05
    Montreal—Rousseau (Duff, Backstrom) 11:22
    Detroit—Ullman (Henderson, Bathgate) 14:22
THIRD PERIOD
    Montreal—Duff (Richard) 5:31

SIXTH GAME (May 5, at Detroit)
Canadiens 3, Red Wings 2

FIRST PERIOD
    Montreal—Beliveau (Provost, G. Tremblay) . . . 9:08
SECOND PERIOD
    Montreal—Rochefort (Richard, Balon) 10:11
    Detroit—Ullman (Delvecchio, Howe) 11:55
THIRD PERIOD
    Detroit—Smith (McDonald, Bergman) 10:30
OVERTIME
    Montreal—Richard (Balon, Roberts) 2:30

Detroit goaltender
Roger Crozier, a knee
wrenched, is helped off
the ice during the fourth
game. His leaving
seemed to dishearten
the Red Wings, who didn't
get a shot at the
Canadien cage for the
next 13 minutes.

223

MONTREAL CANADIENS
TORONTO MAPLE LEAFS
1967

"Some Nights You Stop Them, and Some Nights You Don't"

I got one thing to say, gentlemen. I didn't have a good night.

—Toronto goalkeeper Terry Sawchuk
after giving up six goals in the first game

You know what they say: Goalkeeping is like pitching, which is 75 percent of baseball. If Sawchuk is Koufax tonight, we win. If he isn't . . .

—Toronto defenseman Tim Horton
on the eve of the sixth game

The Chicago Black Hawks won the Prince of Wales Trophy for the first time in their history, scoring a record 264 goals as they glided home 17 points ahead of the second-place Canadiens. Bobby Hull scored 52 goals during the season but he was limping as the playoffs began. "It would be nice to enter the playoffs just once without an injury," he told a friend. "I haven't been sound for the playoffs in years."

In the semifinal Bobby and the Hawks were frustrated by 38-year-old Terry Sawchuk, doing sleight-of-hand tricks in goal for the third-place Maple Leafs. "I saw him make those saves but I still can't believe it," Hull said after the Maple Leafs beat the Black Hawks in six games.

Sawchuk was one of seven Maple Leafs who were 36 or older. Defenseman Allan Stanley was 41, goalkeeper Johnny Bower at least 42. Leonard ("Red") Kelly, 39, and a Member of the Canadian Parliament, was playing in his 19th playoff, more than anyone else in the NHL. (As a Red Wing Gordie Howe played in his 19th in 1970.) Around the league the Maple Leafs were known as Punch's Old Folks Home.

Youth was represented among the "old folks" by the line of Jim Pappin, Bob Pulford, and Pete Stemkowski. The other top-gunning line was centered by little Dave Keon with Frank ("Big M")

Mahovlich on one wing and George ("Chief") Armstrong, the team captain, on the other. The Big M and a few others sometimes seemed to play in a sullen fashion under George ("Punch") Imlach—none of his players was close to Punch—but the Imlach record was undeniably brilliant: nine playoff years in his nine years as coach and general manager.

Hector ("Toe") Blake's Canadiens had bumped along as low as fourth during the season. Near the end of the season Toe replaced Lorne ("Gump") Worsley with Rogatien Vachon, a 22-year-old goalkeeper from a Junior B team. The Canadiens hopped to second, wiped out the fourth-place Rangers in four straight playoff games, and came to the final winging along on a ten-game winning streak.

This was another typical Blake team: quick, poised, experienced (Jean Beliveau was playing in his 14th successive playoff). "Rugged-checking teams used to bother our skaters," Blake said. "But no more. Since we got some big guys ourselves—John Ferguson, Terry Harper, and Ted Harris—we can handle our own in any brawls."

The oddsmakers made Montreal a heavy favorite over Punch's "old-timers." But Punch grabbed most of the pre-playoff attention. Discussing young Rogatien Vachon, he told a reporter: "You can tell that Junior B goaltender he won't be playing against a bunch of peashooters. When he plays against the Leafs, we'll take his head off with our first shot."

Vachon's head was still atop his neck after the first game, won 6-2 by the Canadiens. Asked about Vachon, Imlach commented: "I haven't changed my opinion. He's still Junior B. But he's the best damn Junior B in the country."

In that first game Sawchuk had fanned on sev-

Maskless Montreal goaltender Rogatien Vachon watches the bouncing puck evade the crossed sticks of Toronto's Tim Horton (No. 7 in white) and a Canadien. The tension, which shows on Vachon's face during this second game, had wilted his nerves by the fifth game.

Montreal's John Ferguson and Toronto's
Larry Hillman (No. 2) clash sticks as
they try to collect a puck whose
proximity is of some concern to Toronto
goaltender Terry Sawchuk, the
concern showing through Terry's
tight-fitting mask.

eral pucks he should have stopped. For the second game Punch replaced him with Johnny Bower (together Bower and Sawchuk had won the Vezina Trophy in 1965, the first to win that goal-tending award as a twosome). During the game Canadien John Ferguson smashed Bower's nose with his stick, but Bower hung on to shut out Montreal, 3-0. "Next year I'm going to get a mask," Bower said. "Those curved sticks are too dangerous when a guy is down."

In Toronto for the third game, Bower kicked away an awesome total of 60 shots, 20 in 28 minutes of overtime. The end came when the Maple Leafs' Pete Stemkowski snapped a pass from behind the Montreal cage to Jim Pappin, who slid the puck to Bob Pulford in front of the net. Pulford shot the rubber by Vachon before the goaltender could move. The Maple Leafs had won a sudden-death 3-2 victory to lead two games to one. "Bower's saves gave the whole team a lift," Punch Imlach said. "That Pulford goal gave me a lift," said the cherub-faced Bower.

His age betrayed Bower before the fourth game: warming up, he pulled a muscle. Sawchuk strapped on his pads and trundled into action. Again he was terrible, the Canadiens pasting him, 6-2, to even the series at two games apiece. "Sometimes," said Sawchuk, ever the fatalist, "you can't keep the puck out with a snowplow."

Punch had to stick with Sawchuk; Bower was finished for the season. Early in the fifth game Sawchuk stopped a shot by Ralph Backstrom from point-blank range. The save seemed to transform Sawchuk. Suddenly he was batting away rubber, while at the other end Vachon missed on a couple of 40-footers and juggled a few others, the strain of going from Junior B to the Stanley Cup final beginning to show. Toe Blake rushed out his veteran, Gump Worsley, to take over for Vachon, but by then Toronto had locked up a 4-1 victory to lead three games to two. "I got lucky," said Sawchuk, explaining his transformation. "Some nights you stop them, and some nights you don't."

The sixth game was a battle of two veteran goalkeepers—Sawchuk for Toronto, Worsley for Montreal. Sawchuk was slightly better, stopping 46 shots to 36 by Worsley. With a minute left to play, the Leafs led, 2-1.

Blake took out Worsley and sent out six of his fastest skaters. Punch called on the oldest of his "old folks" to protect the lead: Allan Stanley, Tim Horton, Red Kelly, and Chief Armstrong. On the face-off, Stanley pinned Beliveau's stick while Kelly whisked in and stole the puck. It was passed to Armstrong, who glided toward the blue line, coolly aimed at the open Montreal net, then swatted the puck into the center of the cage.

Punch's Senior Citizens were 3-1 winners, and seconds after the siren sounded, Chief Armstrong was escorting the Cup around the Maple Leaf Gardens to tumultuous applause. It was Toronto's first Cup since 1964 and the fourth of Punch's nine years at Toronto.

"This was my most satisfying Cup," Punch said as his athletes drank champagne from the Cup in their dressing room. "Everybody said I'd never win another Cup with these old guys. Well, maybe that makes this the biggest kick of all for me because we sure shoved it down everybody's throats. These guys have always been champs for me. With expansion coming up, I won't be able to keep them all. But now they're going out as champs, and that's the way it should be."

Bob Pulford:
When opportunity knocks, an old head helps

One of Punch's younger Senior Citizens, Bob Pulford now coaches the Los Angeles Kings of the NHL. He talked about his most satisfying Stanley Cup win.

It was a real team effort in 1967. I'm not sure we had the best team but we won. We might not have had as talented a team as we had in the early 1960s when we won the Cup three years in a row—a lot of us were near the end of our careers by 1967—and Montreal had a better team personnel-wise. But experience is very helpful in a playoff, and we may have had a little more experience than some of the Canadiens, even though they'd won the past two years.

In 1964 I had scored a goal when we were shorthanded. Detroit lost the puck at the blue line. I picked it up and came in on Terry Sawchuk and beat him. But a bigger goal to me was the one I scored in 1967 in double overtime to win that third game. Jim Pappin got the puck to me in

228

front of the net and here, again, it was experience that may have helped. In Stanley Cup playoffs I've seen younger players who don't react properly to opportunity because they're nervous. When the opportunity came I had the experience to react properly and we scored. Winning that Cup, it was one of the most satisfying experiences of my life because it was truly a team effort. Everyone had a hand on the Cup, and when Imlach put out his old guys at the end to protect the lead, it was something I'll never forget.

FIRST GAME (April 20, at Montreal)
Canadiens 6, Maple Leafs 2

FIRST PERIOD
Montreal—Cournoyer (Beliveau, Rousseau)... 6:25
Toronto—Hillman (Pappin)................. 6:40
Montreal—Richard (Rochefort, Balon)....... 1:19
SECOND PERIOD
Montreal—Cournoyer (Rousseau, Richard)... 5:03
Montreal—Beliveau (G. Tremblay)........... 6:36
Toronto—Pappin (Horton, Pulford).........12:59
THIRD PERIOD
Montreal—Richard (Balon)................. 4:53
Montreal—Richard (J. C. Tremblay)........ 8:21

SECOND GAME (April 22, at Montreal)
Maple Leafs 3, Canadiens 0

FIRST PERIOD
Toronto—Stemkowski (Pulford, Walton)......12:14
SECOND PERIOD
Toronto—Walton (Pappin, Mahovlich)....... 9:12
Toronto—Horton (Stemkowski, Conacher)....16:57
THIRD PERIOD
No scoring

THIRD GAME (April 25, at Toronto)
Maple Leafs 3, Canadiens 2

FIRST PERIOD
Montreal—Beliveau (Rousseau, Duff)....... 2:37
Toronto—Stemkowski (Hillman, Pappin)..... 8:39
SECOND PERIOD
Toronto—Pappin (Horton, Pulford).........10:34
Montreal—Ferguson (Beliveau).............18:10
THIRD PERIOD
No scoring
FIRST OVERTIME
No scoring
SECOND OVERTIME
Toronto—Pulford (Stemkowski, Pappin)...... 8:26

FOURTH GAME (April 27, at Toronto)
Canadiens 6, Maple Leafs 2

FIRST PERIOD
Montreal—Cournoyer (Beliveau, Rousseau)... 6:25
Toronto—Hillman (Pappin)................. 6:40
Montreal—Richard (Rochefort, Balon)......11:19
SECOND PERIOD
Montreal—Cournoyer (Rousseau, Richard)... 5:03
Montreal—Beliveau (G. Tremblay)........... 6:36
Toronto—Pappin (Horton, Pulford).........12:59
THIRD PERIOD
Montreal—Richard (Balon)................. 4:53
Montreal—Richard (J. C. Tremblay)........ 8:21

FIFTH GAME (April 29, at Montreal)
Maple Leafs 4, Canadiens 1

FIRST PERIOD
Montreal—Rochefort (Duff, Richard)....... 6:03
Toronto—Pappin (Keon, Mahovlich).........15:06
SECOND PERIOD
Toronto—Conacher (Kelly, Hillman)........ 3:07
Toronto—Pronovost......................12:02
Toronto—Keon (Horton)..................19:27
THIRD PERIOD
No scoring

SIXTH GAME (May 2, at Toronto)
Maple Leafs 3, Canadiens 1

FIRST PERIOD
No scoring
SECOND PERIOD
Toronto—Ellis (Kelly, Stanley)............. 6:25
Toronto—Pappin (Stemkowski, Pulford)......19:28
THIRD PERIOD
Montreal—Duff (Harris)................... 5:28
Toronto—Armstrong (Pulford, Kelly).......19:11

Bob Pulford: "A lot of us were near the end of our careers by 1967—and Montreal had a better team personnel-wise. But experience is very helpful in a playoff."

MONTREAL CANADIENS
ST. LOUIS BLUES
1968

Sing No Sad Songs
for These St. Louis Blues

You could see what was sometimes laughingly called big league hockey in six new cities during the 1967–68 NHL season as the league expanded from six teams to twelve. The six new teams were looped together, Philadelphia to Los Angeles, in a Western Division while the six old-line teams formed the Eastern Division. In the Western Division, for the most part, were players too young, too old, or simply not good enough for the East. St. Louis Blues general manager Lynn Patrick, in building his new team, sought age and Stanley Cup experience. He drafted six former Canadiens, including Dickie Moore and Doug Harvey, plus ex-Black Hawk goaltender Glenn Hall. "There are guys on that team," someone cracked, "who remember Betty Boop."

The Blues' old-timers finished third in a Western Division that couldn't even be called mediocre: its top team, the Philadelphia Flyers, lost more games than it won. Playoff experience paid off for the Blues as they beat the Flyers in seven games and outlasted the Minnesota North Stars in another exhausting seven-game series.

Montreal had won the Prince of Wales Trophy and took on a high-scoring, roughneck Boston Bruin crew led by Phil Esposito and Bobby Orr. The Big Bad Bruins tried to knock down their opponents, but seldom could stay with the fast-skating Canadiens long enough to level them. Montreal won in four games. In the other Eastern semifinal, the Black Hawks bounced back after losing the first two games to the Rangers to win four straight. In the Eastern final—the "real" Stanley Cup playoff to most devotees of the sport—the Canadiens won three straight, lost a 2-1 game, then eliminated the Black Hawks in the fifth game, 3-2, on an overtime goal by rookie Jacques Lemaire. Hector ("Toe") Blake and his

team entered their fourth straight Stanley Cup final, looking to win the Cup for the third time in those four years.

For the first year since 1926, a Stanley Cup game would be played west of the Mississippi. Probably no Stanley Cup finalist ever was more lightly regarded than this St. Louis Blues team, which had lost three of four games to the Canadiens during the season, managing only a tie. "I'd be out of my mind," conceded Lynn Patrick, "if I didn't admit that our chances of beating Montreal are practically nil."

Blues coach Scotty Bowman tried to rally his team with the news that big Jean Beliveau would miss the final (he had a chipped bone in his ankle). "Without him," maintained Scotty, "they are not the same team," which was clearly true, of course. But even without Big Jean, Montreal still seemed to tower over the Blues. "Without Beliveau," someone joked, "the Canadiens will need four games to win. With him they'd win it in three."

Only 10,231 fans showed up for the first game in St. Louis Arena, the home folks expecting the worst. This was the smallest crowd at a Stanley Cup game in 23 years. The fans were happily surprised to see the Blues leading, 2-1, late in the second period. Then Yvan Cournoyer scored for Montreal, and the game went into overtime where it was won, 3-2, by Montreal on a close-in shot by Lemaire.

In the second game Glenn Hall leaped, dived, split, and otherwise contorted himself, but Montreal's Serge Savard got a puck by him early in the third period. Lorne ("Gump") Worsley, in goal for the Canadiens, fended off a couple of breakaways, and the Canadiens won, 1-0. "A goalie's gotta do something, after all you don't score

Montreal's Jacques Lemaire (No. 25) cranks up a left-handed shot as a Blues player arrives a trifle too late to check him. The puck bounces into the corner of the cage, goaltender Glenn Hall frozen and helpless against the shot's close-in velocity. Immediately Lemaire is mobbed, the overtime goal winning the first game for Montreal.

231

Montreal's Gump Worsley fends off a
St. Louis shot (opposite page), but the
puck bounces into the path of the Blues'
Gary Sabourin, who blasts it right back
at Gump from close range. The sprawling
Worsley makes an amazing stop (above),
blocking the puck, encircled in white,
with his upraised stick.

goals," the Gumper later remarked. "I think we played to the best of our capabilities tonight," said Scotty Bowman, "and we lost."

Late in the third game, with Montreal ahead 3-2, ex-Canadien Gordon ("Red") Berenson slapped the puck by Worsley and the teams went into the second overtime of the series. Again, St. Louis lost by a single goal, Bobby Rousseau winging a puck by Hall for a third straight Canadien victory.

On Sunday, May 11, in the 40th game of the playoffs—the most ever in a single season—the Canadiens scored two goals in the third period, coming from behind to post their fourth straight victory, 3-2, all the games won by a one-goal margin.

At the siren, Toe Blake came out on the ice to hug Worsley. He walked with his goalkeeper toward a red carpet where the Cup was perched on a table. "Blake kept trying to tell me something," Gump said later, "but he was crying so hard he couldn't get the words out."

What Toe Blake was trying to say was that he was through. After 13 seasons, in which his team had won nine Prince of Wales trophies and eight Stanley Cups, Blake announced, "I've had enough. The pressure is too much."

Glenn Hall got some compensation for his miracle-working in goal for St. Louis. He won the Conn Smythe Trophy as the playoffs' Most Valuable Player. As Hall packed his bags to re-turn to his 500-acre farm, he looked around the empty Blues dressing room and said, "We had nothing to be ashamed of."

Jacques Lemaire:
"Jacques, you can do it again . . ."

At his home in Montreal, Canadien center Jacques Lemaire remembered his first Stanley Cup final.

I was very nervous when we started the play-offs. You know in a playoff that every team has a chance to win because in a short series every goal is important and if you make one mistake, it can cost you a goal. Just a few mistakes and a good team can lose to a team that isn't as good.

You keep telling yourself when you are young: Don't make a mistake, don't make a mistake. During the season we had a lot of centermen: Beliveau, Richard, Backstrom, Rousseau, and I was a centerman too. But in the playoffs they shifted Rousseau to wing with me at center and Dickie Duff on the other wing. I got to play more. In the semifinal against Chicago I scored two overtime goals, one the goal that won the series, and you know it was funny, but after that I wasn't so nervous anymore. After that goal I told myself: Jacques, you belong. You can do it again. And I did. In the final I beat St. Louis with another goal in overtime.

In the third game, Montreal's Serge Savard—shown here in a sequence from a movie of the game—collects a loose puck, feints with his stick against the blurred St. Louis goaltender, Glenn Hall, then puts the puck by Hall for a 2-1 Canadien lead.

FIRST GAME (May 5, at St. Louis)
Canadiens 3, Blues 2

FIRST PERIOD
St. Louis—B. Plager........................ 9:19
Montreal—Richard (Larose)............... 9:42
SECOND PERIOD
St. Louis—Moore (Berenson, B. Plager)...... 8:16
Montreal—Cournoyer (Ferguson, Harris).....18:14
THIRD PERIOD
No scoring
OVERTIME
Montreal—Lemaire........................ 1:41

SECOND GAME (May 7, at St. Louis)
Canadiens 1, Blues 0

FIRST PERIOD
No scoring
SECOND PERIOD
No scoring
THIRD PERIOD
Montreal—Savard (Provost)................ 2:17

THIRD GAME (May 9, at Montreal)
Canadiens 4, Blues 3

FIRST PERIOD
St. Louis—St. Marseille (Picard, Harvey).....10:22
Montreal—Cournoyer (Richard, Ferguson)....14:24
SECOND PERIOD
Montreal—Savard......................... 1:23
St. Louis—Berenson (Talbot)............... 3:37
THIRD PERIOD
Montreal—Backstrom (Cournoyer, Ferguson)..11:43
St. Louis—Berenson.......................17:25
OVERTIME
Montreal—Rousseau (Duff)................. 1:13

FOURTH GAME (May 11, at Montreal)
Canadiens 3, Blues 2

FIRST PERIOD
Montreal—Duff (Lemaire).................16:47
SECOND PERIOD
St. Louis—Cameron (Ecclestone)........... 6:53
St. Louis—Sabourin (Veneruzzo)........... 7:50
THIRD PERIOD
Montreal—Richard (J. C. Tremblay)........ 7:24
Montreal—J. C. Tremblay (Backstrom,
    Cournoyer)...........................11:40

MONTREAL CANADIENS
ST. LOUIS BLUES
1969

Only for Claude
Did the Cup Come Hard

...You've got to remember that we don't fool around when there's a lot of jack at stake. And almost everybody [on our team] has some kind of bonus that depends on how we do in the playoffs. People talk about the magic of Montreal and things like that. Well, we're all in this thing to make money, and when we've got a chance to do it, we're not going to blow it.

—Montreal's John Ferguson
on the eve of the 1969 final

Young Bobby Orr danced the length of the ice like a butterfly, playing keep-away with the puck until he flashed it to a teammate or ripped it by a goaltender. Big Phil Esposito shouldered his way to the cage mouth, stretched out tentacular arms for the puck while muscling away defensemen, then blasted 15-footers past helpless goaltenders. When Orr, Espy, and all the other Big Bad Boston Bruins didn't have the puck, they bounced opposing players into the boards. "Nobody wants the puck when we play them," Orr said with a toothy grin.

Until the coming of Orr and Esposito—and a new coach, Harry Sinden—the Bruins had been the doormats of the league, out of the playoffs for nine of the past ten years. Under Sinden they were revolutionizing hockey offense, their five-man end-to-end rushes leaving their goalkeeper unprotected. They were willing to yield one goal if they could score two. At a time when 3-1 and 4-2 scores were the norm in hockey, these new Bruins were winning—and sometimes losing—by scores of 7-5 and 8-6. They won 42 games in this 1968–69 season, finishing second in the Eastern Division behind the Canadiens.

In an Eastern quarterfinal against Toronto, Boston played better defense than usual and hu-

miliated the Maple Leafs, 10-0 and 7-0, and went on to win in four straight games, prompting the immediate firing of Toronto general manager-coach George ("Punch") Imlach. In the other Eastern quarterfinal, Montreal disposed of New York, also in four games, and the Bruins and the Canadiens met for the Eastern Division championship, a confrontation between the two teams that would dominate the NHL during the next few years.

With the Stanley Cup at stake in most minds—no one was taking the Western Division champion, whoever it might be, seriously—the Canadiens won the first two games, which were played in Montreal. In both games Boston had clearly outplayed Montreal. "How do you explain it?" grumbled Boston's outspoken center, Derek Sanderson. "They don't have the team, the defense, the talent, or the guts. But they get the goals."

"In the playoffs," smiled Jean Beliveau, "the Canadiens are lucky."

In Boston the Bruins won the next two games to even the series. In the fifth game, at Montreal Forum, the Bruins outshot Montreal 42 to 25, but lost on the scoreboard, 4-2. During the season, Montreal's chunky, sideburned goaltender, Rogatien Vachon, had played so loosely that the Canadiens considered giving him a plane ticket to the minors. But during one stretch of the sixth game, with the score tied, Vachon leaped, split, and dived to stop 22 straight Bruin shots while Montreal whacked only eight at Gerry Cheevers. In overtime Beliveau stopped a pass at the goal mouth and hit a whizzing liner over goalkeeper Cheevers' shoulder for a 2-1 victory that put the Canadiens in the final for the fifth straight year.

Out West the expansion teams were deciding

Montreal's potent power play strikes again as Serge Savard (No. 18) passes the puck to Jean Beliveau (No. 4) at the face-off circle. Beliveau feeds the puck to Dick Duff, who scores against Glenn Hall and a divided St. Louis defense in the second game.

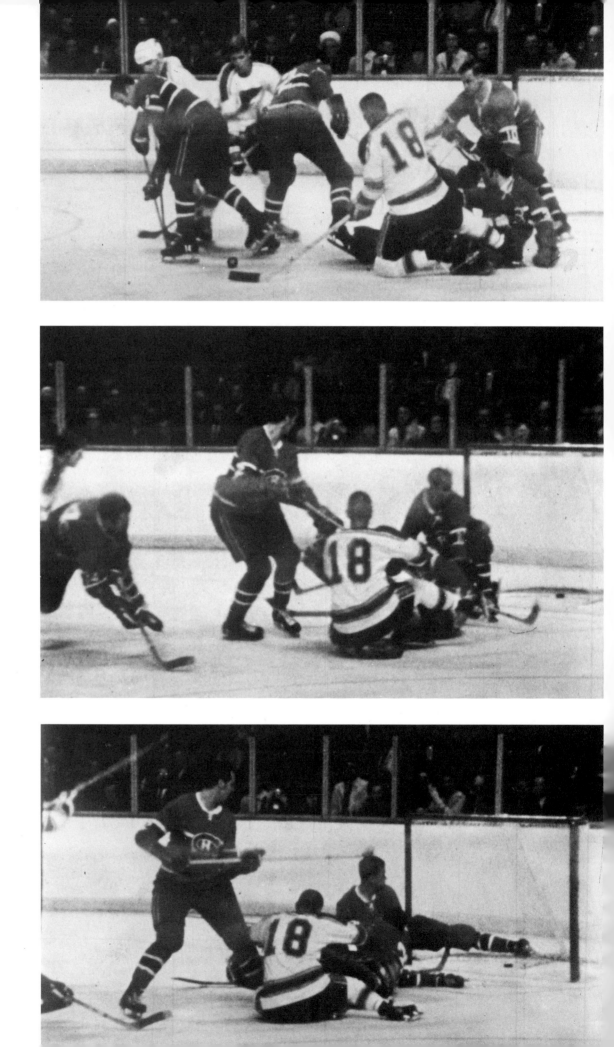

No. 18, St. Louis' Larry Keenan, swings as he is falling down and swats the puck into the Montreal cage in the second game. Before the final, St. Louis coach Scotty Bowman compared the underdog Blues to the underdog New York Jets, who had won in the Super Bowl a few months earlier: "We stand as good a chance as the Jets against the Colts—and you know who won that." But history, Scotty would find, does not always repeat itself.

who would be fodder for the Canadiens. The Blues, with two veteran goalkeepers, Jacques Plante and Glenn Hall, finished first. In eight straight games they wiped out Philadelphia and Los Angeles. For a second successive year they would meet the Canadiens in the final.

"I figure," said the Blues' ebulient coach, Scotty Bowman, "that we're 25 percent better than last year when we lost four games to the Canadiens by only one goal."

"First Western Team to Reach the Final, First Western Team to Win the Cup."

That was the St. Louis slogan as the Blues flew to Montreal for the first two games. Behind the airy slogan was this hard truth: in 14 meetings between St. Louis and Montreal over the past two years, St. Louis had yet to win a game (there were two ties). For a so-called championship series, this seemed hardly a meeting between equals. The final appeared to be a formality at best, a customer-cheating charade at worst.

The Blues, however, professed to have personal reasons for wanting to dethrone Montreal. "It amazed me," said Scotty Bowman, "the way some of them lorded over us after winning four straight last year. They say that to be great you must be hungry and humble. The Montreal team is hungry but not humble. They are haughty."

The Canadiens also claimed that they had a personal score to settle with former Canadien Jacques Plante. "He didn't leave many friends here," said one Canadien. "Plante talks about us," said defenseman Jacques Laperriere. "He talks too much. It starts when he leaves us . . . he talks and talks."

"When I see those eyes looking out from behind the mask," said Yvan Cournoyer, "I want my shots to come from cannons."

The Canadiens boomed three goals by Plante to win the first game, 3-1. They knocked in another three against Hall to win the second game by an identical score. "To beat Montreal," said Boston coach Harry Sinden, "you have to press them, rush them, hit them in their own end—like we did. But to do that you have to have the players—and right now we're the only club with nearly the players Montreal has. No expansion club is close."

A crowd of 16,338, a record for St. Louis, filled the Arena for the third game, expecting to see a close match like those of a year earlier. By the end of the game the few die-hards who remained were booing, Montreal an easy 4-0 winner over Plante.

Before the fourth game the Canadiens relaxed in the sunshine of a Missouri spring, playing golf, watching the Cardinals, betting on horses at the track, and planning a victory party in Montreal the day after the game.

Only their rookie coach, portly Claude Ruel, looked worried. At four o'clock on the morning before the fourth game he was seen sitting in the lobby of his hotel, unable to sleep. "Nothing ever came easy to me," he said, a worried look in his eyes: "I don't expect a Stanley Cup to come easy."

He had reason to worry a little as the Blues led 1-0 at the start of the third period. But Ted Harris slipped a puck past Glenn Hall to tie the score, and two and a half minutes later John Ferguson lashed in another puck to win the game, 2-1. The Canadiens flew home to their victory party with a second successive Stanley Cup, their fourth in the past five years, their 15th since they began the hunt in 1917. If they seemed haughty, they had a right.

Barclay Plager:
It's not the best that wins the Cup

A defenseman with the St. Louis Blues since their first year, Barclay Plager talked at his home in St. Louis about the Blues of 1969 and another expansion team that also made it to the Stanley Cup finals—the Philadelphia Flyers of 1974.

We were in awe of Montreal. They were a great hockey team. We had one good player—Red Berenson. They had five or six—Beliveau, Cournoyer, all those guys. That first game. If we had won that game in Montreal . . . we lost it 3-1 when Ferguson put a puck into the open net near the end of the game . . . we wouldn't have beaten the Canadiens, but it might have turned our way of thinking around and we might have won a couple of games. But there's a big difference between the Philadelphia Flyers of today and the St. Louis Blues of seven years ago. They have a lot more good hockey players than we did. And

they are just working hard, out-working every-body on the Boston Bruins. We worked hard the first year [1968] because we were proud of being the first expansion team in the finals. We didn't work as hard the second time. Philadelphia was not as good talent-wise as Boston—or New York —but they had Bobby Clarke and good goaltend-ing and they worked hard. They proved again that it's not the best team that wins the Cup, it's the hardest-working team.

FIRST GAME (April 27, at Montreal)
Canadiens 3, Blues 1

FIRST PERIOD
Montreal—Duff (Cournoyer, Beliveau) 3:39
Montreal—Rousseau (Provost) 4:17
St. Louis—St. Marseille (McCreary, Picard) . . .18:24
SECOND PERIOD
No scoring
THIRD PERIOD
Montreal—Ferguson (Richard) 19:46

SECOND GAME (April 29, at Montreal)
Canadiens 3, Blues 1

FIRST PERIOD
Montreal—Backstrom (Tremblay) 17:26
SECOND PERIOD
Montreal—Duff (Beliveau, Savard) 9:07
Montreal—Cournoyer (Beliveau) 14:11
THIRD PERIOD
St. Louis—Keenan (Roberts, B. Plager) 9:20

THIRD GAME (May 1, at St. Louis)
Canadiens 4, Blues 0

FIRST PERIOD
Montreal—Savard (Duff) 12:34
SECOND PERIOD
Montreal—Lemaire (Redmond) 8:16
Montreal—Duff (Cournoyer, Beliveau) 13:38
THIRD PERIOD
Montreal—Duff (Beliveau, Cournoyer) 18:35

FOURTH GAME (May 4, at St. Louis)
Canadiens 2, Blues 1

FIRST PERIOD
St. Louis—Gray (St. Marseille, Crisp) 10:50
SECOND PERIOD
No scoring
THIRD PERIOD
Montreal—Harris (Duff, Tremblay) 0:43
Montreal—Ferguson (Backstrom) 3:03

On a pretty pass play, the Blues' Frank St. Marseille (No. 9 in dark jersey) tosses a pass ahead of a Montreal defender onto the stick of Terry Gray, who drives in on goaltender Rogatien Vachon to score for St. Louis in the fourth game, won by Montreal, 2-1.

BOSTON BRUINS
ST. LOUIS BLUES
1970

"Never Mind Winning a Game . . . Win a Period!"

We practiced covering Bobby Orr for six hours today, but the only trouble is, we don't have a Bobby Orr to practice against.

—Blues coach Scotty Bowman
on eve of the final

The Great Boston Scoring Machine strafed opposing goalkeepers with 40 and 45 shots a game, 15 or 20 more than most other teams, as the Bruins set a batch of scoring records. Twenty-two-year-old Bobby Orr led the league in scoring, the first defenseman ever to win scoring honors, and many were hailing him as the greatest all-around hockey player in history.

The Bruins, muscular and aggressive, assigned their heavyweight forwards and mean defensemen to flatten opponents. They rushed out of their end, Orr often leading the charge, swarming in on goalkeepers, their best defense a whirlwind offense. At Boston Garden, Bruin fans screeched happily as kayoed opponents were carted off the ice, eyes glazed. Away from Boston, fans and some opposing players despised the Bruins for their tactics, the most hated Bruin being Derek ("Turk") Sanderson, who prided himself on being called a dirty player.

Although he was shy off the ice, on-ice the most colorful Bruin was Orr, who twirled with a ballet dancer's grace, a blond whirling dervish who electrified crowds with his dashes. With him were players every bit as flamboyant as baseball's Gas House Gang of the 1930s; in fact, the Bruins soon became known as the Ice House Gang. On TV talk shows and in Boston saloons, Sanderson mouthed all sorts of absurd statements that tickled his fans. Johnny ("Chief") Bucyk and the cherub-faced John ("Pie") McKenzie lifted fans to their feet when they blasted opposing players into the

boards. Defenseman Teddy Green, his slitted eyes measuring people, his stick poised menacingly, was as fascinating as a cobra ready to strike.

In a pre-season game Green's skull was fractured during a stick-swinging duel, and he was out for the season. But what Green had planted in this club—its on-ice meanness—flourished despite his absence, or perhaps because of it. "If you didn't fight," a teammate once said of him, "Greenie would fight you." All during the season Orr would tap each player with his stick in the dressing room just before the Bruins went out to combat. The last player he tapped would be the player sitting at Greenie's locker. Terrible Teddy had not been forgotten.

The sad-eyed, wise-cracking, 210-pound Phil Esposito cruised over blue lines like some huge shark and was as tough as a boulder to dislodge from the goal mouth, where he took passes to rip shots past the goaltender. This season he was second only to Orr in NHL scoring, and he would go on to lead the league in scoring for the next four years, pumping in goals at a faster rate than any other hockey player in history.

The Bruins and Chicago tied for first place in the East, each with 99 points, but the Black Hawks won the Prince of Wales Trophy on the basis of having won more games than Boston. Detroit finished third, New York fourth, the defending champion Canadiens missing the playoffs for the first time since 1948.

The Bruins erased the Rangers in six games while the Black Hawks were sweeping the Red Wings in four. Hockey fans waited eagerly for the Eastern final (to most minds the Stanley Cup final), expecting two momentous battles: the battle of the Bobbys between Chicago's Hull and Boston's Orr; and the battle of the Espositos be-

Blues' goaltender Jacques Plante is struck between the eyes by a puck and goes down in the first game. "My mask saved my life," he said in the hospital. "I always said I would put my face in front of a shot. But [after this] I don't think that way any more."

243

Bobby Orr is tripped and soars across the cage mouth, grinning even as he flies. "I thought I was going to fly right out of the building," Orr said later. Before the game Bobby told a friend: "No one on this team has ever won the Stanley Cup. As we get closer, we are all getting more and more excited. If we win that Cup, the top of my head is going to pop like a champagne cork."

tween Boston's Phil and his brother Tony, Chicago's intense rookie goalkeeper. Tony, the younger Esposito, had won the Calder Memorial Trophy as rookie of the year, as well as the Vezina award as goalkeeper of the year, posting a record 15 shutouts.

Both battles were no-contests. Boston's Eddie Westfall clung so securely to Bobby Hull that the "Golden Jet" could shoot only eight times in the series, and he didn't score a goal. Bobby Orr whizzed all over the ice, feeding teammates. As for the Esposito battle, Tony yielded 20 goals, 5 of them knocked in by brother Phil, and Boston swept by Chicago in four games.

The Bruins were entering their first final since 1958, looking to win their first Cup since 1941. Opposing them were the St. Louis Blues, who finished first in the West and went on to overcome the Minnesota North Stars in six games and the Pittsburgh Penguins in six, entering their third final in only their third year in the league.

But the Blues had not won a Stanley Cup final game. "The immediate challenge," wrote *St. Louis Post-Dispatch* sports editor Bob Broeg, "is to win a game, not the Stanley Cup. Crawl before you walk."

"We don't have a chance unless we stop Bobby Orr," coach Scotty Bowman told the Blues. "We'll rise or fall on that strategy."

He assigned Jimmy Roberts to shadow Orr. Roberts stuck so close to Orr in the first game that Bobby said later: "I could have gone out to lunch for all the chance I got to play. So I just stayed out of things."

While the Blues hemmed in Orr, the other Bruins ran wild. Chief Bucyk scored the hat trick and Esposito, Turk Sanderson, and Wayne ("Swoops") Carleton each tossed in a goal in a 6-1 rout. "It proved," said Sanderson, "that we have a lot of hockey players besides Bobby Orr."

In the second game Bowman gave up trying to shadow Orr, but his veterans—their average age was 30—could not keep up with the young Bruins, who won 6-2. In the first two games, Boston outscored the Blues in two of three periods and tied them in a third, which prompted a Blues fan to comment: "Never mind winning a game—the question is, will we win a period?"

For the first time in three years, Scotty Bowman talked realistically about the Cup chances of his or any other Western team. "We're getting thrown to the lions," he said. "I've known for a long time that we can't compete with the Eastern teams with what we've got. But if you think we feel bad, what about the five teams that finished behind us in the West? They have to be getting the message, too."

"We're the best of a very poor lot," conceded Blues owner Sid Salomon.

In the third game at Boston, the Bruins slammed 46 shots at a besieged Glenn Hall and won, 4-1. "We were scoring on second and third rebounds," said one Bruin.

"We got to go out fighting or we won't be able to hold up our heads," the Blues' Jimmy Roberts said before the fourth game. The Blues fought back. After tying the score 1-1, they led 2-1, then 3-2, but both times the Bruins scored to tie the game.

The game went into overtime, Bruin fans in the packed Garden hoping to see the Cup won in Boston. Some 30 seconds into overtime Turk Sanderson collected the puck at the side of the cage, fended off two Blues, then passed to Orr, who was dashing toward the cage. Orr batted at the puck as a defenseman tripped him. As Bobby soared through the air he saw the puck bounce into the cage for the goal that brought the Stanley Cup back to Boston for the first time in 29 years.

Phil Esposito had broken two playoff records with 27 points and 13 goals. He said what was on everyone's mind: "We've got too good a club for any team in the West. The final is anticlimactic." Or, he might have added, a joke.

Al Arbour:
The best thing for hockey

Al Arbour played on four Stanley Cup winners before coming to the Blues in 1967. He is now the coach of the New York Islanders.

We didn't think our chances were hopeless against Boston, but we realized we had to hope for a lot of luck against that club because they were quite a machine, eh? We had to have everything on our side. We were outmanned. But we fought right to the end. We could have packed our bags in Boston for that last game. Boston wanted to win that game bad—it was in front of their home-town fans and they wanted to win the Cup at home. Everybody played their hearts out and it ended up in overtime. I told the younger guys after it was over: Any time you give your best, you don't have to be ashamed of anything.

I know there was a lot of criticism about the new teams that were playing in the finals. I thought it was the best thing for hockey at the time. It was good for the younger players, knowing that a club that had just started was in a Stanley Cup final. It gave hope to all the expansion teams, seeing the St. Louis Blues in the final, and it gave hope to kids in the minor leagues, knowing that if they went to an expansion club, they could still have a chance to play for the Cup. It was a real shot in the arm for the expansion teams. I said that in seven to ten years an expansion team would win the Stanley Cup and that's what happened.

FIRST GAME (May 3, at St. Louis)
Bruins 6, Blues 1
FIRST PERIOD
Boston—Bucyk (Stanfield).................19:45
SECOND PERIOD
St. Louis—Roberts (McCreary).............. 1:52
Boston—Bucyk (McKenzie, Esposito)....... 5:16
THIRD PERIOD
Boston—Carleton (Sanderson, Awrey)........ 4:59
Boston—Bucyk (R. Smith, McKenzie)....... 5:31
Boston—Sanderson (Orr).................17:20
Boston—Esposito........................18:58

SECOND GAME (May 5, at St. Louis)
Bruins 6, Blues 2
FIRST PERIOD
Boston—Stanfield (Orr, Esposito)........... 8:10
Boston—Westfall (R. Smith)...............13:38
Boston—Westfall (Orr).....................19:15
SECOND PERIOD
Boston—Sanderson (Carleton, Esposito)...... 9:37
St. Louis—Gray (Picard)...................17:26
THIRD PERIOD
Boston—Sanderson (R. Smith, Westfall)...... 0:58
St. Louis—St. Marseille (Goyette, McDonald). 4:15
Boston—Bucyk (McKenzie).................15:00

THIRD GAME (May 7, at Boston)
Bruins 4, Blues 1
FIRST PERIOD
St. Louis—St. Marseille.................... 5:32
Boston—Bucyk (Esposito, Stanfield).........13:23
Boston—McKenzie (Orr, Stanfield)..........18:23
SECOND PERIOD
No scoring
THIRD PERIOD
Boston—Cashman (Hodge, Esposito)........ 3:20
Boston—Cashman (Hodge, Esposito)........14:46

FOURTH GAME (May 10, at Boston)
Bruins 4, Blues 3
FIRST PERIOD
Boston—R. Smith (Sanderson).............. 5:28
St. Louis—Berenson (R. Plager, Ecclestone)...19:17
SECOND PERIOD
St. Louis—Sabourin (St. Marseille).......... 3:22
Boston—Esposito (Hodge).................14:22
THIRD PERIOD
St. Louis—Keenan (Goyette, Roberts)........ 0:19
Boston—Bucyk (McKenzie, R. Smith).......13:28
OVERTIME
Boston—Orr (Sanderson)................... 0:40

Al Arbour: "It gave hope to kids in the minor leagues, knowing that if they went to an expansion club, they could still have a chance to play for the Cup."

CHICAGO BLACK HAWKS ── 1971
MONTREAL CANADIENS

For Peanuts and the Law Student,
a Come-from-Behind Victory

The NHL expanded to 14 teams for the 1970–71 season. So that there would be no more of those lopsided mismatches between a weak West team and a strong East team in the final, the two new teams were added to the Eastern Division and Chicago was shifted to the West, giving that division a team the equal of the best in the East. The league also changed the playoff rules: The two best teams in the West would have to meet the two best teams in the East before entering the final. No longer was "the best of a bad lot" in the West an automatic finalist.

In the Eastern Division the Great Boston Scoring Machine steamrollered to its first Prince of Wales Trophy in 30 years, smashing some 40 records, with Phil Esposito and Bobby Orr ranking one-two in scoring. The Rangers finished second, Montreal third, and Toronto fourth.

In the East quarterfinals, the defending champion Bruins were heavy favorites against an erratic Canadien team. In goal for Montreal was a lanky law student, Ken Dryden, who had played only six games all season. The Boston sharpshooters licked their lips in anticipation of a feast of goals, this kid goalkeeper only a year out of college. They beat him, 3-1, in the first game, and were shellacking him 5-1 midway through the second game. Suddenly Dryden stiffened, rising to pluck down rubber, and the Canadiens rallied to win, 7-5.

The series came down to a seventh game, played in Boston before howling Bruin fans. Early in the game the Boston triggermen fired a burst of shots, Dryden stopping them all (frustrating Phil Esposito to a point where he smashed his stick against the partition). The Canadiens

won, 4-2, eliminating the defending champions in one of the biggest upsets of Stanley Cup history.

New York and Toronto brawled through the other Eastern quarterfinal. At one point a Ranger tossed goalkeeper Bernie Parent's mask into the crowd, where it disappeared. Parent didn't have a second mask; Toronto had to replace him with Jacques Plante. Later both teams paid nearly $17,000 in fines for their delinquencies. New York won in six games, the first victory in a playoff series since 1950 for the Rangers.

In the West, Chicago's Black Hawks finished first, then swept over Philadelphia in four games. In the other series the Minnesota North Stars sent the St. Louis Blues marching back home in six games.

In the semifinals the East's Rangers were matched against the West's Black Hawks, the East's Canadiens against the West's North Stars. Rangers and Black Hawks fought to a seventh game. With the score 2-2 in the third period there was a face-off in Ranger ice. Lou Angotti shoveled the puck to Bobby Hull, who rifled it by Ed Giacomin before the Ranger goalkeeper could make a move. The Black Hawks, 3-2 winners, skated into their first final since 1965.

In the Canadien-North Star semifinal, meanwhile, an expansion team beat an old-line team for the first time in Stanley Cup play when the North Stars twice stopped Montreal, tying the series at two games apiece. But Montreal won the next two, and for the first time since 1967 there was an old-timey feeling to the finals: Montreal against Chicago.

Montreal coach Al MacNeil assigned Rejean

Montreal captain Jean Beliveau grasps the Cup, presented by Clarence Campbell moments after the Canadien triumph. For *Le Gros Bill* ("The Big Guy"), this was his 162nd playoff game—and his last. He had scored 79 goals and 97 assists, a Stanley Cup record for points (176) and assists that still stood in 1975.

Chicago's Jim Pappin (No. 8) slips the puck through the legs of a Montreal defender and skates in alone on Montreal goaltender Ken Dryden. Faking Dryden to his knees, Pappin pokes the puck into the cage for an unassisted goal and a 1-0 Chicago lead in the first period of the sixth game. During the playoffs someone asked Bobby Rousseau, then with the Minnesota North Stars, what motivated players in the playoffs. His answer: ''Pride, insecurity, emotion, and greed.''

251

Cheering Canadien fans,
some wearing team
jerseys and one dressed
as a masked goalie, line
a parade route through
Montreal to salute the
Cup winners. The players
sit in open cars that
nose through the crowds.
While some fans wave
from on high, one delivers
her salutation close up.

Houle to shadow Hull, even though "Peanuts," as the Canadiens called Houle, was a skinny 165-pound lightweight skating next to the ponderous 200-pound Bobby. "Stopping Bobby is the key to beating the Hawks," said Montreal defenseman J. C. Tremblay. "When Bobby scores a lot, it seems all the other Hawks score a lot. And when he doesn't score much, they don't score much."

Gamblers made the Hawks the favorites. This Chicago club was nicely balanced with players like Bobby and Dennis Hull and Stan Mikita on offense, and on defense Pat Stapleton and Bill White posted in front of the previous year's Vezina Trophy winner, Tony Esposito.

Montreal could match the Chicago offense with shooters like Jean Beliveau, Henri ("Pocket") Richard, and the Mahovlich brothers, big Frank and "little" Pete, who at 6-foot-4 and 220 pounds was four inches taller and ten pounds heavier than his brawny older brother, "Big M." But could Montreal's high-scoring offense tally more goals than young Dryden would give up?

Dryden stood tough in the first game, yielding only one goal during 60 minutes of regulation play and an additional 20 minutes of overtime. But Esposito was just as unyielding, and in the second overtime Chicago's Jim Pappin tipped in a pass at the goal mouth for a 2-1 Black Hawk victory. Little Lou Angotti punched two pucks by Dryden in the second game, the Hawks won 5-3, and left for Montreal two games ahead.

The Canadiens evened the series by winning the two games in Montreal. Back in Chicago, Esposito shut out the Canadiens, 2-0. During that game coach Al MacNeil shuffled some of his lines, angering veterans who resented playing with unfamiliar linemates. After the game the silvery-haired Pocket Richard stormed to a reporter: "How can you hope to win with such an incompetent behind the bench?"

His words, when they appeared in headlines across Canada, angered even some of the Canadiens who agreed with Henri. "Why couldn't he wait until after the series to say that?" said one. "This could ruin us."

"I should have kept my mouth shut until the finals were over," Henri agreed. "Now I'm so nervous. There is so much pressure on me and the coach—we have to win."

253

Richard's angry words did seem to arouse the Canadiens to an even greater need to win: They did not want to be accused of losing because of dissension. With the two Mahovlich brothers bulling their way through the Chicago defense to fire at Esposito from close up, Montreal rallied with two goals in the third period of the sixth game to win, 4-3, and square the series at three games apiece.

Millions across Canada and the U.S. watched on TV as the teams skated onto the ice at Chicago Stadium for the seventh game. The Black Hawks had history on their side: Only once before, way back in 1945, had a visiting team won a seventh game.

The Canadiens seemed doomed to relive history as Chicago assumed a 2-0 lead near the game's halfway point. Late in the second period Montreal's Jacques Lemaire zipped across the blue line and snapped a long 40-foot shot. Tony Esposito had been flagging down shorter drives all game long—and this shot he saw coming right at him. But for reasons he couldn't explain years later, he lost sight of the puck and it clanged into the cage behind him. Up in a TV booth his brother Phil told millions: "He should have stopped that one."

That goal seemed to numb the Hawks. Later in the second period Henri Richard took some of the pressure off himself by tying the game, 2-2. And in the third period little Henri made himself a hero by beating Esposito to the corner for a 3-2 lead.

The Black Hawks rallied, circling Dryden with skaters, but he picked off their shots with seeming nonchalance—"like a kid plucking apples off a tree," someone said. At the siren, the roar of the Chicago crowd faded to a wail; moments later the Canadiens' Beliveau was skating around the rink with the glittering Cup, the last for the soon-to-retire Jean, the third in 4 years for Montreal, and the team's tenth in 16 years.

At center ice Richard hugged MacNeil, their feuding forgotten for the moment (but MacNeil would not come back the next season). "Maurice Richard" had been written on the Cup eight times, and Henri had already topped his more famous brother. Now the name "Henri Richard" would be written on the Cup for the tenth time, more often than the name of any other player with the exception of Jean Beliveau, his teammate in those ten Cup triumphs (Henri would top Jean in 1973).

Dryden won the Conn Smythe Trophy as the playoff's Most Valuable Player. The unsung hero was Rejean Houle, who had held Hull to only one goal while the teams were at even strength. Little Houle confessed he'd sometimes harried Hull illegally. "He could handle me like he handles his stick," Peanuts said. "But he is very fair, thank God."

The next morning the Canadiens arrived at the Montreal airport. "Monsieur, what do you have to declare?" a customs officer asked one Canadien.

"Only the Stanley Cup, monsieur."

"There is no problem," said the officer, recalling the previous year's triumph by Boston. "We will just classify that as Canadian Goods Returned."

Bill White:
The puck that got away

A gangling defenseman for the Black Hawks, Bill White had never attended a Stanley Cup final until he played in his first—in 1971.

There is one thing about losing a Stanley Cup game: You are going to hear about it all summer long. You could lose an exciting game during the season but it is forgotten by summer. You forget it yourself. But you play even a dull game in the finals of the Stanley Cup and all season long people will ask you about this play or that play.

I forget about most goals that are scored against us during the season. You have to. But I can still see a goal that Frank Mahovlich scored against us in the playoffs. There was a face-off. Stash [Mikita] won the face-off and drew the puck back toward me. But it hopped right over my stick. Frank came in between me and the cage— I had my back to the cage—and took the puck. He was no more than ten feet away. I turned and couldn't do a thing, Tony had no chance to stop him, and he scored.

You can watch on TV and sense some of the excitement at a Stanley Cup final. But you can't feel all of the excitement that is there. The excitement is tremendous.

FIRST GAME (May 4, at Chicago)
Black Hawks 2, Canadiens 1

FIRST PERIOD
  No scoring
SECOND PERIOD
  Montreal—Lemaire (Tremblay, P. Mahovlich).12:29
THIRD PERIOD
  Chicago—R. Hull (Pappin, Stapleton)........ 7:54
FIRST OVERTIME
  No scoring
SECOND OVERTIME
  Chicago—Pappin (Mikita, White)............ 1:11

SECOND GAME (May 6, at Chicago)
Black Hawks 5, Canadiens 3

FIRST PERIOD
  Chicago—R. Hull (Angotti, Maki)........... 4:39
  Montreal—Lemaire (Tremblay)............. 9:06
  Montreal—P. Mahovlich (Tremblay,
    Laperriere)............................17:58
SECOND PERIOD
  Chicago—Maki (Angotti, R. Hull)..........11:58
  Chicago—Pappin (O'Shea, Foley)...........13:00
THIRD PERIOD
  Chicago—Angotti.......................... 7:27
  Montreal—F. Mahovlich................... 8:56
  Chicago—Angotti.........................16:47

THIRD GAME (May 9, at Montreal)
Canadiens 4, Black Hawks 2

FIRST PERIOD
  Chicago—Koroll (R. Hull, Mikita).......... 4:56
  Chicago—R. Hull (Pappin, Martin)........13:38
SECOND PERIOD
  Montreal—P. Mahovlich................... 5:56
  Montreal—F. Mahovlich (Beliveau,
    Cournoyer)............................ 7:34
THIRD PERIOD
  Montreal—Cournoyer (Harper)............. 6:23
  Montreal—F. Mahovlich (Lapointe).........12:13

FOURTH GAME (May 11, at Montreal)
Canadiens 5, Black Hawks 2

FIRST PERIOD
  Montreal—P. Mahovlich (Harper, Laperriere). 1:00
  Chicago—Mikita (Koroll, Stapleton)........ 3:09
  Montreal—Beliveau (Cournoyer,
    F. Mahovlich)......................... 6:54
  Montreal—Lapointe (Richard, Houle)........16:33
SECOND PERIOD
  Montreal—Cournoyer..................... 9:07
  Chicago—D. Hull (Mikita)................17:30
  Montreal—Cournoyer (F. Mahovlich,
    P. Mahovlich)........................15:33
THIRD PERIOD
  No scoring

FIFTH GAME (May 13, at Chicago)
Black Hawks 2, Canadiens 0

FIRST PERIOD
  Chicago—D. Hull (Koroll, R. Hull).........10:57
SECOND PERIOD
  Chicago—Koroll (D. Hull, Mikita)..........11:26
THIRD PERIOD
  No scoring

SIXTH GAME (May 16, at Montreal)
Canadiens 4, Black Hawks 3

FIRST PERIOD
  Chicago—Pappin.......................11:25
  Montreal—Cournoyer (Beliveau,
    F. Mahovlich)........................12:13
SECOND PERIOD
  Montreal—P. Mahovlich (Houle, Ferguson)... 5:04
  Chicago—Maki (White, R. Hull)............17:40
  Chicago—Pappin (Jarrett, R. Hull)..........18:48
THIRD PERIOD
  Montreal—F. Mahovlich (Beliveau)......... 5:10
  Montreal—P. Mahovlich (F. Mahovlich)...... 8:56

SEVENTH GAME (May 18, at Chicago)
Canadiens 3, Black Hawks 2

FIRST PERIOD
  Chicago—D. Hull (Koroll, R. Hull).........19:12
SECOND PERIOD
  Chicago—O'Shea (Martin)................. 7:33
  Montreal—Lemaire (Laperriere)............14:18
  Montreal—Richard (Lemaire)...............18:20
THIRD PERIOD
  Montreal—Richard (Houle, Lapointe)....... 2:34

BOSTON BRUINS
NEW YORK RANGERS —1972

"Don't Sell the Bearskin Before You Kill the Bear"

This series is going to be one of those love-hate things. There is no love between the Bruins and the Rangers. A lot of hate, maybe, but no love ...
— Boston's John ("Pie") McKenzie
before the final

Boston and New York had last crossed sticks in a final in 1929. In recent years the simmering animosity between the teams had come to a boiling point when some of the players got personal. In a 1971 game, claimed Boston firebrand Derek ("Turk") Sanderson, Ranger goalkeeper Ed Giacomin told him: "We're not here to win, we're here to get you." Minutes later fists were bloodying noses. In a recent book Ranger defenseman Brad Park had called several Bruins gutless, and that was one of Brad's more complimentary appraisals. Replied Sanderson: "He has no concept of hockey ethics."

Boston's 1971–72 Scoring Machine trailed only the previous year's record-busting model in total goals. Phil Esposito flashed in 76 goals in 78 games, and Bobby Orr, second to Phil in scoring, led the league in assists. In the East, that Boston powerhouse finished first, New York second, Montreal third, and Toronto fourth. The Bruins sent the Maple Leafs home to their wives and kiddies early, winning in five games. The Rangers dismissed the Canadiens, now without the strength of Jean Beliveau at center, in six games.

Chicago again finished first in the still-weak Western Division. Minnesota came in second, St. Louis third, and Pittsburgh fourth. The Black Hawks wiped out the Penguins in four straight and the Blues outlasted the North Stars in seven.

In the semifinal Boston walloped St. Louis in four straight, the Blues yet to beat an Eastern team in Stanley Cup play. The Rangers shocked the Black Hawks, whisking 17 goals through Chicago's proud defense in four games, that sweep propelling New York into its first Stanley Cup final since 1950.

The Rangers skated in swift and precise patterns under the discipline of coach Emile Francis. Their top line—Jean Ratelle, Vic Hadfield, and Rod Gilbert—was dubbed the Gag (Goal-a-Game) Line; the three ranked third, fourth, and fifth in league scoring behind Esposito and Orr. But the injured Ratelle had been replaced on the line for the playoffs by little Bobby Rousseau. Although Hadfield, Walt Tkaczuk, and a few other Rangers were brawny, most were smaller than the Bruins.

Loose under the easy-riding ways of coach Tom Johnson, a laughing bunch off the ice, the Big Bad Bruins had defeated the Rangers five straight times during the season (by a combined score of 24-4). The Bruin technique had been as primitive as a punch in the nose: They had bowled over the Rangers at the blue line, not allowing them to penetrate the Boston defense and set up their dizzying passing patterns.

Boston came into the playoffs with two handicaps: Orr was limping on a left knee that would require surgery at the end of the season; and the Bruins still ached mentally from their collapse in the quarterfinal against Montreal the previous season. "We let up and we got our tails kicked in," Orr told his teammates. "We got to keep telling ourselves we can't let up."

Midway through the third period of the first game it looked like 1971 all over again for the Bruins. Leading 5-1 in the second period, they seemed to let up. New York fired in a burst of goals to tie the game, 5-5, midway through the third period. But there was no Boston collapse:

Boston's Johnny ("Chief") Bucyk carries the Cup around the ice at New York's Madison Square Garden through rings of photographers. Of the big Bruins, Ranger coach Emile Francis said: "You can't overemphasize the importance of brawny players. Not with the long season we have now."

Crouching Ranger (No. 16 in dark shirt) drops to his knees to block a shot by Boston's Ken Hodge. The blocked puck skitters to the left of the Ranger cage, where Hodge retrieves it and shoots from a nearly impossible angle. The puck streaks between Ed Giacomin's pads as he kicks out a left skate, and as he falls the puck is behind him for a Bruin goal.

Garnet ("Ace") Bailey feinted around Brad Park and rammed the puck between Ed Giacomin's pads and the near post for the goal that won the game, 6-5.

The Bruins won the second game, 2-1, the Boston goals being scored against New York goalkeeper Gilles Villemure while the Rangers were short a man. "Both teams," said Bruin winger Ken Hodge, who scored the game-winner, "have guys who can put the puck in the net. Tonight proved neither one of us can take too many penalties."

In New York's Madison Square Garden for the third game, Ranger fans tried to dent Bruin skulls with sluglike transistor batteries. "They're as courageous as a lynch mob," *New York Post* writer Hugh Delano wrote of the fans. The mob streamed home happily after Brad Park scored two goals and assisted Gilbert to score on another power play, New York winning 5-2. "You win or lose in the Stanley Cup on power plays and face-offs," Park said later. "As much as I hate to admit it," growled Phil Esposito, "Park was the difference."

But another difference might have been the slowed-up Orr. "His knee must really be bad," said Park. "He didn't rush the puck from his end very often."

Orr's face showed pain early in the fourth game. Twice he left the bench to go to the dressing room, where a trainer strapped fresh ice-packs on his swollen knee. Once, skating to the bench, his knee locked and the sudden pain bent him over. But a minute later he dipsy-doodled his way through the New York defense to punch the puck by Giacomin to put Boston ahead, 1-0. Later in the first period he scored again. In the second period Don Marcotte dropped him a pass. As Marcotte burst toward the cage, Orr wound up to shoot. Giacomin crouched, waiting. Orr threw a lightning-bolt pass to Marcotte, standing at the cage mouth, and Marcotte flipped it by Giacomin for a 3-0 lead.

The Rangers stormed back to push two pucks by Ed Johnston, but lost, 3-2. "Orr was playing real hurt," said Emile Francis, "but he did the job." Added Brad Park: "I wish I was hurt the way he is."

With the Bruins ahead three games to one and

259

playing the fifth game in Boston Garden, the Rangers heard—falsely, as it turned out—that champagne was being delivered to the Boston dressing room for a Stanley Cup victory party after the game. "You shouldn't sell the bearskin," snapped the Rangers' Bobby Rousseau, "before you kill the bear." That night this bear was still alive, the Rangers winning the game, 3-2.

Going back to New York the Rangers talked of sweeping the next two games and winning the team's first Stanley Cup since 1940, the longest time between drinks from the Cup for any NHL team. "Imagine the ticker tape parade we'd get down Broadway," said Rod Gilbert, the Rangers' swinging bachelor, eyes gleaming. "It'd be bigger than anything they gave the Mets."

Big Phil Esposito counseled the Rangers to suppress such dreams. "If the Rangers think they are going to beat us in the next two games," he said, "they're full of Park spelled backward."

Ranger fans—"Those mangy lions," according to one New York reporter—roared with hopes high, nevertheless, as the sixth game began at Madison Square Garden. Early in the game Orr cozied the puck near the blue line. The Rangers' Bruce MacGregor came running at him. If MacGregor poked away that puck, he'd face only ice between himself and Bruin goalkeeper Gerry Cheevers.

Orr pushed out the puck, invitingly. MacGregor lunged for it with his stick. Orr pulled back the puck, pirouetted on that aching knee, and dashed in toward Villemure. He slapped a low line drive that whizzed by Gilles Villemure's left skate. Boston 1, New York 0.

During the next two periods Orr skated in obvious pain—yet he was 100% Orr when he had to be. During one stretch the Bruins were shy a man, then two men, then a man. Orr hugged the puck to his stick and skated in circles, killing time for as long as 30 seconds. Ranger fans shrieked, "Kill 'im," but no Ranger was quick enough to penetrate his twirls and seize the puck.

"Orr is better on one and a half legs," said a journalist, "than most people are on two."

During the intermission before the third period, the Bruins still ahead by that thin 1-0 margin, Orr talked with knife-slim winger Wayne Cashman. "I've been shooting to Villemure's right too

often," Orr told Cashman. "When I shoot, set yourself on the left side and be ready for a tip-in."

Early in the third period Esposito, who had failed to score a single goal in the six games, shoveled the puck to Orr. Bobby snapped a shot at Villemure's left side. Cashman, stationed on the left side, stuck out a skate, the puck ricocheting off the skate and into the cage. Boston led 2-0. "That was the real killer," Park said later.

The Bruins won 3-0. Johnny ("Chief") Bucyk skated around Madison Square Garden with Boston's second Stanley Cup in three years. Someone asked Vic Hadfield the difference between the two teams. "That's easy," Hadfield said. "Bobby Orr."

Bobby Orr:
What he feels like, you couldn't print

Often called the greatest hockey player ever, Bobby Orr—with Phil Esposito—led the Bruins from the NHL basement to two Stanley Cups and the playoffs in every year but one since he came into the league in 1966. In a loser's quiet clubhouse after the final game of the 1974 playoffs, he talked about being a Cup winner and a loser.

Playing in the finals takes a tremendous second effort because you are so tired after the season and the playoff rounds. But one thing that has helped me to get up when I am tired is remembering what it will be like all summer. You know, we have had tremendous years in Boston—setting scoring records, winning like 57 of 78 games one season. But when you get beat in the Stanley Cup playoffs, what they remember all summer is that you didn't win the Cup. That's all you hear back home: What happened? Not: Gee you had a great year. But: What happened? And you can talk all you want to them, say how tired you were and all that, but you can't change it: You didn't win the Cup. Everytime I've lost in a Stanley Cup playoff, I've felt just the way I feel right now—like a piece of . . . well, you couldn't print that.

FIRST GAME (April 30, at Boston)
Bruins 6, Rangers 5

FIRST PERIOD
New York—Rolfe (Gilbert, Park)............ 3:52
Boston—Stanfield (McKenzie)............... 5:07
Boston—Hodge (Esposito, Walton).........15:48
Boston—Sanderson (Westfall)...............17:29
Boston—Hodge (Esposito)..................18:14
SECOND PERIOD
Boston—Hodge (Esposito, Orr)..............10:46
New York—Gilbert (Ratelle, Hadfield)......11:54
THIRD PERIOD
New York—Hadfield (Tkaczuk, Gilbert)...... 1:56
New York—Tkaczuk....................... 7:48
New York—MacGregor (Irvine, Stemkowski).. 9:17
Boston—Bailey (Walton, Westfall)..........17:44

SECOND GAME (May 2, at Boston)
Bruins 2, Rangers 1

FIRST PERIOD
Boston—Bucyk (Orr, Stanfield)..............16:15
SECOND PERIOD
New York—Gilbert (Neilson, Hadfield)....... 7:23
THIRD PERIOD
Boston—Hodge (Walton, Esposito)..........11:53

THIRD GAME (May 4, at New York)
Rangers 5, Bruins 2

FIRST PERIOD
New York—Park (Hadfield, Fairbairn)....... 1:22
New York—Gilbert (Park, Rousseau)........11:19
New York—Park (Gilbert).................13:00
Boston—Walton (Vadnais).................14:04
SECOND PERIOD
Boston—Orr (Smith, Cashman)............. 1:10
New York—Gilbert (Rousseau, Park)....... 3:46
New York—Stemkowski (MacGregor, Irvine)..19:23
THIRD PERIOD
No scoring

FOURTH GAME (May 7, at New York)
Bruins 3, Rangers 2

FIRST PERIOD
Boston—Orr (Walton)..................... 5:26
Boston—Orr (McKenzie, Bucyk)............. 8:17
SECOND PERIOD
Boston—Marcotte (Orr)...................16:33
New York—Irvine (Stemkowski, Seiling)......18:38
THIRD PERIOD
New York—Seiling (Irvine, Stemkowski)......18:35

FIFTH GAME (May 9, at Boston)
Rangers 3, Bruins 2

FIRST PERIOD
Boston—Cashman (Hodge, Esposito)......... 3:55
New York—Rolfe (Tkaczuk, Fairbairn)......13:45
Boston—Hodge (Stanfield, Esposito)........16:07
SECOND PERIOD
No scoring
THIRD PERIOD
New York—Rousseau (Park, MacGregor).... 2:56
New York—Rousseau (Irvine)...............12:45

SIXTH GAME (May 11, at New York)
Bruins 3, Rangers 0

FIRST PERIOD
Boston—Orr (Hodge, Bucyk)...............11:18
SECOND PERIOD
No scoring
THIRD PERIOD
Boston—Cashman (Orr, Esposito)........... 5:10
Boston—Cashman (Esposito, Hodge)........18:11

261

CHICAGO BLACK HAWKS
MONTREAL CANADIENS — 1973

Beep-Beep the Roadrunner—
Proof Enough That Speed Kills

Kevin Leahy, by his own admission a "hockey nut," settled into his seat in St. Paul to watch the Minnesota Fighting Saints play the Winnipeg Jets. The Fighting Saints and Jets were two teams in a new hockey league, the World Hockey Association, which had lured some past and present stars away from the National Hockey League. It drew Gordie Howe out of retirement for a reported one million dollars, and it signed Bobby Hull for another million or more. Hull's Winnipeg Jets led the Fighting Saints in the opening round of the WHA's first playoffs.

"There probably won't be too large a crowd here tonight," Leahy was telling Mark Mulvoy of *Sports Illustrated*. "The [NHL] North Stars are televising their Stanley Cup game back from Philadelphia. Besides that, a lot of people around here still don't buy the argument that the WHA is major league."

Kevin Leahy was indisputably right on one count—only 5,000 people showed up to watch Hull's Jets lose to the Fighting Saints. And he was probably correct when he said that a lot of people did not think the WHA was big league. For despite the presence of magic names like Hull and Howe, the WHA did not possess one magic name the NHL owned—the Stanley Cup.

Chicago finished first in the West for the third successive year, Philadelphia second, Minnesota third, and St. Louis fourth. The Black Hawks eliminated the Blues in five games, and the Flyers took out the North Stars in six.

In the East, Montreal won its 15th Prince of Wales Trophy in 30 years. The Canadiens opposed the fourth-place Buffalo Sabres, the first expansion team to enter the Eastern playoffs. Montreal won, but only after six gruelling games. In

the other quarterfinal, the second-place Bruins faced off against the third-place Rangers. The Rangers won in five games—the first time since 1940 that New York had defeated Boston in a Stanley Cup series.

In the semifinals—East winners against West winners—Montreal toppled Philadelphia in five games while Chicago, after losing the first game to New York, won the next four. For the fifth time going back to 1931, Chicago met Montreal in the final. The record so far: Montreal the winner of four Stanley Cups, Chicago none.

"I am here to watch the two best goaltenders in the world," said Valeri Kharlamov, a member of the USSR team that had lost to an NHL All-Star team, called Team Canada, after a fierce, close struggle the previous fall. In the Montreal cage stood Ken Dryden, the rangy law student who had won the 1972–73 Vezina Trophy as the league's top goalie. In goal for Chicago crouched chunky Tony Esposito, co-winner—with his teammate Gary Smith—of the Vezina award for 1971–72.

Esposito, a church-goer before games, had a special reason for prayer. He was facing a horde of Montreal sharpshooters: brawny Frank and Pete Mahovlich; clever little Henri ("Pocket") Richard; Tony's *bête noire* from 1971, Jacques Lemaire; and will-o'-the-wisp, 5-foot-7 Yvan Cournoyer, called "Beep-Beep the Roadrunner" in tribute to the way he flew around the rink.

"No team can match the Canadiens in depth," Chicago coach Billy Reay said before the first game. "Their fourth line . . . tops the first line of many teams."

Against that blitzkrieg of shooters Reay would send out All-Star defensemen Pat Stapleton and Bill White to stand sentry for Esposito. And he

Henri Richard and the Cup: On it he could see his name written 11 times, a Cup winner more often than any other man.

263

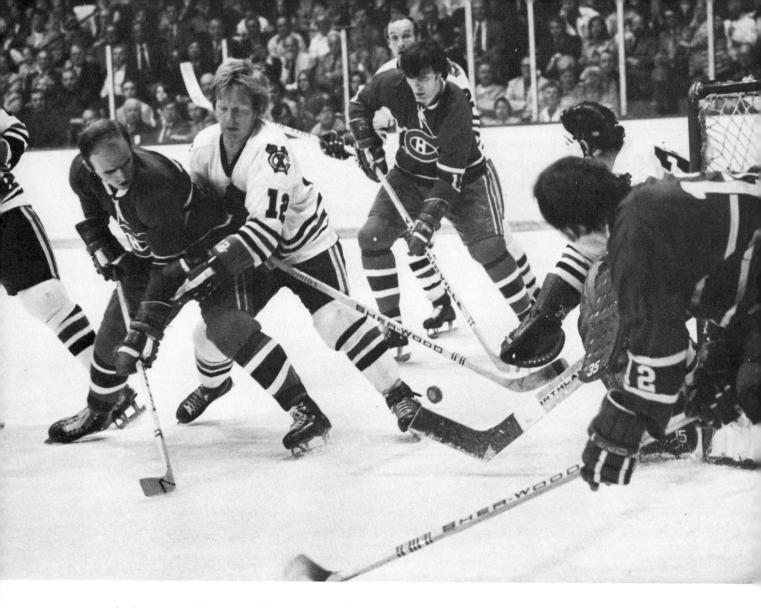

had some artillery to roll out against Dryden: Jim Pappin; Dennis Hull; quick, play-making center Hubert ("Pit") Martin; four-time league scoring leader Stan Mikita; Ronald ("Chico") Maki; Cliff Koroll; and ex-Canadien veteran Ralph Backstrom. But for the first time in a decade a club could oppose the Black Hawks in a playoff without having to shadow Bobby Hull.

Neither goalkeeper looked like the world's greatest in the first game, the Black Hawks ramming two early goals past Dryden, then the Canadiens smacking six straight by Esposito on the way to an 8-3 triumph. In that game Mikita's finger was smashed by a stick. "The finger," said a teammate, "looks like an overboiled knockwurst."

Mikita sat on the bench in the second game and Montreal won easily, 4-1. Down two games

to none, the Black Hawk cause seemed hopeless if Mikita could not come back. "Even the comeback of Bobby Hull wouldn't help them now," someone said.

What did help, however, was the return to the mushy ice of Chicago Stadium for the third and fourth games. The ice slowed the quick Canadiens to Black Hawk speed. "It was like skating uphill," said Montreal's Chuck Lefley.

The Black Hawks, with Mikita now playing despite the sore finger, leaped out to a 5-0 lead. But the Canadiens began to catch up and with a minute to play, the score was Chicago 5, Montreal 4.

Dryden went to the bench, leaving the Canadien cage empty, and six Montreal skaters attacked. A Canadien shot. The puck bounced off Esposito's pads and dropped onto the ice at the feet of Montreal's Frank Mahovlich. With Espo-

Opposite page: Montreal's Jacques Lemaire,
he of the thinning hair at left, backhands
the puck at the masked Tony Esposito,
who stopped it. But Canadien Marc Tardif
slapped in a rebound, the final goal for
the Canadiens in their 6-4 triumph in the
final game. Clutching Lemaire is Chicago's
Pat Stapleton (No. 12).
Above: In the fourth game, helmeted
Stan Mikita of the Black Hawks tries to
swipe the puck by Ken Dryden, who
stopped the shot and the Black Hawks, 4-0.

sito off-balance and out of position, an open cage yawned in front of Mahovlich. One swing and he could tie this game.

Mahovlich swatted at the puck. It rolled toward the corner, missed, and kept rolling to the boards. Chicago's Dennis Hull stopped it and whacked it 150 feet down-ice—into the empty Montreal net. Moments later the Hawks scored again to win, 7-4. "I could have kissed Frank," said Mikita. "I don't know how he missed."

In the fourth game Dryden finally looked like one of the world's two best goalkeepers, shutting out the Black Hawks, 4-0. The Canadiens led three games to one with the fifth game to be played at the Forum in Montreal.

With victory at hand, Dryden crumbled—but so did Esposito. During the season Esposito and Dryden had batted away 16 of every 17 pucks thrown at them. In this game one of every four was going in. The two teams slapped in eight goals during the second period, a Stanley Cup record. The Black Hawks won, 8-7, the 15 goals another Cup record (the old record of 13 had been set in 1936).

Back on the slow ice of Chicago Stadium for the sixth game, the Black Hawks took an early 2-0 lead. But by the third period the under-manned and weary Black Hawks could no longer keep up with the speedy Canadiens, even on the slushy Stadium ice. "I've never seen speed like that before," Chicago rookie defenseman Phil Russell said of Roadrunner Cournoyer. "I'm not used to that."

The teams were tied, 4-4, in the third period when the Roadrunner blew by a Chicago defenseman and poked the puck past Esposito for his 15th goal of the playoffs—a record. Four minutes later, on the Canadien power play that had scored so many Stanley Cup goals, Cournoyer passed to Marc Tardif for another goal, sealing a 6-4 victory and giving Montreal its 11th Cup in 18 years, its 18th since 1916.

"We have the speed," said Tardif between sips from the Cup. "And speed, as they say, kills. Speed will do it every time."

Two days earlier the New England Whalers had beaten Bobby Hull's Winnipeg Jets for the WHA championship. The Whalers challenged the Canadiens to a one-game winner-take-all match for the Cup. The NHL ignored the challenge. But the presence of the WHA—and the strong showing of the Russian National Team against the NHL's Team Canada—made more likely the coming of a time when there would be a round-robin series among the NHL champion, the WHA champion, the Russian National Team, and perhaps a Swedish National Team for the Stanley Cup and the true world championship of hockey.

Yvan Cournoyer:
The best parts of being MVP and a record-breaker

The speedy Canadien, Yvan Cournoyer, talked at his home in Montreal about his record-breaking series.

Oh, that was a good year for me. My 15 goals broke the record for a single playoff year. The old record was 14, which had been set by Frank Mahovlich a couple of years earlier. And I won the Conn Smythe Trophy as the most valuable player in the playoffs. When they told me in the clubhouse after the last game that I had won the Smythe, all the guys on the team came over and said you deserved it, and that was the best part about winning it. The best part of that 15th goal was that it was the winning goal of the last game. Jacques Lemaire let go a slap shot from the blue line that bounced off the glass and came right back in front of me as I was coming in on net at full speed and I shot for the top of the net and put it in.

They say I am fast. Look at how small I am. You have to be fast when you are my size or otherwise those big guys will catch up with you . . .

FIRST GAME (April 29, at Montreal)
Canadiens 8, Black Hawks 3

FIRST PERIOD
Chicago—Martin (Stapleton, Hull)........... 0:35
Chicago—Backstrom (Stapleton)............. 1:02
Montreal—Laperriere...................... 2:28
Montreal—Tardif (Lafleur, Houle).......... 8:07
Chicago—Martin (Stapleton, White)........12:07
SECOND PERIOD
Montreal—Lefley (Cournoyer, Lemaire)..... 3:01
Montreal—Lemaire (Richard, Tardif)........16:23
THIRD PERIOD
Montreal—Lemaire (F. Mahovlich).......... 8:38
Montreal—P. Mahovlich....................12:36
Montreal—F. Mahovlich (Lafleur, Houle).....13:34
Montreal—Lefley (Lemaire, Cournoyer)......14:35

SECOND GAME (May 1, at Montreal)
Canadiens 4, Black Hawks 1

FIRST PERIOD
Montreal—Bouchard (Larose, P. Mahovlich).. 5:36
SECOND PERIOD
Chicago—Koroll (Redmond, Angotti)........ 7:28
Montreal—Cournoyer (F. Mahovlich).......12:18
THIRD PERIOD
Montreal—Cournoyer (Lapointe, Lemaire).... 5:01
Montreal—F. Mahovlich 19:26

THIRD GAME (May 3, at Chicago)
Black Hawks 7, Canadiens 4

FIRST PERIOD
Chicago—Hull (Pappin, Stapleton)........... 1:59
Chicago—Bordeleau (Mikita, Koroll)........11:44
Chicago—White (Stapleton, Backstrom)......13:20
Chicago—Mikita (Koroll, White)...........14:20
SECOND PERIOD
Chicago—Marks (Frig, Mikita)............. 2:08
Montreal—F. Mahovlich (Robinson,
   P. Mahovlich).........................10:25
THIRD PERIOD
Montreal—Cournoyer (Lemaire, Lefley)...... 1:20
Montreal—Lapointe (F. Mahovlich, Larose)... 7:15
Montreal—Lemaire (Cournoyer, Tardif)...... 8:01
Chicago—Hull............................19:29
Chicago—Pappin (Hull)...................19:49

FOURTH GAME (May 6, at Chicago)
Canadiens 4, Black Hawks 0

FIRST PERIOD
Montreal—Tardif (Cournoyer, Lemaire)...... 1:08
SECOND PERIOD
Montreal—Cournoyer (Tardif).............14:13
Montreal—Lefley (P. Mahovlich, Larose).....15:43
THIRD PERIOD
Montreal—Larose (Lemaire)............... 3:45

FIFTH GAME (May 8, at Montreal)
Black Hawks 8, Canadiens 7

FIRST PERIOD
Montreal—F. Mahovlich................... 2:47
Chicago—Hull (Jarrett, Russell)............. 9:34
Chicago—Mikita (Stapleton)...............11:24
Montreal—P. Mahovlich (F. Mahovlich,
   Robinson)............................14:32
SECOND PERIOD
Montreal—Larose....................... 0:37
Chicago—Kryskow (Maki, Backstrom)...... 3:10
Montreal—Larose (Wilson)............... 4:23
Chicago—Mikita (Stapleton, Marks)........ 6:21
Montreal—Cournoyer (Lemaire, Lapointe).... 7:09
Chicago—Pappin........................11:24
Chicago—Frig (Mikita)...................16:12
Chicago—Pappin (Mikita, Hull)...........19:03
THIRD PERIOD
Montreal—Savard (Wilson, Larose).......... 1:15
Chicago—Angotti (White)................. 4:04
Montreal—Richard (F. Mahovlich).........11:43

SIXTH GAME (May 10, at Chicago)
Canadiens 6, Black Hawks 4

FIRST PERIOD
Chicago—Martin (Mikita, Stapleton)........10:35
Chicago—Martin (Pappin)................11:31
Montreal—Richard (F. Mahovlich).........19:48
SECOND PERIOD
Montreal—P. Mahovlich (Laperriere, Lefley).. 5:05
Montreal—Houle (P. Mahovlich, Lefley)...... 6:37
Chicago—Kryskow (Maki, Backstrom)....... 8:32
Montreal—F. Mahovlich (Lapointe,
   Cournoyer)...........................10:54
Chicago—Martin (Hull)..................17:05
THIRD PERIOD
Montreal—Cournoyer (Lemaire)............ 8:13
Montreal—Tardif (Cournoyer, Lemaire)......12:42

BOSTON BRUINS
PHILADELPHIA FLYERS
1974

God Bless Kate Smith

I don't think she'll have a damn thing to do with it. Kate Smith doesn't score pucks.

> —Boston's Bobby Orr
> before the sixth game

Get to the puck by the shortest route and arrive there in ill-humor.

> —Sign posted by coach Fred Shero
> in the Philadelphia dressing room

The 1973–74 Bruins scored more goals than any other NHL team ever, with the exception of the 1971 Boston Scoring Machine. Bruins ranked one, two, three, four in league scoring, with Phil Esposito the leader, followed by Bobby Orr and Phil's wingmates, Ken Hodge and Wayne Cashman. The Bruins cruised home first in the East by a wide margin over the defenders of the Cup, Montreal, with the Rangers third and the Maple Leafs fourth.

In their confrontation with the Bruins, the Maple Leafs thought they saw a hole in the Boston defense: 25-year-old Bruin goalkeeper Gilles Gilbert, who had appeared in only one playoff game (with Minnesota) in his life. But he stood solid in the first game, flagging down 35 pucks in a 1-0 Boston triumph, and the Bruins went on to sweep the Maple Leafs in four games.

The two teams in the other Eastern playoff— the Canadiens and the Rangers—had been burdened by problems stemming from the same root: money. Missing from the Canadien goal mouth was Ken Dryden, who sat out the year as a clerk in a law office after the Canadiens refused to meet his salary demand of $100,000. The Canadiens found no one near as good and gave up more goals than any other team in the proud history of the Flying Frenchmen.

The pride was also missing, insisted veteran Henri ("Pocket") Richard. "Our pride has gone down the drain," he said. "This year the guys get behind by a couple of goals and then they quit. The guys know if they do not play for the Canadiens, they can play somewhere else in the league and still make big money."

That big money had been ladled out to the New York Rangers' stars by general manager Emile Francis to keep them from departing to the World Hockey Association. Chicago coach Billy Reay alleged that "New York is trying to buy the Stanley Cup." When the Rangers looked bad in the early part of the season, Francis took back the coaching job he'd given to Larry Popein. Ranger fans jeered their one-time idols as "fat cats." Instead of shouting "Dee-fense, dee-fense," as was their custom, the fans were chanting, "Ree-fund, ree-fund . . ."

Against Montreal, Francis got unexpected help from Ron Harris, a beefy defenseman who was one of the lower-paid performers on this team of moguls and who had scored only two goals all season. Pressed into service at right wing, Harris scored in overtime to win the fifth game, 3-2, and put New York ahead, three games to two.

Before the sixth game, a spotlighted Kate Smith carols "God Bless America" at the Spectrum. The former owner of a pro basketball team called the Celtics in the 1930s, Kate once was also part-owner of a pro football team, the New York Yankees, now the Baltimore Colts. "But ever since the Flyers adopted me," she said, "I am a hockey fan."

269

With the score tied 2-2 in the sixth game, the Canadiens failed to score while New York was short-handed for almost four minutes. The Rangers whipped in three goals to win the game, 5-2, and the series. The Canadiens went home to ruminate about whether the pride really had gone after 6 Cups in the past 10 years, 11 in the past 19, and 18 since 1916.

In the West the Philadelphia Flyers finished on top after a season of earning such sobriquets as the Broad Street Bullies and the Animals. The Flyers spent more minutes looking out of penalty boxes than any other team in the history of the NHL. "It's not hockey," said one critic of the Flyers, "it's warfare."

Finishing behind the Flyers were the Chicago Black Hawks and two newcomers to the playoffs: the Los Angeles Kings and the Atlanta Flames. The Flyers put out the Flames in four games, and the Black Hawks disposed of the Kings in five. So much for the *nouveau riche*.

For the semifinal round against Boston, Chicago had Tony Esposito in goal and not all that much else, the offense crippled by injuries (in one game against the Kings, a 1-0 victory, the Black Hawks could get off only 10 shots on goal). Although Phil Esposito had a reputation for scoring almost at will against Tony, this season he had scored only two of his league-leading 68 goals against his brother. And in five clashes with the Bruins, the Black Hawks had not lost a game, tying three and winning two.

The Black Hawks surprised the Bruins at Boston Garden, winning the first game, 4-2, as Tony batted away 46 shots. Boston won the second game, in Boston, Chicago the third in overtime, in Chicago. In the fourth game, also in Chicago, the Boston "big line" of Esposito, Ken Hodge, and Wayne Cashman each registered a goal in a 5-2 victory, tying the series at two games apiece. Back in Boston for the fifth game, Phil whistled two more pucks by Tony's ears in a 6-2 rout, the mangled Chicago attack tossing only 21 pucks at the Boston net. Down three games to two, the Black Hawks rallied in the third period of the sixth game to tie, 2-2. With fewer than 90 seconds remaining, Boston's Gregg Sheppard scooped up a pass from Dallas Smith and beat Tony with a bullet to the corner. A little later Phil tapped the puck into an empty Chicago net for a 4-2 victory

that sent the Bruins into their 13th final looking for their sixth Stanley Cup.

"There are three things that make a hockey player," said Philadelphia coach Fred Shero, speaking of Dave ("Hammer") Schultz, the most penalized of the Flyers. "Speed, skill, and strength. Schultz realizes he doesn't have speed or skill but he knows what he is here for: to beat up the other guy."

Soft-spoken and mild-mannered off the ice, a former Bible student, the 24-year-old Schultz frowned at such talk. "I scored over 20 goals this season," he said, stroking a walrus mustache. "People don't notice because I get in so many fights." But he conceded: "I'd be lost on a finesse team or if I stopped playing the way I do. Hockey is a contact sport for me. It's not the Ice Follies."

The best fighter on the team was Bob ("Hound") Kelly. "They don't pay me to score goals—I got only four all season," he told reporters. "But I don't lose many fights." "Kelly," said Flyer centerman Bobby Clarke, "is so fast he gets in three or four punches before the other guy even realizes he is in a fight."

From the start of their semifinal with the Rangers, the Flyers tried to tense up a Ranger team that had the reputation of not caring for the game's bruising aspects. In the first game Flyer bully boy Andre ("Moose") Dupont kayoed Ranger forward Walt Tkaczuk, and the Flyers won, 4-0. In the second game Hound Kelly punched winger Jerry Butler out of the game, and the Flyers won, 5-2.

In New York the Rangers won the next two, 5-3, and then 2-1 on an overtime goal by Rod Gilbert. Before the fifth game, back at Philadelphia's Spectrum, the public-address system blared a recording of Kate Smith's "God Bless America" instead of the "Star Spangled Banner." In the seven years that the Flyers had occasionally subbed Kate for the national anthem, the Flyers had won 32, tied 1, lost only 3. Kate came through again, the Flyers winning, 4-1, to lead three games to two.

Flyer goaltender Bernie Parent, who liked to laugh—for no apparent reason—behind his mask during games, had been rated not too mobile. So far, however, he had stopped 143 of 153 Ranger shots. But in the sixth game, at Madison Square

Garden, the last laugh was on Bernie, and the Rangers won, 4-1, to force a seventh game.

"Something has to give," noted Parton Keese in the *New York Times.* "Never has an expansion team [like the Flyers] won a round in the NHL playoffs against a non-expansion team [like the Rangers], and never have the Rangers won a seventh game in a Stanley Cup series."

Flyer fans filled the Spectrum, sang along with Kate's recording of "God Bless America," then watched the Flyers cozy a 3-1 lead into the third period. New York's Steve Vickers golfed a puck by Parent to narrow the gap, but Philadelphia's Gary Dornhoefer scored only 12 seconds later for a 4-2 Philadelphia lead. Minutes later the Rangers' Pete Stemkowski tapped a rebound by Parent. But the Rangers could come no closer, losing 4-3, the door to a Stanley Cup they had not won in 34 years shutting in their faces. Flashed the Spectrum scoreboard: GOD BLESS KATE.

In the final against Boston, Philadelphia seemed to be outclassed. The Flyers had not won a game at Boston Garden since 1967. They had won only once over Boston in their last 28 games.

"We're a hitting team," Shero told his Flyers. "But we've always made the mistake of treating Orr and Esposito as untouchables. As a result, they have killed us, particularly Orr . . . Orr is not God, and we've got to stop treating him like God." Shero instructed the Flyers to give Orr the puck, "then hit him, make him work, and hit him again."

Slim, intense Bobby Clarke, Philadelphia's top scorer, was assigned to face off against Esposito. In their first 66 face-offs, Clarke won 48, and when he lost he tied up Boston's premier scorer. "When Clarke loses a face-off," said Boston coach Armand ("Bep") Guidolin, "you don't move because he's got his stick between your legs or else he's grabbed your stick. He doesn't let you move until he moves."

None of these stratagems seemed to upset the Bruins at the beginning of the first game as they jumped out to a 2-0 lead. But after that most of the Bruins appeared to sleep on their skates, and the Flyers came back to tie the game, 2-2. With an overtime almost certain, Bobby Orr brought the crowd in Boston Garden to its feet by slipping through the Flyer defense with less than 30 sec-

onds to play and scorching the puck by Parent for a 3-2 Bruin victory.

Orr was not happy in victory. "We got that lead," he snapped, "and we stopped skating."

Two nights later, again in Boston, the Bruins stepped out to another 2-0 lead. Although Clarke scored in the second period, Boston still led, 2-1, with less than a minute remaining, the tall Gilles Gilbert fending off one Flyer foray after another. But he was screened as the Flyers' Moose Dupont veered in on the cage and shot. The puck slid by Gilbert for a last-minute goal that tied the game, 2-2, and strangled the roaring of Boston fans expecting momentary victory.

That roaring flared again in the overtime as Boston's Johnny ("Chief") Bucyk skimmed in alone on Parent. But Bucyk stumbled, then let fly a weak shot that Parent caught at his waist. Two minutes later the Flyers' Clarke backhanded a puck that bounced off Gilbert's pads and hopped back onto Clarke's stick. In stopping the shot Gilbert had toppled out of position, and Clarke was staring at a wide-open side of the cage. The Bruins' Terry O'Reilly dived into the gap but Clarke lofted the puck over him for the goal that won the game 3-2. For the first time in seven years the Flyers departed Boston as victors.

Back in Philadelphia the Flyers won, 4-1, to lead two games to one. "Only three Bruins are skating," growled Boston coach Bep Guidolin, "Orr, Cashman, and Gregg Sheppard. If saying that is going to get me fired, I don't care."

"The Bruins are willing to be physical, but not for sixty minutes," said Fred Shero, commenting on observations by some writers that the Bruins looked tired. "They'll be physical for ten or twenty minutes and if you can withstand that, you can beat them."

With fewer than six minutes remaining of the fourth game, the score tied at 2-2, the Flyers' Bill Barber streaked by the face-off circle and clipped a rising liner at Gilbert in the Boston cage. "I went down to take a better look," Gilbert said afterward, "and as I went down it flew over my shoulder." Two minutes later Moose Dupont slugged another puck by Gilbert, and the Flyers skated off the Spectrum ice 4-2 winners and ahead in the series three games to one. For the first time since 1927, a team from a city other than Montreal, Toronto, New York, Boston, Chicago, or

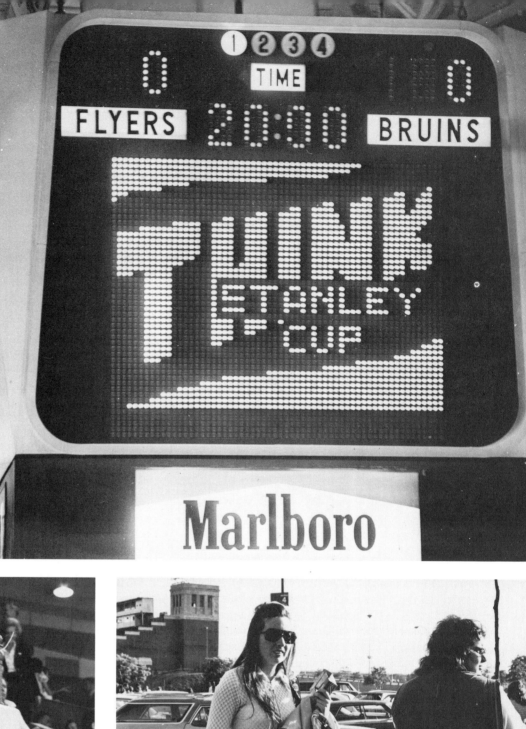

In Philadelphia and Boston, the enthusiasm of crowds was whipped on by messages like the one flashed at right on the Spectrum scoreboard, by a placard in Boston Garden (below l.) that told of Bruin fans' love for Gilles Gilbert, and by a sign outside the Spectrum (below r.) predicting the best for the Western champion Flyers. On the opposite page (top): Veteran Boston Garden organist John Kiley pumps out chords to rally the Bruins. Bottom: Some of the overflow crowd in the Spectrum hanging onto the action.

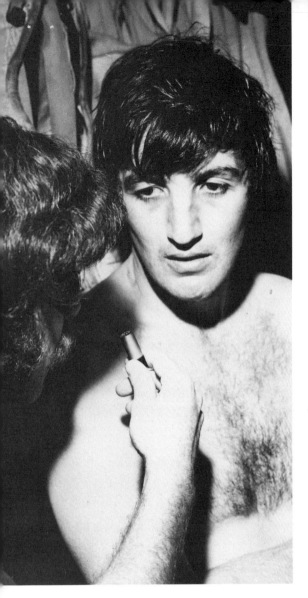

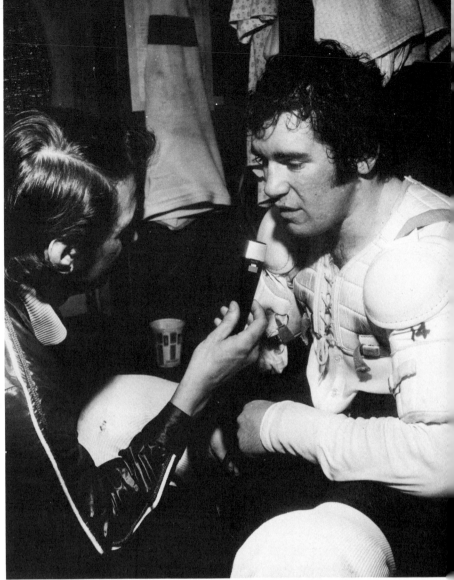

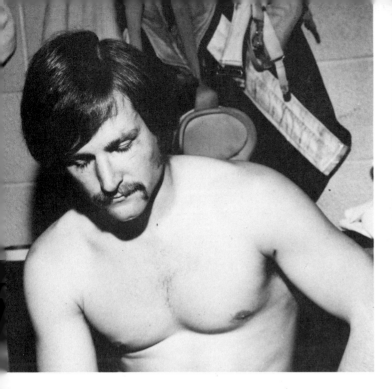

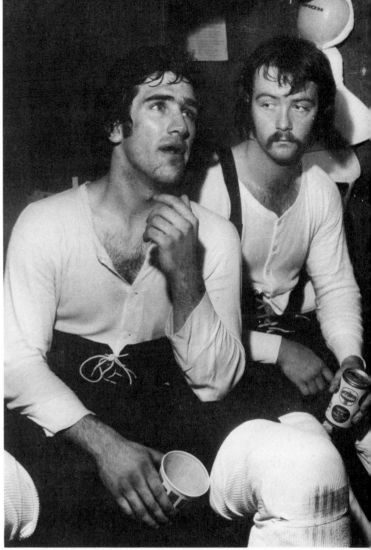

Privacy is impossible during a Stanley
Cup final, reporters, photographers, and
TV and radio men poking into the dressing
rooms. Opposite page (top): Boston's Carol
Vadnais (l.) and Flyers' Joe Watson tell it
as they saw it. Bottom: A player's reminder
to himself of the money to be won. Top:
Bruin Greg Sheppard (l.) and Flyers Joe
Watson and Bruce Cowick (r.) in thoughtful
moments. Above: Winning coach Fred Shero
ruminates. At right: Belongings of the
Bruins, kept to ward off evil spirits.

Detroit stood within a game of winning the Cup.

Abused by their fans and their coach, the Big Bad Bruins snapped back at the Broad Street Bullies in the fifth game, played at Boston Garden. Blood splotched the ice during six separate fistfights. Officials called 43 penalties, an NHL record for playoff and regular-season play, with Bruins and Flyers sent to the penalty boxes for such niceties as slashing, spearing, and butt-ending. In between the blood spilling, Bobby Orr scored twice to erect a 5-1 Boston lead. Near the end of the game the now-appeased Boston fans serenaded the beaten Flyers with "God Bless America"—sung boisterously and derisively.

In Philadelphia for the sixth game, the Flyers decided the stakes were too high to rely on a recording; they called on the real thing, a flesh-and-blood Kate Smith. She swept onto the ice in a glittering gown and thundered out "God Bless America" so joyously that even the Bruins, though aware of her 36-3-1 record for the Flyers, applauded. "Super song, Kate," Esposito whispered, shaking her hand.

Kate seemed to have lifted the dormant Bruins higher than the Flyers, who appeared defensive in the early portion of the game, battling in their own zone against wave after wave of Boston rushes. In the first period the Bruins flung 16 shots at Parent while Gilbert saw only eight. Some observers began to suspect that if the Bruins won

this game, tying the series at three victories apiece, they would almost certainly win the seventh game in Boston. But about three-quarters of the way through that first period, with one Flyer and two Bruins in the penalty boxes, Philadelphia's Rick MacLeish won a face-off in the Boston zone and shuttled the puck backward to Moose Dupont. MacLeish zigzagged toward the Boston cage as Dupont swung at the puck. The flying puck hit MacLeish's leg, ticked off his skate, and tumbled by Gilbert. Philadelphia led, 1-0, the Spectrum suddenly one big boiler room of noise.

That goal seemed only an opening bang with some 45 minutes of play stretching ahead; the Bruins had not been shut out all season. But as time went on the Bruins' attack lost speed and cohesiveness, turning to water in the Flyers' zone. When the Bruins did manage a shot, there stood Parent to grab it.

During the final five minutes, the Flyers still ahead 1-0, a sustained roaring filled the Spectrum. When Orr let fly a last long drive that Parent snared, the game ended with one climactic roar. Sweaty-faced Flyers hugged each other. Parent and Clarke carried the Cup around the rink, chased on the slushy ice by mobs of spectators and photographers.

While Philadelphia celebrated with streakers gamboling on downtown streets and car horns blaring in impromptu parades, Bep Guidolin was telling reporters:

"There were just too many of our guys relying on No. 4 (Orr). He was out there playing his heart out when he shouldn't have been while guys who weighed 200 pounds weren't getting their hair mussed." Later he said that the 210-pound Esposito had been thinking too much about a $2-million offer from the WHA . . . and later still Guidolin quit.

"This club has more courage than any club I've ever coached," Fred Shero said. "A team like this comes along once in a lifetime. But I'll tell you: If someone had asked me at the beginning of this season if I thought this team would win the Stanley Cup, I'd have said they were crazy."

Bernie Parent:
Nobody needs telling

The first player to jump from the NHL to the WHA, the mustached, genial Bernard Parent later jumped back and shared the 1974 Vezina with Tony Esposito. In the playoffs he won the Conn Smythe as the most valuable player.

They ask me: Is it different for a goaltender in the playoffs? If you came into the clubhouse before one of these final games, you would know it was different. I can't tell you exactly how it is different, but look around this clubhouse. You see 20 guys and not one of them has ever had his name on the Stanley Cup—and that is something every boy dreams of when he grows up in Canada. Now we have played 104 games so far in this preseason and in this season and in this playoff, and we are only one game away from winning the Stanley Cup. When you have come that far, nobody has to tell us where we are and what we have to do.

FIRST GAME (May 7, at Boston)
    Bruins 3, Flyers 2

FIRST PERIOD
    Boston—Cashman (Orr, Vadnais)...........12:08
    Boston—Sheppard (Forbes, Smith)..........13:01
SECOND PERIOD
    Philadelphia—Kindrachuk
        (Joe Watson, Saleski).................... 7:47
THIRD PERIOD
    Philadelphia—Clarke (Joe Watson, Nolet)..... 5:32
    Boston—Orr (Hodge, Cashman).............19:38

SECOND GAME (May 9, at Boston)
    Flyers 3, Bruins 2

FIRST PERIOD
    Boston—Cashman (Esposito, Vadnais)........14:24
    Boston—Esposito (Hodge, Cashman)........17:42
SECOND PERIOD
    Philadelphia—Clarke (Flett, Schultz)........ 1:08
THIRD PERIOD
    Philadelphia—Dupont (MacLeish, Clarke)....19:08
OVERTIME
    Philadelphia—Clarke (Flett, Schultz)........12:01

THIRD GAME (May 12, at Philadelphia)
    Flyers 4, Bruins 1

FIRST PERIOD
    Boston—Bucyk (Sheppard, Orr)............. 1:03
    Philadelphia—Bladon (Clarke, MacLeish).....10:27
    Philadelphia—Crisp......................15:43
SECOND PERIOD
    No scoring
THIRD PERIOD
    Philadelphia—Kindrachuk (Saleski, Barber)... 7:53
    Philadelphia—Lonsberry (MacLeish)........14:19

FOURTH GAME (May 14, at Philadelphia)
    Flyers 4, Bruins 2

FIRST PERIOD
    Philadelphia—MacLeish (Bladon)............ 4:40
    Philadelphia—Schultz (Saleski, Van Impe).... 5:30
    Boston—Esposito (Bucyk, Hodge).......... 7:12
    Boston—Savard (Orr, Vadnais).............11:24
SECOND PERIOD
    No scoring
THIRD PERIOD
    Philadelphia—Barber
        (Lonsberry, Jim Watson).................14:35
    Philadelphia—Dupont (Clarke, Crisp)........16:40

FIFTH GAME (May 16, at Boston)
    Bruins 5, Flyers 1

FIRST PERIOD
    Boston—Sheppard (Orr).................... 8:14
SECOND PERIOD
    Philadelphia—Clement (Flett, Van Impe)..... 6:04
    Boston—Orr (Sheppard, Bucyk)............12:06
    Boston—Orr (Hodge, Smith)...............16:55
THIRD PERIOD
    Boston—Hodge (Sheppard, Bucyk).......... 0:39
    Boston—Marcotte (Savard, O'Reilly)........18:59

SIXTH GAME (May 19, at Philadelphia)
    Flyers 1, Bruins 0

FIRST PERIOD
    Philadelphia—MacLeish (Dupont)..........14:48
SECOND PERIOD
    No scoring
THIRD PERIOD
    No scoring

Signs in Boston (opposite page) are hung by fans of Gilbert, Orr, Hodge, Sims, and Esposito. At left (top), Bruin fans urge their heroes to send the Flyers packing. But a sign hoisted in the Spectrum before the sixth game (bottom) proved to be prophetic almost to the minute and gave Flyer fans the last word.

Robert B. Shaver

United Press International

BUFFALO SABRES
PHILADELPHIA FLYERS

1975

Out of the Fog Came Bernie with "That Bleeping Stanley Cup"

Hockey has been revolutionized by Shero's system. But it doesn't hurt to have a Bernie Parent playing goal for you, either.
—Flyer center Bobby Clarke

The 1975 playoffs lingered longer into spring than any other playoff in Cup history. Two games were played as summery 87-degree heat slopped the ice with puddles, clouds of steam rising off the melting ice to obscure the puck. Players pleaded for the playoffs to start earlier before hockey became a summer sport.

But there were few complaints about the NHL's new playoff system. It was necessitated by the addition of two teams, the Kansas City Scouts and the Washington Capitals, raising the number of clubs in the league to 18. Twelve of the 18 teams qualified for the playoffs, a two-thirds ratio that hadn't changed from the years when there had been six teams in the league and four qualified for the playoffs.

The 12 qualifiers were the top three teams in each of the league's four new divisions. That was simple enough. Things got less simple when the playoffs began.

The four teams that finished in first place in each division sat out the opening round of the playoffs. The remaining eight teams were matched against each other. The team that totaled the most points during the season—two points for each victory, one for each tie—faced the team with the fewest points. The team with the next-highest number of points played the team with the next-fewest number of points, and so on. Each series in this opening round was a best-of-three affair.

Four teams survived the opening round. They joined the four division champions who sat out the opening round, in the best-of-seven quarter-final series. The eight teams were ranked—or, to use a tennis term, "seeded"—again according to the total number of points scored during the season. The No. 1-seeded team played the No. 8-seeded team, the No. 2-seeded team played the No. 7 team, and so on. The four survivors advanced to the semifinals, the two semifinal winners meeting in the finals, each duel a best-of-seven series.

What made this playoff system unique was the seeding feature. It motivated teams to keep on winning—and thus amassing points—even after clinching a playoff spot. The more points a team had, the higher it would be seeded. And the higher it was seeded, the weaker a team it played. Perhaps most important, the higher-seeded team got the "home-ice advantage"; that is, if a seventh game were necessary in a best-of-seven series, it would be played on the higher-seeded team's ice.

The 12 qualifying teams, in the order of finish in each division, were: Montreal, Los Angeles, and Pittsburgh from the James Norris Division; Buffalo, Boston, and Toronto from the Charles F. Adams Division; Philadelphia, New York Rangers, and New York Islanders from the Lester Patrick Division; Vancouver, St. Louis, and Chicago from the Conn Smythe Division.

OPENING ROUND

Toronto vs. Los Angeles. The Maple Leafs, with only 78 points, were a journeyman bunch.

The Flyers' Bernie Parent flops onto the foggy ice as the puck skitters through him for the sudden-death goal that won the third game for the Sabres, 5–4. Bottom: Moments later, Parent and Ross Lonsberry leave as the Sabres' Danny Gare hoists hands and stick.

Fastest-ever goal in overtime of Cup play is scored by Islander Jean-Paul Parise (No. 12), who rammed the puck by Ranger defenseman Brad Park and goalie Ed Giacomin, then collapsed atop them. Bottom: Islander hero Glenn Resch, better known as Chico.

Joe Bereswill

Of Maple Leaf goalie Gord McRae, coach Red Kelly said, "He's the best I have," and he might have said the same about most of the other Leafs.

The Kings called themselves Team Castoff. Sixteen of the 20 had been discarded by other NHL clubs. They played a tightly disciplined, close-checking game, making the best use of their talent. They had finished with 105 points, fourth highest in the league.

The teams split the first two games, each winning at home, 3–2, in overtime. After the second game, in Toronto, the players had to hop across the continent to play the third and final game the next night in Los Angeles. The weary teams slapped only 45 shots at both goals. The Maple Leafs scored early, then cosseted that lead to win, 2–1, upsetting the Kings, two games to one.

Chicago vs. Boston. As usual, the Bruins could brag of a lusty offense. Bobby Orr led the league in scoring, Phil Esposito ranking second. But opposing shooters put the red light on above Gilles Gilbert, the Bruins' goalie, so often that the Bruins could amass no more than 94 points.

The Black Hawks, with 82 points, looked mostly to little Stan Mikita for their offense and

to goalie Tony Esposito for their defense. The Bruins counted on scoring against Tony E., as they had in previous playoffs. That was what happened in the first game, the Bruins humiliating Tony by an 8–2 score. But Tony shut the door in the second game, the Black Hawks winning, 4–3, in overtime.

At Boston for the third game, the Bruins whacked 56 shots at Tony, while the Black Hawks could hit only 19 at Gilbert. But the puck was as slippery as soap for Gilbert, and the Black Hawks won, 6–4, to oust the Bruins, two games to one, in another upset.

Pittsburgh vs. St. Louis. Each team was a "homer." The St. Louis Blues (84 points) had won 11 straight at home; the Pittsburgh Penguins (89 points) had lost only five times in 40 home games. Neither team had great goaltending. The St. Louis defense seemed especially weak against an array of excellent Pittsburgh shooters. But in the first game, St. Louis raced out to a 3–1 lead. Then that weak defense collapsed. In the third period, the Pittsburgh shooters whistled three pucks by St. Louis goalie John Davidson for a 4–3 victory.

280

Joe Bereswill

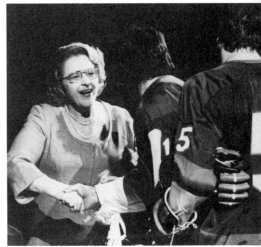

United Press International

The Islanders shake hands (l.) after beating the Rangers, lined up for the ritual ceremony at the end of every series; and later (above), they "welcome" Kate Smith to the Spectrum, a counter-hex ploy—before the seventh game of the Flyer series—that failed.

In the second game, at St. Louis, with the score 3–3 in the third period, Pittsburgh's Colin Campbell and Vic Hadfield rapped pucks by Ed Johnston for a 5–3 Pittsburgh victory, erasing St. Louis in two straight.

N.Y. Islanders vs. N.Y. Rangers. Each team had 88 points, but the Rangers got the home-ice advantage, having won 37 games to 33 for the Islanders. The young Islanders—most were under 25 and only four had been in a playoff—concentrated on defense. They led the league in tie games. "If we could score," one Islander said, "we'd be great."

The Rangers, most of them highly paid veterans, seemed to take the Islanders lightly. Playing with bearded faces, having vowed not to shave until they won the Cup, the Rangers streaked to a 2–0 lead in the first game. But the Islanders squeezed three pucks by Ed Giacomin in the third period for a 3–2 victory.

Embarrassed and angry, the Rangers spilled that anger onto the Islanders in the second game at the Nassau Coliseum, swinging sticks and fists. The Islanders fought back and 50 penalties were called, a playoff record. In fighting back, the

Islanders forgot to do what they did best, play defense, and the Rangers won, 8–3.

At Madison Square Garden for the third game, the Islanders forged out to a 3–0 lead but the Rangers blasted three pucks by Billy Smith in the third period to send the game into overtime. On the face-off at the start of the overtime, the Islanders won the draw and flicked the puck to Jean-Paul Parise at the goal mouth. Parise slammed the puck by Giacomin, and the Islanders won the game, 4–3, and the series, two games to one. The goal was the fastest in overtime in Cup history—11 seconds.

THE QUARTERFINALS

Philadelphia vs. Toronto. After surprising the Bruins to win the Cup the year before, the Flyers had proven they were no one-year flash by amassing 113 points, with the league's best record—51–18–11. The Flyers had already made other coaches—notably Los Angeles' Bob Pulford and Montreal's Scotty Bowman—disciples of coach Freddy Shero's "system hockey."

Shero had picked up the system from a Russian, Anatoli Tarasov, who advocated short shifts of no more than a minute and carefully staged attacks instead of the freewheeling end-to-end rushes of the type popularized in the NHL by the Rocket Richards and the Bobby Orrs.

"Put very simply," Shero said, "my system recognizes that on a hockey rink there are four corners and two pits, the pits being the areas in front of the cage. You throw the puck into the corner, then dig it out and get it to the guys in the pit. To win a game you got to win the corners and the pits. You give punishment there, and you take it, which is why we have more fights than other teams.

"With a team like Montreal everything is one on one. We set up two on one and three on one. That takes discipline and self-sacrifice. It won't work where players want to put the puck in the net themselves. I'm lucky there isn't a selfish man on this team.

"Once we are on the move with the puck, no defenseman can be more than one zone—or two stick lengths—behind the puck carrier. In other words, once Clarke gets to center ice, I want my defenseman, say Ed Van Impe, to be at the blue line. When Clarke reaches the far blue line, I want Van Impe at the red line. Once Clarke is ten feet inside the zone, Van Impe must be stationed at the point."

With that mixture of precision and muscle, the Broad Street Bullies swept over the Maple Leafs in four straight games, winning 6–3, 3–0, 2–0, and, in overtime, 4–3. Flyer captain Bobby Clarke talked of sweeping the next two series and winning the Cup in 12 straight games.

Buffalo vs. Chicago. Buffalo's French Connection Line—Gil Perreault, Rick Martin, and René Robert—had been the league's most prolific scoring line. As a team, only Montreal had scored more goals than the Sabres, who totaled 113 points, with a 49–16–15 record. The Sabres stationed boulders like Jerry ("King Kong") Korab on defense in front of the cage, but neither young Gary Bromley nor veteran Roger Crozier had been satisfactory in goal. Just before the season ended, Gerry Desjardins hopped from the World Hockey Association to take over as the No. 1 netminder for the Sabres.

The Sabres won the first two games, 4–1 and 3–1. Chicago won the third game, 5–4, in overtime. But the French Connection exploded for

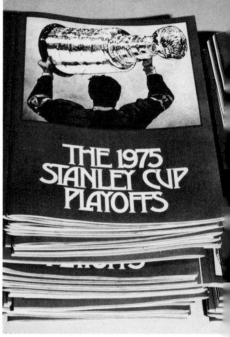

Inside the Spectrum (top to bottom): Stacks of programs; TV commentators Ted Lindsay (l.) and Phil Esposito; and Bernie Parent in the winners' clubhouse.

Barbara Devane

John Devaney

John Devaney

DAVE SCHULTZ "The Penalty Box" on SALE at the concession stand

Right: A Spectrum poster advertises Dave Schultz' recording, "The Penalty Box," a place he knew something about. He led the league in penalties during the season, then broke John Ferguson's career record of 260 minutes in the box during playoffs. Far right: Spectrum usherettes. Below: Flyer banner taunts the Sabres' No. 1 line (shown at bottom, l. to r.)— René Robert, Gil Perreault, and Rick Martin.

John Devaney

John Devaney

Robert B. Shaver

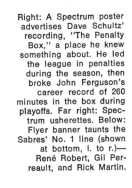

THE FRENCH CONNECTION HAS BLOWN A FUSE

John Devaney

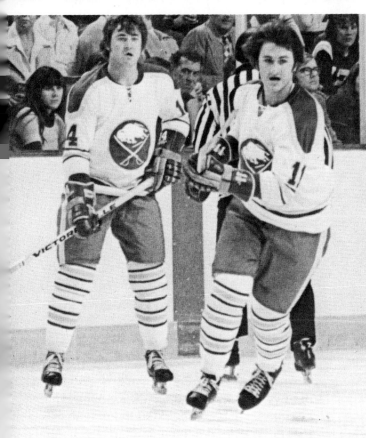

three goals to win the fourth game, 6–2. And Perreault set up Robert for a goal that clinched the fifth game, 3–1, the Sabres eliminating the Black Hawks in five games.

Montreal vs. Vancouver. This was a duel of first-place teams. The Canadiens had led the James Norris Division, with 113 points, the Canucks the weaker Conn Smythe Division, with only 86. "We don't score a lot of goals," said Canuck forward Chris Oddleifson, who had racked up only 16 himself, "but we work our heads off."

The Canucks figured to butt those heads against a Canadien offense that had scored more goals—almost five a game—than any other NHL team this season and any other Canadien team in history. And on defense for Montreal was goalie Ken Dryden, who after a year's retirement had returned with a million-dollar contract.

Montreal won the first game, 6–2, but Vancouver took the second, 2–1, its first playoff victory in only its second try. Montreal won the next three games, 4–1, 4–0, and 5–4 (in overtime), to send the Canucks home for the summer, four games to one.

N.Y. Islanders vs. Pittsburgh. Some Rangers, after being eliminated by the Islanders in the opening round, had growled that the Islanders had been lucky. Predicted Derek Sanderson: "They won't win another game."

His prediction appeared accurate as the Penguins won the first three games, 5–4, 3–1, and 6–4. For the fourth game, Islander coach Al Arbour replaced goalie Billy Smith with Glenn Resch, a rookie who was called Chico by the Islanders because of his constant chatter and a black mustache that reminded them of TV's Chico. Chico became The Man in the fourth game, the Islanders winning, 3–1.

They also won the next two games, 4–2 and 4–1, to tie the series at three games apiece. They were only the fourth team in Cup history to tie a series after being three games down. The others were the 1939 Rangers, 1942 Maple Leafs, and 1945 Red Wings (but only the 1942 Maple Leafs had won their series).

In the seventh game, at Pittsburgh, Chico stopped one puck with his head, and his "two best friends, the goalposts," stopped two more. With the score 0–0 in the closing minutes, the Islanders' Bert Marshall intercepted a pass in the Penguin end. He whisked it to Ed Westfall, who lifted a ten-footer by Gary Inness. The Islanders won, 1–0, to duplicate for the first time in 33 years (albeit not in a final) what the Maple Leafs had wrought in 1942.

THE SEMIFINALS

Philadelphia vs. N.Y. Islanders. The Flyers won the first three games, 4–0, 5–4 (in overtime), and 1–0. "Now we got 'em where we want 'em," joked the Islanders' general manager, Bill Torrey. "We play best when we're down three games to nothing."

But the Islanders did not seem likely to bounce back against the Flyers, who hadn't lost a game in their last 21. Indeed the Flyers appeared to have made it a four-game sweep when Reggie Leach stroked the puck by Chico Resch as the buzzer sounded in the fourth game for a 4–3 victory. But officials ruled that the puck had crossed the line after the buzzer went off. In overtime, Jude Drouin put the puck past Bernie Parent for a 4–3 New York victory. Though down three games to one, the Islanders were still breathing.

They were exultant a few days later after winning the next two games, 5–1 and 2–1, to tie the series at three games apiece. The Islanders had come within one game of accomplishing twice in four weeks what only one other team had done in NHL history.

For the seventh game, the Flyers called on their good-luck charm. They asked Kate Smith to come in person to the Spectrum to sing "God Bless America." The Flyers were now 42–3–1 when Kate, in person or on a record, had sung the Irving Berlin classic. Someone asked a club official why the Flyers didn't play the record at all home games. "Then," he explained, "it wouldn't be a good-luck charm. We only play it when we need her."

She was as lucky as ever for the Flyers. Moments after Kate left the ice after singing "God Bless America"—in fact, at the 19-second mark—the Flyers' Gary Dornhoefer banged the puck by Chico Resch. Then playing their methodical waiting game for the rest of the night, the Flyers won, 4–1, to go into their second straight Stanley Cup final.

284

Buffalo vs. Montreal. Each team had totaled 113 points during the season, but the Canadiens hadn't beaten the Sabres in a year and a half. Montreal coach Scotty Bowman assigned a checking line to lean on the French Connection. The Sabres won the first two games, 6–5 (in overtime) and 4–2, but at home the Canadiens soared to 7–0 and 8–2 victories. In the last ten periods the French Connection had not scored.

"If the French Connection can't do the job," said Buffalo coach Floyd Smith, "we're in trouble, because they're our best."

The fifth game, at Buffalo, went into overtime with the teams in a 4–4 tie. On a face-off Gil Perreault stole the puck from Jacques Lemaire and backhanded it to French Connection linemate René Robert, who had broken free from a Montreal shadow. Robert skimmed the puck by Dryden for a 5–4 Sabre victory. In the sixth game, the French Connection powered another goal by Dryden, and the Sabres then cozied a 2–0 lead into a 4–3 triumph to win the series, four games to two. Buffalo went into the final against Philadelphia, and for the first time since 1923 there would be no team representing Montreal, Boston, Detroit, Chicago, New York, or Toronto in a Stanley Cup final.

FINAL ROUND

Philadelphia vs. Buffalo. On paper this matchup of the No. 1-seeded Flyers against the No. 2-seeded Sabres seemed a triumph for the new playoff system in that the two top-rated teams had reached the finals. But other statistics indicated a mismatch. The Sabres had not won a game in Philadelphia in five years of trying, their record 0–11–2. The Sabres hadn't beaten the Flyers all this season nor in 13 straight games going back a couple of seasons, and they had never, ever beaten Bernie Parent.

Yet the clash had at least two intriguing elements. It was a battle between a good offense, the Sabres', against a good defense, the Flyers'. And it was a battle between the old and the new, the Sabres' free-wheeling attack *à la* Richard against the Flyers' machine-like system *à la* Shero.

Shero assigned Bobby Clarke to harass the shifty Gil Perreault. No center in the league was more adept a fore-checker than Clarke, who slowed opponents by thrusting his stick between their legs, at their middles, or across their ankles. "Perreault holds that French Connection together," Shero said. "And Buffalo depends too much on that line. Stop them and we win."

Clarke and the Broad Street Bullies, however, could not contain the French Connection and the other Sabres in the first two periods of the first game. The Sabres swept out of their end to drill twice as many shots at Bernie Parent as the Flyers could trigger at Gerry Desjardins. But Parent stopped everything that came at him, and the two teams entered the third period tied 0–0.

Then Desjardins made two fatal errors. On a Flyer shot that hit the boards behind the cage, he turned to his right. The puck bounced out on his left. The Flyers' Bill Barber shoved it into the yawning left side, and Philadelphia led, 1–0.

A little later, Philadelphia's Ross Lonsberry drove in on Desjardins, who flopped to the ice too soon. Lonsberry slipped the puck between Desjardins' pads for a 2–0 Flyer lead. The Flyers kept the puck in the Sabre end for much of the rest of the game and won, 4–1.

"Parent won it for them," Desjardins said. "He came up with the big saves and I didn't. Aside from him it was an even game."

The second game, also at the Spectrum, was tied 1–1 early in the third period. While a Sabre sat in the penalty box, the Flyers unleashed their power play. They encircled Desjardins and whirled the puck around him like kids playing keep-away. From the left, Bill Barber faked a shot, then slid the puck to Bobby Clarke on the right side of Desjardins. With a backhand swipe, Clarke lashed the puck into the cage. The Flyers won, 2–1, and led two games to none.

During the season, the Sabres had averaged 37 shots a game on goal. In this game, they had hit only 19; in two games the French Connection had scored only one goal.

A heat wave baked Buffalo before the third game. In the non-air-conditioned Memorial Auditorium, thermometers at rinkside read 87 degrees. The date, May 20th, was the latest ever for a Stanley Cup game.

Desjardins looked shaky during the opening minutes. Of the first five shots the Flyers winged at him, three went in. After the first period Desjardins asked to be replaced. With Roger Crozier in the cage, the Sabres rallied, but still trailed 4–3 in the third period.

Parent stopped a shot, then fell to the ice. Sabre defenseman Bill Hajt cruised in and cracked the puck over the fallen Parent to tie the game, 4–4.

By now layers of steam were floating over the melting ice. Twelve times the referee stopped the game and asked the weary players to skate around the rink to blow away the fog. "Maybe," said one player, "they should put electric fans on our backs."

The score still tied after three periods, the players panted into overtime. For 18 minutes they labored through the mist and the choking fumes of chlorine rising off the ice. Shifts had to come off every 30 seconds instead of every minute or two.

With a second overtime looming, the French Connection's Perreault drove the puck against the boards behind the Philadelphia cage. It bounced back on the left side. Perreault's French Connection linemate René Robert outraced a Flyer to the puck. From a sharp angle, Robert hit the puck into the rising mist. Parent, perhaps surprised that Robert shot from such a difficult angle, said he lost sight of the puck. It slammed into his right leg, then squirmed between his pads for the 5–4 game-winner.

After the game, Desjardins explained that he had quit because "I was too nervous to continue and I didn't want to let the guys down." He came back for the fourth game, the heat again oppressive inside the "Aud." This time he gave up a goal in the first period, but the Sabres bounced back in the second to take the lead, 3–2. With three minutes left, the Flyers' Ross Lonsberry veered through the steamy air and shot at Desjardins from close range. Desjardins knocked away the shot that would have tied the game. In the last minute, Don Luce poked a puck into an empty net to give the Sabres a 4–2 win and tie the series at two games apiece.

That save on Lonsberry, the Sabres hoped, might restore Desjardins' confidence. But on home ice in the fifth game, after listening to Kate's record, the Flyers scored early when a low shot by Dave ("Hammer") Schultz ticked a stick and flew over Desjardins' shoulder. The goal seemed to unnerve Desjardins once more. The Flyers socked four more goals by him before the game was half-over, winning 5–1 to lead now three games to two.

The Sabres replaced the downcast Desjardins ("I hate this game") with Crozier for the sixth game, in Buffalo. In the first two periods, the Sabres fired 26 shots at Parent and he blocked them all. Crozier saw almost as many pucks and was just as effective. Early in the third period,

United Press International

An ice crew flaps sheets around Buffalo's Memorial Auditorium rink during the fourth game to sweep away the fog. Of Parent, picked as the playoffs' outstanding player, Buffalo's Jerry ("King Kong") Korab said: "In Philadelphia, they say that only God saves more than Parent. Ah, but God should have a season so good, eh?"

with the game tied 0–0, the Flyers' Bob ("Hound") Kelly chased the puck along the boards behind the Buffalo cage. Buffalo's King Kong Korab rammed Kelly into the boards. Like a ball, Kelly bounced off the boards and whirled to a stop in the crease of the goal to the right of Crozier. From the boards a Flyer shoved the puck to Kelly. Crozier lunged toward Kelly, but the Hound backhanded the puck past him, and the Flyers led, 1–0. "No other team," Shero said later, "can come out of the corner with the puck like the Flyers."

Late in the game, Philadelphia's Orest Kindrachuk darted from the blue line to scoop up the puck near the left boards. Two Sabres converged on him. He pushed the puck between them to teammate Bill Clement, who rode in alone on Crozier. Clement beat Crozier with a slap shot to the corner. With the Flyers leading 2–0, Sabre fans in the "Aud" knew that the dream was over. To a team that had come to the pinnacle in only five years, the Buffalo fans began to chant, "Thank you, Sabres. . ."

Some two minutes later Parent and Clarke were toting the Cup around the ice, trailed by red-shirted, grinning Flyers. The Flyers were the first team to win the Cup two years in a row since the 1969 Canadiens.

In their dressing room, the Flyers roared "Bernie! Bernie! . . ." when their goaltender appeared with the Conn Smythe Trophy, awarded to him as the playoffs' Most Valuable Player. It was his second straight Smythe. But Bernie wouldn't pose for long with the trophy. "If you want to take a picture of me with a trophy," he said, "take me with that bleeping Stanley Cup. That's what this game is all about."

FIRST GAME (May 15, at Philadelphia)
Flyers 4, Sabres 1

FIRST PERIOD
  No scoring
SECOND PERIOD
  No scoring
THIRD PERIOD
  Philadelphia—Barber (Van Impe, MacLeish)...3:42
  Philadelphia—Lonsberry (Bladon, Clarke)......7:29
  Buffalo—Martin (Lorentz)................11:07
  Philadelphia—Clarke.....................11:41
  Philadelphia—Barber (Clarke)..............19:02

SECOND GAME (May 18, at Philadelphia)
Flyers 2, Sabres 1

FIRST PERIOD
  No scoring
SECOND PERIOD
  Philadelphia—Leach (Clarke, Lonsberry)......8:24
THIRD PERIOD
  Buffalo—Korab (Lorentz, Spencer)..........2:18
  Philadelphia—Clarke (Barber, MacLeish)......6:43

THIRD GAME (May 20, at Buffalo)
Sabres 5, Flyers 4

FIRST PERIOD
  Philadelphia—Dornhoefer (Barber)...........0:39
  Philadelphia—Saleski (Harris)...............3:09
  Buffalo—Gare (Ramsay, Luce).............11:46
  Buffalo—Martin (Guevremont).............12:03
  Philadelphia—MacLeish (Barber)..........14:13
SECOND PERIOD
  Buffalo—Luce (Korab)....................0:29
  Philadelphia—Leach (Kelly, Crisp)..........14:30
THIRD PERIOD
  Buffalo—Hajt (Martin, Luce)................9:56
OVERTIME
  Buffalo—Robert (Perreault, Martin).........18:29

FOURTH GAME (May 22, at Buffalo)
Sabres 4, Flyers 2

FIRST PERIOD
  Philadelphia—Dupont (Kelly, Crisp)........11:28
SECOND PERIOD
  Buffalo—Korab (Robert, Martin)............3:46
  Philadelphia—Lonsberry (MacLeish).........4:20
  Buffalo—Perreault (Martin, Robert).........10:07
  Buffalo—Lorentz (Dudley, Schoenfeld)......15:07
THIRD PERIOD
  Buffalo—Gare (Luce, Schoenfeld)...........19:28

FIFTH GAME (May 25, at Philadelphia)
Flyers 5, Sabres 1

FIRST PERIOD
  Philadelphia—Schultz (Saleski, Kindrachuk)....3:12
  Philadelphia—Dornhoefer (Crisp, Van Impe)..12:31
  Philadelphia—Kelly (Crisp, Jim Watson)......12:50
SECOND PERIOD
  Philadelphia—Leach (Barber, Goodenough)....1:55
  Philadelphia—Schultz (Goodenough, Harris)...9:56
THIRD PERIOD
  Buffalo—Luce (Ramsay, Gare).............14:02

SIXTH GAME (May 27, at Buffalo)
Flyers 2, Sabres 0

FIRST PERIOD
  No scoring
SECOND PERIOD
  No scoring
THIRD PERIOD
  Philadelphia—Kelly (Leach, Jim Watson)......0:11
  Philadelphia—Clement (Kindrachuk)........17:13

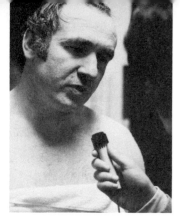

Ed Van Impe:
From Lord Stanley, a kitchen

The blunt-nosed veteran defenseman of the Flyers, Ed Van Impe, talked about being in a second straight Stanley Cup final shortly after the Flyers won the second game.

I started playing pro hockey in 1960, and it was 14 years later before I was in a Stanley Cup final. I started out in the National Hockey League in 1966 with the Black Hawks and then I went to Philadelphia, an expansion team, so there were times when I thought I would never play for the Cup, especially when I got past the age of 30 and I knew that any season could be my final season. When you're my age, which is almost 35, and you finally get into one Stanley Cup final and you win it, and then you get into another final the next year . . . well, it's like the guy who has been playing the Irish Sweepstakes all his life and has never won anything, then suddenly he wins a million dollars. And the next year, when he plays it again, he wins another million dollars.

And certainly there is no decrease in your desire to win the Cup the second time around. You know that there have been a lot of teams that have won the Cup once. But there are damn few that have won it two times in a row.

Oh, sure, you also think of the money. Last year we each won $19,000 for winning the Cup. I have a real quaint, old house in a suburb outside Philadelphia. Both my wife, Diane, and I love old houses. But the kitchens in old houses can often be a real problem, being out of date. Last year we used part of the check to bring it and the dining room up to date. Now we call it the Lord Stanley Memorial Kitchen.

Robert B. Shaver

United Press International

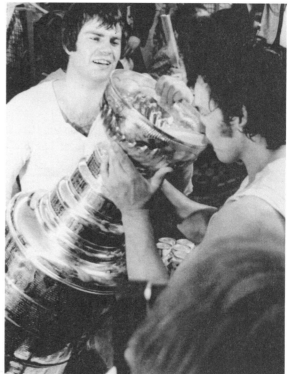

The gleaming Cup floats off the ice one more time (l.), grasped by the gap-toothed Bobby Clarke and the half-hidden Bernie Parent, the other smiling Flyers trailing behind. Above: Flyer Reggie Leach drinks from the Cup tipped by Tom Bladon, a ritual shared since 1893 by the hundreds whose names are inscribed on the side of what is still the best-known trophy in sport—Lord Stanley's Cup.